Studies in the History of Medieval Religion

VOLUME XXXIX

ENGLISH NUNS AND THE LAW IN THE MIDDLE AGES

CLOISTERED NUNS AND THEIR LAWYERS, 1293–1540

Studies in the History of Medieval Religion

ISSN 0955–2480

Founding Editor
Christopher Harper-Bill

Series Editor
Frances Andrews

Previously published titles in the series
are listed at the back of this volume

ENGLISH NUNS AND THE LAW IN THE MIDDLE AGES

CLOISTERED NUNS AND THEIR LAWYERS, 1293–1540

ELIZABETH MAKOWSKI

THE BOYDELL PRESS

First published 2011
The Boydell Press, Woodbridge

ISBN 978–1–84383–786–2

The Boydell Press is an imprint of Boydell & Brewer Ltd
PO Box 9, Woodbridge, Suffolk IP12 3DF, UK
and of Boydell & Brewer Inc.
668 Mt Hope Avenue, Rochester, NY 14620, USA
website: www.boydellandbrewer.com

A catalogue record for this book is available from the British Library

Printed and bound in Great Britain by
CPI Group (UK) Ltd, Croydon, CR0 4YY

For Maggie

Contents

Preface

This book is about cloistered nuns and the lawyers who worked for them. It links the rise of legal professionalism in late medieval England with the successful institutionalization of an old ideal – the fully enclosed yet economically self-sustaining nunnery. Crafted in antiquity and legislated about for centuries thereafter, this ideal had almost never before been realized in England prior to the arrival of mendicant and Bridgettine nuns in the late Middle Ages. Like their continental sisters, English nuns in traditional orders had long resisted hierarchically imposed cloister regulations, but these latecomers to the English scene embraced them. Dominican, Franciscan, and Bridgettine nuns saw strict enclosure as conducive to the special brand of devotion, the contemplative spirituality, characteristic of their orders. Lay founders and patrons shared their vision and made their bequests with an eye to spiritual rather than practical, temporal rewards. Finally, and most importantly for their institutional survival, these cloistered nuns did not have to compromise their spiritual ideals in the interests of economic security; their endowments were safeguarded and augmented by the professional lawyers whom they hired to act for them in the courts of Church and Crown.

Thanks to the largess of founders, each of the five monasteries considered here had extensive endowments in the form of far-flung tracts of arable land, rental properties, immunities, and privileges. The latter included rights to hold manorial courts and retain the fees of justice that they generated, and to offer unique indulgences to pilgrims who would leave behind pious donations. In addition, each new generation of nuns profited from the ongoing generosity of lesser benefactors. While alive such benefactors made modest gifts of cash, chattels, food and drink. When they died lay patrons made provision for 'their' monasteries in wills. Generally this meant leaving gifts of money but less straightforward donations were also possible. For example, a testator could decide that any debts owed him at the time of his demise would, once collected, become pious donations to the sisters.

Such diverse monastic portfolios provided security against economic downturns and disasters, but they clearly needed a great deal of management. For the routine collection of rents and taxes, cloistered nuns employed servants, bailiffs, and other laymen who had traditionally acted as agents for religious women. For the conduct of litigation to which their landed holdings and bequests gave rise, they hired professional lawyers, agents who had not been available to their predecessors. Before the middle of the thirteenth century, members of the landed classes, whether secular or religious, had been expected to personally oversee litigation in which they were interested parties, or to act through amateurs: friends, patrons, servants, or relatives. But, by the time mendicant and Bridgettine nuns arrived in England, the growing complexity of the law had dictated a major change. It was a change that benefited cloistered nuns enormously.

When personal attention to litigation had been the norm, strictly cloistered nuns would have been at a disadvantage since rules of enclosure prohibited even the heads of houses from going to court. In late medieval England, however, the filing of lawsuits, as well as routine legal business, had become the work of professionals, so those consequences were minimal. Speaking of the revolution in legal practice that took place at this time, the historian Paul Brand put it succinctly: "A litigant who was foolish enough to try to present his own case or make his own defence (unless he was a former royal justice or very expert attorney) was an amateur up against a professional or rather a group of professionals. Few litigants were willing to put themselves at such a disadvantage."[1]

English cloistered nuns were definitely not among those reckless few, and the story of their involvement in the law courts is a vital one, the details of which are intriguing, piquant, and sometimes funny. It is an important story for two reasons. First, unlike their sisters in traditional Benedictine or Augustinian monasteries, mendicant and Bridgettine nuns left few traces in the sources ordinarily mined for the study of religious women; consequently, they have become almost invisible in the history of English monasticism. By investigating evidence gleaned from public records such as court rolls and memoranda books, I have tried to redress the situation. Second, although scholars have devoted considerable attention to the origins of the legal profession in England as well as on the continent, they have not observed what this development meant for cloistered religious. I have made and documented such observations.

As an investigation of female agency in religious communities, *English Nuns and the Law* follows in the wake of books like Anne Winston-Allen's *Convent Chronicles: Women Writing about Women and Reform in the Late Middle Ages*, Sean Field's *Isabelle of France: Capetian Sanctity and Franciscan Identity in the Thirteenth Century*, and Maiju Lehmijoki-Gardner's *Worldly Saints*. As a contribution to the history of women's monasticism in

1 Paul Brand, "Inside the Courtroom: Lawyers, Litigants and Justices in England in the Late Middle Ages," in *The Moral World of the Law*, ed. Peter Coss (Cambridge: Cambridge University Press, 2000), p. 95.

England it greatly profits from the scholarship of Marilyn Oliva, Bernice Kerr, Paul Lee, Nancy Bradley Warren, and the many others who have attempted to add dimension to a landscape so long populated exclusively by monks and friars.

Like the history of monasticism in England, English legal history has been steadily broadened to include discussion of women at law and the evidence that I have assembled here is in keeping with that trend. My case studies featuring nuns as litigants and consumers of legal services complement the work of Barbara Hanawalt, Sue Sheridan Walker, Emma Hawkes, and Noël James Menuge, who have tended to focus on wives, widows, and single laywomen. As a study of English legal professionals and their work, *English Nuns and the Law* rests squarely on the path-breaking labors of John Baker, Paul Brand, and James Brundage. My debt to other scholars too numerous to mention here will soon become apparent.

The cases presented in this book were extracted from highly technical legal records, those required for what F. W. Maitland called "a whole scheme of actions with repulsive names."[2] The process was not always easy, but the results are worth the effort. Formal pleadings and procedures, whether in the ecclesiastical or common law courts, document the actions of cloistered nuns in the defense of their property and privileges, and they illustrate a broad spectrum of very human motives and needs – reminding us of something else that Maitland said: "legal documents, documents of the most technical kind, are the best, often the only evidence that we have for social and economic history, for the history of morality, for the history of practical religion."

2 F. W. Maitland, "Why the History of English Law Is Not Written," in *The Collected Papers of Frederic William Maitland*, ed. H. A. L. Fisher (Cambridge: Cambridge University Press, 1911) vol. 1, p. 486.

Acknowledgments

I am very grateful for the research opportunities and financial assistance afforded me by the Ingram Professorship of History at Texas State University, and two university-sponsored Research Enhancement grants. I thank the former dean of Liberal Arts, Ann Marie Ellis, for her consistent appreciation of faculty efforts and the current dean, Mike Hennessy, for keeping up that wonderful tradition. I gratefully acknowledge all of my colleagues in the History Department for maintaining the congenial ambience that has long been the hallmark of the department. It is that atmosphere that fuels creativity and makes cooperative labor possible and enjoyable. Special thanks to three friends and colleagues extraordinaire, historians Mary Brennan and Lynn Denton, and fellow medievalist Susan Morrison – creative, remarkable women, and such fun to be around.

Research grants from Texas State University's Alkek Library have allowed me to purchase digital images of manuscripts and the interlibrary loan staff, particularly Michelle Williams and Jerry Weathers, have been zealous in their efforts to obtain some very arcane materials as well. I thankfully acknowledge the expert assistance and generosity of library staff farther afield, at the National Archives, Public Records Office, Cambridge University Library, King's College Archive Centre, Cambridge, and the British Library. Special thanks to Bernard Mulcahy, OP, Head Librarian, Dominican Theological Library, Washington, DC.

Throughout the years devoted to research and writing of this book I have profited from the insightful comments and suggestions of many other historians engaged in research on religious women. Thanks especially to Jennifer Kolpacoff Deane, Sean Field, Letha Böhringer, Hildo van Engen, Alison Beach, Anne Winston-Allen, and Connie Berman; to Isabelle Heullant-Donat, Julie Claustre and Elisabeth Lusset, organizers of an international colloquium on enclosure held at Troyes, France, October 22–24, 2009; and to Carmen Mangion, Caroline Bowden, and Louise O'Reilly, who organized the conference of Historians of Women Religious of Britain and Ireland, Queen Mary College, London, June 23–25, 2011. Thanks also to participants at a meeting of the American Catholic Historical Society, New York, January 5, 2009 and those attending the special session in honor of Susan Mosher Stuard at the 43rd International Congress on Medieval Studies, Kalamazoo, Michigan, May 10, 2008, for their helpful comments and questions.

I happily acknowledge long-standing debts of gratitude to James A. Brundage and Robert Somerville whose instruction, support, and guidance have shaped my career as an historian. Essays written in their honor, "*Deus est procurator fatuorum*: Cloistered Nuns and Equitable Decision-Making in the Court of Chancery," in *Law as Profession and Practice in Medieval Europe: Essays in Honor of James A. Brundage*, edited by Ken Pennington and Melodie Harris Eichbauer, Farnham, UK: Ashgate Press, 2011, and "Canon Law and the Spirituality of Cloistered English Nuns," in *Canon Law, Religion, and Politics:* Liber Amicorum *Robert Somerville. Festschrift*, edited by Uta-Renate Bluemental and Anders Winroth, Washington DC: Catholic University of America Press, 2012, have evolved into chapters of this book.

I appreciate the informed criticisms of an anonymous reader which helped me to improve the draft of this manuscript and the consummate professionalism and solicitude of my editor, Caroline Palmer. Finally, I thank my husband, Roger Boylan, who has always believed in me, and my daughter, Margaret Mary Boylan, whose love sustains me. I dedicate this book to her.

Abbreviations

BF	Konrad Eubel, *Bullarium Franciscanum*, 3 vols. 1842–1922.
BRUC	A. B. Emden, *A Biographical Register of the University of Cambridge to 1500*. Cambridge: Cambridge University Press, 1963.
BRUO	A. B. Emden, *A Biographical Register of the University of Oxford to* AD *1500*. Oxford: Clarendon Press, 1957–1959.
BRUO 1501	A. B. Emden, *A Biographical Register of the University of Oxford,* AD *1501 to 1540*. Oxford: Clarendon Press, 1974.
Bull. O.P.	E. T. Ripoll, *Bullarium ordinis fratrum praedicatorum*, 8 vols. Rome, 1729–1740.
C	Early Chancery proceedings: Equity suits before 1558. National Archives.
CCR	William Henry Bird, *Calendar of the Close Rolls Preserved in the Public Record Office. Henry VI*. Nendeln: Kraus Reprint, 1971.
CPL	William Henry Bliss, *Calendar of Entries in the Papal Registers Relating to Great Britain and Ireland: Papal Letters*. London: HMSO, 1893.
CPP	William Henry Bliss, *Calendar of Entries in the Papal Registers Relating to Great Britain and Ireland: Petitions to the Pope,* AD *1342–1419*. London: Eyre and Spottiswoode, 1896.
CPR	*Calendar of Patent Rolls Preserved in the Public Record Office*. London, 1891–.
DDC	*Dictionnaire de droit canonique*, ed. R. Naz, 7 vols. Paris, 1935–1965.
DMA	*Dictionary of the Middle Ages*, ed. Joseph Strayer. 13 vols. New York: Scribner's, 1982–89.
DNB	*Dictionary of National Biography*, ed. Leslie Stephen and Sidney Lee. Oxford: Oxford University Press, 1917–.
E	Records of the Exchequer, and its related bodies, with those of the Office of First Fruits and Tenths, and the Court of Augmentations. National Archives.
Hain	Ludwig F. T. Hain *Repertorium bibliographicum*. 1822.
LR	Records of the Auditors of Land Revenues. National Archives.

Misc. Roll	Miscellaneous Roll. *London Assize of Nuisance 1301–1431. A Calendar* (British History Online)
ODNB	*Oxford Dictionary of National Biography*. Oxford: Oxford University Press, 2004. Online edition, 2008, www.oxforddnb
OED	*Oxford English Dictionary*
PL	Records of the Palatinate of Lancaster. National Archives
Schulte, *QL*	J. Friedrich von Schulte. *Die Geschichte der Quellen und Literatur des canonischen Rechts von Gratian bis auf die Gegenwart*. 3 vols. Stuttgart: F. Enke, 1875–77; Rpt. Graz: Akademische Druck u. Verlagsanstalt, 1956.
Seipp	*Printed Year Book Reports, 1268–1535*, compiled by David J. Seipp (Seipp's Abridgement) available online at www.bu.edu/phpbin/lawyearbooks/display.php?id=13519 (accessed August 10, 2009)
SYO	Syon Abbey Documents. Cambridge, King's College.
VCH	*Victoria History of the Counties of England*
VE	*Valor Ecclesiasticus*

Introduction

The Topic

In 1293, the first two communities of Franciscan nuns, referred to as *Sorores Minores* or Minoresses, were established in England. One was the Abbey of Waterbeach in Cambridgeshire, the other the London Minories. The rule in both monasteries required strict enclosure, and, unlike those English nuns upon whom cloister regulations were externally imposed, the Minoresses appear to have observed it. In subsequent years, three other mendicant houses, two more Franciscan and one Dominican, as well as the Bridgettine community of Syon, also observing strict enclosure, were founded. With the exception of Waterbeach, which was subsumed into the newly established house of Denney in the late fourteenth century, all of the monasteries survived as vital and economically sound institutions up to the time of the Dissolution, and in the case of Syon, beyond.

Confined to monastic precincts, these nuns depended first and foremost on landed endowments for their livelihood, and, like all substantial property owners in late medieval England, they were forced to engage in nearly constant litigation to defend them. Commenting on the astounding rate with which English men and women went to law in the fifteenth century, E. W. Ives estimated that the central common law courts alone heard 3,000 new suits a year.[1] Because each monastery was a corporation with a multigenerational existence, even outright gifts of land could present legal complications. Kings might repent of grants made by their predecessors, and newly elected bishops might need reminding about an ancient tax exemption. And, subsequent to the foundation of a house, bequests were almost never outright gifts.

Grants of rights and privileges, such as the right to collect rents or tithes, or the right to appoint a cleric to a local parish church, increased the opportunities for legal squabbles exponentially. The standard practice of 'farming' tithes and rents in return for a fixed annual fee – a fee which did not always materialize – added further opportunity for litigation. And then there was the overwhelmingly conditional and contingent nature of lay patronage. For instance, a testator might bequeath the proceeds from property in which a surviving spouse possessed a life interest, or order that

1 E. W. Ives, *The Common Lawyers of Pre-Reformation England: Thomas Kebell, a Case Study* (Cambridge: Cambridge University Press, 1983), p. 7.

his gift be paid out of the debts owed him, leaving it up to the nuns he had endowed to successfully claim those debts.

In such a litigious environment, strictly cloistered nuns might have been at a serious disadvantage. Even half a century before the arrival of the first Minoresses, at the close of Henry III's reign (1216–1272), it was still in the interests of religious communities for heads of houses to give their personal attention to lawsuits. The Abbot of Westminster still occasionally appointed his own monks to represent the abbey in King Henry's courts, and, in a 1230 contest with the Abbot of Peterborough, the Benedictine nuns of St Michael's, Stamford, disavowed their incompetent proctor and sent their prioress to the court of the Archbishop of Canterbury to oversee the case in his stead.[2]

By 1300, however, all that had changed.

> The expansion of royal justice and the increased demand for legal remedies led to a corresponding need for the employment of those who could assist expertly in the complexities of litigation and consequently meet the growing "consumer demand." The services of professionals were required for the selection of writs to initiate proceedings, for making the plaintiff's "count" (setting out the claim or grievance), for putting forward legal argument and presenting evidence to the court and for general advice about how to proceed with litigation.[3]

In short, the emergence of a class of professional lawyers made it unnecessary for an abbot to use his monks as attorneys, and a prioress might save herself a trip to court. Employing amateurs of any sort, be they servants, benefactors, or fellow religious, became downright unwise.

By the time the first mendicant nuns arrived in England, then, the practice of the law was well on its way to becoming the exclusive preserve of professionals. Long recognized as having had a profound effect upon the nature of litigation and the direction of legal change, this development has never been studied with reference to women religious, for whom it was no less significant.[4] Dependence on professional lawyers reduced

2 For the abbots of Westminster, see Barbara Harvey, *The Obedientiaries of Westminster Abbey and Their Financial Records*, c. *1275–1540* (Woodbridge: Boydell Press, 2002), p. xxxv. For the case of the nuns, see *VCH Northampton*, vol. 2, p. 98 and David Bell, *What Nuns Read: Books and Libraries in Medieval English Nunneries* (Kalamazoo, MI: Cistercian Publications, 1995), p. 10.

3 Anthony Musson and W. M. Ormrod, *The Evolution of English Justice: Law Politics and Society in the Fourteenth Century* (New York: St Martin's Press, 1999), p. 139.

4 The most recent, and most comprehensive, study of the phenomenon is James A. Brundage, *The Medieval Origins of the Legal Profession* (Chicago: University of Chicago Press, 2008), but overviews of different aspects of English legal history all devote time to this revolutionary transformation. See, for instance, Richard Helmholz, *Canon Law and Ecclesiastical Jurisdiction from 597 to the 1640* (Oxford: Oxford University Press, 2004); Musson and Ormrod, *Evolution*; John Hamilton Baker, *The Legal Profession and*

the practical significance of cloister regulations for nuns. It narrowed the gender gap (the better word might be chasm) which those regulations had created, since now monks found themselves equally dependent on outside agents for the defense of their land and rights. If religious in open monasteries might still choose to appear personally as litigants, it was seldom expedient to do so.

For example, John Wessington, prior of Durham, was perfectly qualified to personally represent his community in a court of law. Wessington had attended Durham College, Oxford, and as chancellor of his convent had "established his reputation as an astute and energetic defender of the monastery's privileges and liberties against external aggression … by an exceptionally ingenious use of Durham's own historical and legal muniments."[5] Yet, when elected prior in 1416, Wessington put the legal affairs of his house in the hands of a cadre of retained professionals whom he and his convent paid handsomely.

Nuns in open monasteries responded similarly. To judge from the number and kind of episcopal fulminations against the Benedictines of St Helen's in Bishopsgate, prioress and nuns alike took every opportunity, whether for business or pleasure, to mingle with secular society.[6] Yet, in 1363, Prioress Margery de Honylane acted via her attorney, Robert de Watlyngton, even when she was merely lodging a complaint in a local assize.[7] Traveling to attend to the business of one's community, unless that business was to parley with retained "men of law," had by this time became associated with poverty, rather than protection of legal interests: Poor nunneries might simply find that they could not afford the professional services that they would have preferred to have at their disposal.[8]

Because the advent of legal professionalism made religious litigants, whether monks or nuns, similarly dependent upon their lawyers, the topic has obvious comparative potential. We get some idea of the caliber of legal representation available to cloistered nuns, for instance, when we compare the education and career paths of their attorneys with those of counsel retained by contemporary monks and unenclosed nuns. We can also draw comparisons with legal professionals acting for laywomen and

the Common Law (London: Hambledon Press, 1986); Paul Brand, *The Origins of the Legal Profession* (Oxford: Blackwell, 1992).

5 R. B. Dobson, *Durham Priory, 1400–1450* (Cambridge: Cambridge University Press, 1973), p. 91.

6 Eileen Power, *Medieval English Nunneries* c. *1275 to 1535* (Cambridge: Cambridge University Press, 1922), p. 395; *VCH County of London*, vol. 1, p. 457.

7 *Misc. Roll FF.* #519.

8 Power, *Medieval English Nunneries*, p. 201; Bell, *What Nuns Read*, pp. 9–10.

men since the trend toward professionalization certainly affected secular clients as well – the steadily increasing reliance of wives and widows on attorneys in their dower suits, for example, has been charted by scholars like Barbara Hanawalt and Sue Sheridan Walker.[9]

The Sources

As historians of women religious well know, there is a 'source gap' to contend with when studying material aspects of the lives of English Franciscan, Dominican, and Bridgettine nuns. Cartularies, those compilations of deeds, charters, and administrative records archived by and relevant to a specific house, are extant for none of the communities.[10] This means reliance on scattered references such as the very few surviving account rolls and valuations of the houses, supplemented by a source decidedly hostile to monastic interests, Henry VIII's survey of monastic wealth at the time of the Dissolution, the *Valor Ecclesiasticus*.[11]

We also lack visitation records. Because all mendicant nuns were exempt from episcopal jurisdiction, bishops were not required to conduct and record their visits to Franciscan or Dominican houses within their dioceses. Visitation by provincials of the respective orders, as prescribed for mendicants, is scarcely mentioned in the annals of English Franciscans and all pre-Reformation records of the English Dominican province have been lost.[12] Although the Bridgettine constitutions of Syon stated the "the bishop of the place be the visitor," registers of the Bishops of London do not record any visitations having taken place.[13]

9 Barbara Hanawalt, *The Wealth of Wives* (Oxford: Oxford University Press, 2007), see especially the text and notes to pp. 98–99. Sue Sheridan Walker, "Litigant Agency in Dower Pleas in the Royal Common Law Courts in Thirteenth- and Early Fourteenth-Century England," *Journal of Legal History* 24 (2003): 215–236.

10 Paul Lee, *Nunneries, Learning, and Spirituality in Late Medieval English Society: The Dominican Priory of Dartford* (York: York Medieval Press, 2001), p. 7; Anne Francis Claudine Bourdillon, *The Order of Minoresses in England* (Manchester: Manchester University Press, 1926), p. 61; E. M. Tomlinson, *A History of the Minories of London* (London: Smith, Elder, 1907), p. 13; R. Dunning, "The Muniments of Syon Abbey: Their Administration and Migration in the Fifteenth and Sixteenth Centuries," *Bulletin of the Institute of Historical Research* 37, no.95 (1964): 103.

11 Bourdillon, *Minoresses*, pp. 28–29.

12 *Ibid*., p. 55. Marilyn Oliva, *The Convent and the Community in Late Medieval England* (Woodbridge: Boydell Press, 1998), p. 8. William Hinnebusch, *The History of the Dominican Order* (Staten Island, NY: Alba House, 1966), p. 393. No records of the English Dominican province are extant according to Jane E. Sayers, *Law and Records in Medieval England* (London: Ashgate, 1988), p. 168.

13 VCH, *Middlesex*, vol. 1, pp. 182–183; G. J. Aungier, *History and Antiquities of Syon Monastery* (London: J. B. Nichols, 1840), p. 245.

In this situation, public records such as those upon which this book depends take on a special value. Although we might expect that litigation involving ecclesiastical persons always took place in the ecclesiastical courts, this was very often *not* the fact in England. By English custom, 'benefit of clergy,' or the right of clerics to be tried exclusively in church courts, was limited to criminal law. Protests of English bishops to the contrary, in civil matters "the clergy were almost as fully subject to the royal courts in England as the laity was."[14] Since the king claimed complete control over temporal property, which after the Constitutions of Clarendon was considered to include advowsons, disputes involving monastic endowments were regularly pleaded in the central royal courts of law or of equity: King's Bench, Common Pleas, Chancery, and Exchequer.

Because judgments given in the king's courts were set down in writing, with copies obtainable at any time to prove a title to property or privilege, royal courts were "the landowner's supreme muniment."[15] And, as valuable as they proved to disputatious gentry, the voluminous records generated by royal courts make them even more valuable to historians of women religious. Plea and memoranda rolls of the common law courts, including many local assizes, the Year Books, which were unofficial summaries of cases heard in these courts, and the Close and Patent Rolls, which often record suits for the recovery of debts and the appointment of attorneys, all reference the activities of cloistered nuns along with other litigants.

Unlike disputes about landed property and suits for the recovery of debt, at least when no pledge of faith prefaced the promise to repay, litigation about tithes and other lucrative spiritual rights and privileges *was* routinely heard in church courts. Although mostly unpublished, large numbers of the records of these courts survive.[16] They too yield the names of cloistered litigants and their legal agents. Consistory court calendars often list the names of advocates and proctors (the rough equivalent in canon law of the advocate/pleader and the attorney of common law), along with case summaries. Episcopal registers reference suits remanded to higher courts and papal registers, and letter books record suits assigned to local abbots and bishops acting as papal judges delegate. When a case was appealed to the Roman curia, documentation, including legal briefs

14 Helmholz, *The Canon Law*, p. 509.

15 Nigel Ramsey, "Retained Legal Counsel, c. 1275–c. 1475," *Transactions of the Royal Historical Society* 35 (1985): 102.

16 For the most extensive listing to date see Charles Donahue and Working Group on Church Court Records, *The Records of Medieval Ecclesiastical Courts* (Berlin: Duncker & Humblot, 1989).

of advocates who aided the pope in decision-making, could become very rich indeed.

Methodology

This book is as much about religious women as it is about the lawyers they employed, and I have divided it accordingly. Chapter 1 deals with the clients. It contrasts the cloistered spirituality of nuns in traditional English orders with that of mendicant and Bridgettine nuns, and evaluates the ways in which late medieval social and legal change facilitated adherence to the strictly enclosed regime under which the latter lived. Chapter 2 deals with the lawyers employed by these contemplatives. It looks at the ways in which legal professionalism manifested itself in the courts and in the training of individuals who acted in them. It also identifies some of the lawyers who worked for cloistered nuns, and assesses their professional qualifications and the ways in which they were recruited and paid. Chapter 3 brings lawyers and their clients together by presenting examples of the formal warrants which established their working relationships. It also deals with the non-litigious work done by lawyers on retainer.

Chapters 4 and 5 describe selected cases tried in the main courts of state. They are representative of the many legal battles waged in common law courts and Chancery, but they are unique in that lawyers engaged in them on behalf of clients *of*, but not *in*, the world. Chapters 6 and 7 treat of disputes tried before or arbitrated by bishops and popes or their delegated judges. A comparative assessment of the performance of legal professionals representing cloistered clients comprises my conclusion, and the appendix provides an annotated list of some of the lawyers known to have acted for those clients.

The natural backdrop for this study is the burgeoning professionalism of law and its practitioners in late medieval England. But lawsuits are much more than legal exercises, and this was a particularly turbulent era. Prolonged war with France and a plague which reduced the population by at least a third between 1350 and 1400; major transformations in patterns of land tenure and usage; unprecedented opportunities for intimidation and extortion of the landed classes unleashed by the rivalry between York and Lancaster in the mid-fifteenth century; and in the first decades of the next, a king "careful of the law and careless of justice," who ineluctably eroded the foundations of English monasticism.[17] How could such things

17 Clayton Roberts and David Roberts, *History of England*, vol. 1 (Englewood Cliffs, NJ: Prentice Hall, 2002), p. 252.

not affect the lives of nuns dependent on landed bequests and on the noble patrons who made them? While we usually catch only a glimpse of the larger political and social forces at work in these disputes, some of the cases presented here would simply never have existed without them.

I

CLIENTS AND LAWYERS

1

Cloistered Spirituality and English Nuns

Worn down by a long property dispute which had depleted the community's resources, Abbess Joan Keteryche (1459–1479) of the Franciscan Abbey of Denney wrote a letter to her relative and patron, John Paston. It was an importunate letter that ended with this reminder: "Consydre how we be closyd withynne the ston wallys, and may no odyr wyse speke with you but only be wrytynge."[1] Hoping to persuade Paston to assist her, the abbess had needed to strike just the right rhetorical note and did so by mentioning the fact of her strict enclosure. It hardly signified that, by virtue of a papal mandate issued over a century earlier, every abbess in England as well as on the continent *should* have faced similar constraints. To remind her kinsman of the distinctive, strict, nature of enclosure at Denney was to gain much-needed leverage.

As Joan Keteryche knew well, the cloistered spirituality of the mendicant nuns of Denney was not typical of late medieval English nuns, notwithstanding a concerted papal attempt to make it so. That attempt began with the well-known 1298 decree of Pope Boniface VIII, *Periculoso*. Substituting the inflexible papal will for flexible local prerogative, in language reminiscent of his more famous decrees, *Periculoso* applied the law of enclosure to "nuns of every community or order, in every part of the world, both collectively and individually."[2] It sought to restrict both exit from and entrance into monastic precincts – referred to respectively as 'active' and 'passive' enclosure. "Reasonable and obvious cause" might mitigate claustration, but only upon receipt of a "special license" granted by the "appropriate authority."

Boniface VIII was not heedless of the fact that only the possession of adequate worldly goods could ensure this level of separation from worldly affairs. He required nunneries to accept new members only if their communities could "support them with goods or revenues and without

1 *VCH*, *Cambridge*, vol. 2, p. 299. Also see, Bourdillon, *Minoresses*, p. 30; Lee, *Nunneries*, p. 37.

2 For a detailed account of the decree, including Latin text as an appendix, see Elizabeth Makowski, *Canon Law and Cloistered Women:* Periculoso *and Its Commentators, 1298–1545* (Washington, DC: Catholic University of America Press, 1997).

penury." He recognized that bishops, abbots, and other agents responsible for carrying out his measures would incur costs in doing so (for renovation of existing structures, sealing certain doors, constructing walls, etc.), and instructed them to "meet expenses incurred therein from the alms procured from the faithful for this purpose." This having been said, there could be no question that *Periculoso was* to be implemented. Invoking the "threat of divine judgment and the prospect of eternal damnation," he determined that the recalcitrant were to be "constrained through ecclesiastical censure, with no right of appeal."

Boniface included *Periculoso* in his official compilation of canon law, the *Liber Sextus*. He then sent copies of his collection to the law faculties of universities throughout Europe, since it would be the job of academic canon lawyers to interpret and to clarify the laws it contained. Despite its relatively straightforward mandate, the decree left these commentators with a wide range of issues that demanded such clarification.

The earliest interpreters, such as Joannes Monachus (d. 1313) and Johannes Andreae (d. 1348), author of the standard interpretation (ordinary gloss) of *Periculoso*, noted a number of questions that the decree had raised but not resolved. Who, for instance, was the "appropriate authority" empowered to grant licenses to enter or leave the cloister? Were nuns who had already made their profession under a less strict rule of life to be compelled to accept enclosure? Could an abbess conduct visitations of the houses under her supervision without herself violating the law of enclosure? Were the "ecclesiastical censures" which constrained the disobedient to be construed as excommunication?

In each instance, early commentators tended to a strict interpretation of the pope's words. Only the local official, usually a bishop, who had jurisdiction over a monastery of nuns could grant licenses lifting enclosure. A professed nun might indeed be compelled to abide by *Periculoso*, even if that meant living under obligations stricter than those she had vowed to observe. Abbesses, as nuns, were bound by the rules of enclosure, so could not possibly conduct visitations of houses under their jurisdiction. The ecclesiastical sanction with which the pope had threatened violators was to be understood as excommunication.[3]

Later commentators were not, however, so unequivocally supportive of Boniface VIII's hieratic aims; even those who were questioned *Periculoso*'s practical impact. As in his more celebrated fiats, *Clericis laicos* (1296) and *Unam sanctam* (1302), Boniface had asserted comprehensive papal power over far-flung peoples and jurisdictions, in utter disregard of prevailing

3 *Ibid*., pp. 53, 60–61, 75–76.

practice.[4] Academic lawyers could not but debate the newly minted right of the papacy to impose a stricter way of life on unwilling nuns. They also observed that the decree, whatever its intrinsic merits, was simply not being enforced in certain places, Venice being an often-cited example. Practicing canon lawyers, whose clients were occasionally the very nuns affected by *Periculoso*, sometimes went a step further than the theorists. Two examples, from the pens of two of the most renowned advocates of their times, will suffice.

The first, *Consilium XCVI*, is found in the collected opinions of the esteemed canonist and judge of the Roman Rota, Oldradus de Ponte (d. 1343?).[5] In this formal consultation, designed to advise a judge or litigant on complex points of law, Oldradus flatly denied that *Periculoso* could impose strict claustration on an already professed nun if she were unwilling to accept it.

As with so many edited *consilia*, the names of the parties to the case and other introductory *formulae* are missing. The opinion simply begins with a question: Is the pope able to enclose (*includere*) a nun against her will? "Joannes Monachus and Johannes Andreae both say that it is possible for the pope to do so," observes Oldradus, citing *Periculoso* as well as Johannes Andreae's gloss.[6]

> But the opposite prevails, since every entrant to a monastic order is given a probationary year within which to experience the harshness of the rule, and during which he or she might freely leave if it does not suit them [canons from the *Liber Extra* and the *Liber Sextus* are cited here as proof texts]. Therefore it does not seem that a nun should be held to a harsher form of life against her will, or that, at the least, she be given another [probationary] year.[7]

4 Brian Tierney, *The Crisis of Church and State 1050 –1300* (Toronto: University of Toronto Press, 1988 rpt of 1964 edition) contains a succinct overview and translation of both famous decrees.

5 Oldradus de Ponte, *Consilia* (Venice: Apud Franciscum Zilettum, 1571), p. 38. For a discussion of the case see Elizabeth Makowski, "Cloister Contested: *Periculoso* as Authority in Late Medieval *Consilia*," *The Jurist* 71, no. 2 (2011): 334–348. A short and still valuable introduction to the genre as a whole is provided by Peter Riesenberg, "The Consilia Literature: A Prospectus," *Manuscripta* 6 (1962): 3–23.

6 Makowski, *Canon Law*, pp. 51–52, 60–62. As noted earlier, both the commentators whom Oldradus cites had argued that the papacy could bind a nun to obey a rule of life stricter than the one under which she had entered the monastery. In the opinion of Joannes Monachus, this action was defensible because *Periculoso* merely addressed the manner in which any monastic rule should be lived out; it guaranteed that vagrancy and association with secular folk, neither of which fitted the life of a nun, would be avoided. Johannes Andreae had made shorter shrift of the whole issue. Regulars, unlike secular clergy, relinquished personal volition when professed. Professed nuns, therefore, simply had no basis for resisting enclosure.

7 "Sed movet contrarium, nam ab initio datur ingresso annus probationis, ut experiatur

By deciding that compliance with *Periculoso* could not be routinely compelled, Oldradus had subjected *Periculoso* to serious reinterpretation. In doing so, he parted company from Joannes Monachus, Johannes Andreae, and other canonists who had required professed nuns, by virtue of their vow of obedience, to acquiesce to strict enclosure. His contrary point of view was to appeal, however, to at least one prominent jurist of the next generation. In his commentary on *Periculoso*, Petrus de Ancharano (d. 1416) reproduced Oldradus' argument verbatim (albeit without attribution), reminding us of the interdependent relationship between the courts and schools of law.[8]

Oldradus' spare straightforward brief contrasts sharply with our second example, written by the active diplomat and distinguished lawyer, Cardinal Franciscus Zabarella (d. 1417). In this opinion, his *Consilium XLVI*, both the litigant in the case and the specific circumstances of her action come to light.[9] It is an intriguing and perhaps not altogether unique story.

A professed Benedictine nun "about twenty-five years old" and referred to throughout as "Domina L" wanted to transfer to the monastery of Corpus Christi, an Augustinian house under Dominican supervision. When she asked her abbess for a license to do so, she was not only refused that license but also incarcerated. Along with the other nuns, the abbess conspired to deny her the right to make her petition to the pope for such a transfer. They threatened L and tried to alter her decision by defaming the monastery of Corpus Christi. In response to these pressures, L swore an oath to remain where she was and to live under obedience to the abbess. But when as a consequence of her oath she was set free, she changed her mind and secretly left the Benedictine house to enter the monastery of Corpus Christi.

Once she had taken up residence there, L decided to safeguard her new status by hiring a lawyer (*procuratorem iuridicum*) to act for her in obtaining the transfer license that she had requested from her erstwhile abbess. She was requesting one as well from the prioress, and from the ordinary of the Benedictine house, the bishop. The questions posed to Cardinal Zabarella – by a litigant or by the court, we cannot be sure – are two: Is Domina L in fact a nun of Corpus Christi, or was her petition to transfer there nullified by her oath to remain at the Benedictine house? By

asperitates ordinis: infra quem, si ei non placit, potest exire ... Non ergo videtur, quod contra voluntatem suam ad asperiorem vitam debeat astringi, vel saltem quin concedatur sibi alius annus."

8 Petrus de Ancharao, *Super sexto Decretalium* (Bologna, 1583) *de statu regularium c. 1*, 354. See also, Makowski, *Canon Law*, pp. 80–82.

9 Franciscus Zabarella, *Consilia* (Venice: 1581), p. 39.

leaving her first monastery secretly without a license, had L incurred the sentence of excommunication?

The first issue in this case is the one with which Cardinal Zabarella deals most extensively. As promises invoking God to witness, oaths were taken very seriously by medieval jurists. Perjury attended their violation, and the law concerning oaths, their consequences, and the circumstances in which they might be mitigated, was complex.[10] Suffice it to say that Cardinal Zabarella finds the oath to be so mitigated because it was made under duress and on the basis of false information, that is, slanders against the community at Corpus Christi. He then turns his attention to the charge that, by leaving her Benedictine monastery without authorization, L had incurred the sentence of excommunication. If she had, her legal right to engage a proctor to secure her transfer licenses would be in question.

"I am not about to run through all the instances of excommunication *ipso iure*," he testily responds – the materials with which he had been provided evidently failing to include a specific citation.

> If, however, it is *Ut Periculosa* that is being alleged in this instance, it speaks in another case but does nothing [here]. Also, in Venice the nuns whose monasteries are open, and who do not observe the clause in the law concerning unlicensed exits, should not be called excommunicates since both their superiors and the Pope know about and tolerate the situation.[11]

Because it is her right to retain a proctor that is an underlying issue, the cardinal ends his *consilium* by stating that even if she *were* at present an excommunicate, Domina L would be entitled to complete the legal actions she had previously initiated. It is clear from his earlier statements, however, that he was not inclined to view her as one.[12]

Like Oldradus de Ponte, Cardinal Zabarella had seriously challenged cloister regulation – in this case, the routine enforcement of active enclosure as outlined in *Periculoso*. His observation that the nuns of Venice did

10 Richard Helmholz, *The Spirit of Classical Canon Law* (Athens, GA: University of Georgia Press, 1996), pp. 167, 172–173.

11 "Quod autem egrediendo fuerit excommunicata quia non dicitur quo iure, non curo discurrere per iura in quibus quis est excommunicatus ipso iure. Sed si pro hoc allegatur cap. Ut periculoso [tit] ne cler.vel monachi, lib 6. dico quod si bene suspicitur, loquitur in alio casu & nihil facit. Item maxime Venetiis non debet dici moniales fore excommunicatas cum pro maiori parte monasteria monialium sint aperta & non observent clausulam de qua iure disponitur quod superiores & Papa sciunt & tollerantur."

12 On the ability of the excommunicate to follow such a course of action see Elisabeth Vodola, *Excommunication in the Middle Ages* (Berkeley: University of California Press, 1986). Chapter 4.

not observe strict cloister rules was scarcely new since it had been retailed by Johannes Andreae, Petrus de Ancharano, Joannes Koelner de Vanckel, and other commentators on *Periculoso.*[13] Unlike those theorists, however, the cardinal used the example of noncompliance to argue against the imposition of the prescribed penalty of excommunication for unlicensed exit from the cloister. That officials responsible for implementing enclosure of nuns, including popes themselves, acquiesced to this state of affairs made excommunication in other instances of unlicensed exit untenable. Finally, the cardinal strengthened his position with his choice of a proof text.

It will be remembered that academic commentators had routinely interpreted the "ecclesiastical censures" of *Periculoso* as excommunication. Nevertheless, the decree itself did not contain the word. Another Bonifacian fiat, however, one unhelpfully named *Ut periculosa,* did. Also found in the *Liber Sextus*, but under the title *ne clerici vel monachi saecularibus negotiis se immisceant, Ut periculosa* prescribed excommunication as a penalty for professed monks who left their monasteries without permission in order to pursue legal or medical studies.[14] Their unlicensed exit, furthermore, had to have been accompanied by a "casting off" of the religious habit. If this was a less than apposite proof text to cite with respect to the facts of the Domina L case, Cardinal Zabarella made his point by doing so. Even when there was no ambiguity about the designated penalty for leaving the cloister, even when that penalty was clearly prescribed by law, failure to apply it in one well-known instance imperiled the ability of authorities to do so in another.

Like their colleagues on the continent, noted English canonists began to interpret *Periculoso* shortly after its promulgation. In the fourteenth and fifteenth centuries, two of England's most famous canonists, John Acton and William Lyndwood, glossed *Periculoso* in light of previous, specifically English, legatine and episcopal statutes.[15] Both interpreted the papal mandate as augmenting earlier national legislation, and both noted the almost impossible task of enforcing it in England.

At the close of his 1348 commentary, John Acton wrote of that task with uncharacteristic verve:

13 Makowski, *Canon Law*, pp. 74–75, 80, 91.

14 *VI* 3.24.2.

15 Makowski, *Canon Law*, Chapter 7. This chapter deals in greater detail with these English canonists. For essays on famous English canonists see J. H. Baker, *Monuments of Endless Labours: English Canonists and Their Work, 1300–1900* (London: Hambledon Press, 1998).

> the nuns respond to these statutes, or to others concerning their lasciviousness, saying that those who made those laws were putting much confidence in their own highmindedness when they burdened them with these hard and intolerable restrictions. We see that these statutes are never, or badly, observed and so we might ask why the holy fathers bothered to labor so hard only to "beat the air."[16]

Almost a century later, Acton's words were still relevant, echoed as they are in the *Provinciale* (1422–1430) of William Lyndwood. *Periculoso should* have the force of a general law, opined Lyndwood, but it did not. English nunneries subject to monastic superiors were "for the most part" compliant, but those supervised by bishops continued to disregard regulations the legality of which they doubted. Less willing than Acton to concede the failure of the papal initiative, Lyndwood encouraged tepid bishops who had been swayed by recalcitrant nuns to renew their labors and so fulfill their enjoined responsibilities.

Lyndwood's characterization of both bishops and nuns was a negative one, but what in fact was going on? English episcopal registers show that some late medieval bishops were not the ineffectual figures depicted by Lyndwood. Beginning in 1299, the Archbishop of Canterbury Robert Winchelsy (1293–1313) and his suffragans began sending copies of *Periculoso* to nunneries in their dioceses. A few hardy bishops even attended to its implementation by visiting the houses under their jurisdiction. None of these probably regretted his zeal more than Bishop Dalderby of London who, in 1300, was repaid for his eloquent explication of the details of their new cloistered life by having a copy of *Periculoso* hurled at his head by the unhappy nuns of Markyate.[17]

Throwing unwelcome papal directives at them might get their attention, but bishops tended to respond better to reasoned objections, coupled with well-timed shows of local/legal opposition. Nuns who effectively resisted strict enclosure used both of these techniques, and their reasons for rejecting claustration were generally twofold. William Lyndwood had alluded to the first when he mentioned nuns ignoring a papal directive "the legality of which they doubted."

Many sisters asked how they could be legally compelled, even by papal decree, to maintain strict active and passive enclosure when that meant living under obligations stricter than those they had vowed to observe at the time of profession. It was a good question since, as we have seen, even canon lawyers could not agree about the answer. For one thing, monastic

16 Makowski, *Canon Law*, p. 104.

17 Power, *Medieval English Nunneries*, pp. 351–352. See as well, Makowski, *Canon Law*, p. 115.

profession produced some uniform but by no means unilateral results. Profession in an order created reciprocal obligations between regulars and their monasteries. By taking her vows a nun bound herself inviolably to a religious community and that community in turn bound itself to her – each monastery being obliged to provide its members with food and other necessities of life in perpetuity. Nuns were quite well aware of the reciprocal obligations attached to profession and they even took legal action when they felt themselves defrauded of the lifelong economic support they had a right to expect.

In a case that came to the attention of the noted canon lawyer Dominicus de Sancto Geminiano, we see a particularly fine example of such an action. In this instance, a professed nun sued to be readmitted to her monastery and reinstated into the community with all of the rights that entailed. Her suit for restitution was countered by her sister nuns on the grounds that the plaintiff had left voluntarily with all her belongings. There had been no forcible ejection, they claimed, no spoliation; the plaintiff had renounced her rights and therefore had no basis for a suit demanding restitution. Additionally, it was contended that the plaintiff had committed sexual indiscretions which should by themselves have been grounds for her expulsion. Despite this last allegation, Dominicus de Sancto Geminiano argued that the plaintiff's suit for restitution, based on what the monastery owed her, should stand.[18] Exactly what the nun in question, or any professed nun, owed to her monastic community in return was less clear.

Although every statement of profession included the standard vows of poverty, chastity, and obedience, the particular words spoken and the attendant rituals reflected an order's characteristic vision of itself.[19] In Benedictine, Augustinian, Cluniac, and Gilbertine monasteries, that vision did not include strict cloistering and profession formulae consequently made no mention of it. For example, the complete formula of profession at the wealthy and prestigious Benedictine priory of Little Marlow in the county of Buckingham in England is as follows:

> In the name of God, Amen. I, Sister Constance, in the presence of Almighty God and our blessed lady St Mary, patron of this monastery and all angels and saints of heaven, and of you, reverend Father in God, John bishop of Lincoln and ordinary of this diocese, and in the presence of all this honourable witness,

18 Dominicus de Sancto Geminiano, *Consilia* (Lyon: Jacobus Giunta), 1541, fol. 15.

19 Nancy Bradley Warren, *Spiritual Economies: Female Monasticism in Later Medieval England* (Philadelphia: University of Pennsylvania Press, 2001). Chapters 1 and 2 deal particularly with such distinctions among Benedictine, Franciscan, and Bridgettine nuns.

> vow offer and fully give myself to serve Almighty God during my life natural in this monastery of Little Marlow, dedicated in honour of God and of our blessed lady St Mary. And for this intent and purpose here renounce forever and utterly forsake the world, and property of temporal substance and goods of the same and all other worldly delights and pleasures, taking upon me wilful poverty; vowing also and promising ever to live in pure chastity during my life: to change my secular life into regular conversation and religious manners, promising and vowing due and reverent obedience unto you, Reverend Father in God, John bishop of Lincoln and your successors, bishops; and unto my lady and mother Dame Margaret, now prioress of this monastery, and to her successors, prioresses of the same. And utterly from henceforth I forsake mine own proper will, and not to follow the same but to follow the will of my Superior in all lawful and canonical commandments. And to observe this holy order and religion according to the holy rule of St Benedict and all the laudable constitutions of this monastery by the gracious assistance of Our Lord Jesus Christ. In witness whereof I do put and sign with mine own hand to this my profession.[20]

Even when mandates from general chapters required the acceptance of enclosure by nunneries that wished to be officially designated as Cistercian, constitutions and house charters continued to avoid any mention of it in that order as well. For instance, the proposed cloistering of the nominally Cistercian house of Rechentshofen was objected to as being against the wishes of the founders and the earliest Cistercian foundations, including the well-known and aristocratic abbey of Las Huelgas, Spain, were clearly not strictly cloistered foundations.[21] When professed nuns belonging to any of these traditional orders objected to *Periculoso*, or to later Observant reforms which incorporated its strictures, they often did so making explicit reference to such incontrovertible facts. This happened all over Europe.

According to the chronicler of Meaux Abbey, for example, all Yorkshire nuns remained uncloistered nearly a century after attempts to enforce *Periculoso*, since they said that they "refused to be bound by regulations stricter than those that they had undertaken to observe at their profession."[22] When the Benedictine nuns of Rijnsburg Abbey solicited

20 "Houses of Benedictine Nuns: The Priory of Little Marlow," in *A History of the County of Buckingham*, vol. 1 (1905), pp. 357–360. Online at www.british-history.ac.uk/report.aspx?compid=40308 (accessed June 10, 2008).

21 Anne Winston-Allen, *Convent Chronicles: Women Writing about Women and Reform in the Late Middle Ages* (University Park: Pennsylvania State University Press, 2004), p. 132; Louis J. Lekai, *The Cistercians* (Kent, OH: Kent State University Press, 1977), Chapter 22; Constance Berman, *Women and Monasticism in Medieval Europe: Sisters and Patrons of the Cistercian Reform* (Kalamazoo, MI: Medieval Institute Publications, 2002).

22 John Tillotson, "Visitation and Reform of the Yorkshire Nunneries in the Fourteenth Century," *Northern History* 30 (1994): 2.

legal advice to bolster their opposition to the reforms of Nicholas of Cusa, they did so claiming that the cardinal could not impose upon them a stricter rule than that which they had followed "as far back as human memory could recall."[23] Similarly, the lawyer acting on behalf of a group of Perugian tertiaries in their struggle against attempts by Observant Franciscans to cloister them in 1469, argued that the women should keep their "original and accustomed rule."[24] And when the Abbess of Santa Clara of Barcelona refused the observance of strict active and passive enclosure enjoined upon her in 1494, she claimed that it was "contrary to the use, practice, and custom of the monastery."[25]

Nuns in traditional orders throughout Europe also made a convincing case against enclosure on economic grounds. Without continued access to the larger world, they claimed, they would be impoverished. Were they to keep to their cloisters, they would not be able to oversee collection of rents, litigation over property, and sundry other business affairs crucial to the economic health of their houses. If fallen on hard times, they would no longer be able to go out to beg for alms, or make visits to relatives and friends to ask for money. Patrons who would no longer be able to board daughters or wives (for a fee) at their convents, or whose children could not be assured of instruction by the sisters, would not be likely to continue to support the nuns. Likewise, the fees collected for the performance of other 'community services' such as providing hospitality to noble ladies and their retinues, acting as godmothers, and providing secure retirement lodgings, would disappear.

Since it had been anticipated by Boniface VIII, this claim might have been countered if more bishops had acted in accord with papal pragmatism and, like the zealous monastic reformer Johannes Busch, taken pains to secure an ample endowment for a house *before* expecting its members to realize the cloistered ideal.[26] Not that this was an easy task, since both nuns and their lay supporters had been used to very different sorts of economic arrangements.

At the Cistercian monastery of Marienkammer near Halle, for example, Johannes Busch learned that kinsmen willing to provide private support for their daughters who had become nuns were not always willing to give

23 Winston-Allen, *Convent Chronicles*, p. 137.

24 Katherine Gill, "Scandala: Controversies Concerning *clausura* and Women's Religious Communities in Late Medieval Italy," in *Christendom and Its Discontents*. ed. Scott L. Waugh and Peter D. Diehl (Cambridge: Cambridge University Press, 1996), p. 180.

25 Elizabeth Lehfeldt, "Discipline, Vocation, and Patronage: Spanish Religious Women in a Tridentine Microclimate," *Sixteenth Century Journal* 30 no. 4 (1999): 1019.

26 See for example, Johannes Busch, *Chronicon Windeshemense und Liber de reformatione monasteriorum*, ed. Karl Grube (Halle: Otto Hendel, 1886), pp. 572, 588–591, 671.

bequests for general use. Providing endowments for a community as a whole sometimes required him to preach monitory sermons to the locals, or to threaten to move all the nuns in a town to distant houses.[27]

In England, too, established custom and the desires of the laity opposed attempts at economic restructuring, and many nuns argued that it need not be begun. When adequate endowments could not be obtained, English ordinaries agreed. Lay boarders, pensioners, and children schooled within cloister confines continued to supply needed income to nuns while those nuns rendered the services which founders and patrons had long come to rely upon.

At length, legal consultants, sympathetic bishops, and subsequent popes responding to the arguments and actions of nuns in traditional open monasteries, all but undid the papal policy of enclosure that had been inaugurated by Pope Boniface VIII. Compromises between nuns, their diocesan overseers, and popes themselves soon became the norm.[28] Licenses to leave cloister precincts on monastic business, for pilgrimages, and reasons of health, among other things, abounded. Indults for outsiders to enter the cloister were granted with such liberality that the restrictions set out in *Periculoso* had little impact on the majority of late medieval English nuns. An observation from the *Victoria County History* citing the hapless Bishop Dalderby's attempts to impose those restrictions on the Benedictine nuns of Little Marlowe, nicely sums up the larger situation:

> There are no visitations of this house recorded in the episcopal registers except one of Bishop Dalderby in 1300, which was merely for the purpose of explaining to the nuns the Statute of Pope Boniface VIII. *Pro clausura monialium*. This statute was intended to compel the English nuns of all orders to observe a stricter enclosure; but though Bishop Dalderby did his duty conscientiously by explaining it to all the houses under his care – sometimes under rather trying circumstances – it seems to have been quite ineffectual. The English Benedictine nuns and Austin canonesses never had been strictly enclosed, and quietly ignored the new regulations, even though they came from the pope himself. In later episcopal visitations the nuns of these two orders were often ordered not to go out without the consent of their superiors: but there was no established rule or custom before the Reformation to prevent them going out of the cloister at all.[29]

27 *Ibid.*, pp. 571–572. It is also reported in Power, *Medieval English Nunneries*, pp. 673–674.

28 Tillotson, "Visitation and Reform," pp. 20–21. Makowski, *Canon Law*, pp. 115–121. Gill, *Scandala*, pp. 191 ff. She refers to the words which adorn so many fourteenth- and fifteenth-century papal exemptions: "notwithstanding the decisions of our predecessor Boniface VII," as "*Periculoso*'s legal solvent."

29 "Houses of Benedictine Nuns."

But, as Abbess Joan Keteryche's letter reminds us, there *were* strictly cloistered nuns in late medieval England. Those nuns closely approximated the Bonifacian ideal, although they were not the products of papal manipulation. They were the latecomers to the English scene, Franciscan, Dominican, and Bridgettine nuns whose spiritual ideal required, and whose economic circumstances allowed for, adherence to strict active enclosure. The remainder of this chapter will be devoted to analyzing the spirituality at the core of these newer orders, and to assessing how those ideals were able to be realized in practice.

The four nunneries of the Franciscan order in England were products of female initiative and linked to continental developments which accorded a distinctive place to religious women in monastic renewal.[30] The Minories, outside Aldgate in the parish of St Botolph, London, was founded in 1293 by Blanche, Queen of Navarre, with the assistance of her husband, Edmund Earl of Lancaster.[31] The wealthy widow Denise de Munchensey founded Waterbeach in Cambridgeshire in the same year, and Denney was established only a mile away in 1342 by another widow, Mary of St Pol, Countess of Pembroke.[32] Between 1364 and 1367, Bruisyard in Suffolk was founded by Lionel, Duke of Clarence, in memory of his mother-in-law, Maud of Lancaster, granddaughter of Blanche of Navarre.[33]

The nuns in all of these houses observed a version of the Rule of St Clare which was known as the Isabella Rule. Isabelle, sister of King Louis IX of France and founder of the Abbey of Longchamp outside of Paris, was responsible for its distinctive features. Among them was the specification that the nuns of Longchamp, and others who followed her rule, would be known as *Sorores Minores* (Sisters Minor; Minoresses), a name suggesting the close relationship that Isabelle wished her nuns to have to the male Franciscan *Fratres Minores* who would minister to them spiritually.[34] Like

30 Warren, *Spiritual Economies*, p. 13.

31 *VCH London*, vol. 1, pp. 516–519 for an overview of the history of the house; Bourdillon, *Minoresses*, p. 16; Edward Murray Tomlinson, *A History of the Minories, London* (London: Smith, Elder, 1907), p. 12.

32 *VCH Cambridge*, vol. 2, pp. 292–295; pp. 295–302 for overviews; Bourdillon, *Minoresses*, pp. 14–21.

33 *VCH Suffolk*, vol. 2, pp. 131–132 for an overview; Bourdillon, *Minoresses*, pp. 22–25; Loveday Lewes Gee, *Women, Art and Patronage from Henry III to Edward III, 1216–1377* (Woodbridge: Boydell Press, 2002), p. 130.

34 Sean Field, *Isabelle of France* (Notre Dame, IN: University of Notre Dame Press, 2006). Chapters 3 and 4 discuss the composition and content of the rule in detail and reference to its success in England. Also see, Gertrude Mlynarczyk, *Ein Franziskanerinnenkloster im 15. Jahrhundert* (Bonn: Ludwig Röhrscheid Verlag, 1987), pp. 36–41; Bourdillon, *Minoresses*, pp. 8–9; Warren, *Spiritual Economies*, p. 13.

all Franciscan nuns, however, the Minoresses were also referred to in the rule as *sorores inclusae* (enclosed sisters) since they added a fourth vow at the time of profession, namely the vow to live *sub claustra*.[35] To this end, the Isabella Rule provided substantial regulations for servants sent out of the abbey on behalf of the nuns and it regulated the very limited conversations professed nuns might have with visitors. In the parlor there was to be a curtained grille to shield them from view and a *rota*, or wheel, set into a door to allow the sisters to take in food and other necessities without themselves being seen. Outsiders were required to secure papal and not merely episcopal permission for entry into the cloister precincts. In the words of the rule, each nun "shall dwell all the days of her life enclosed, as a treasure kept to the sovereign king."[36]

A firm understanding of, and adherence to, the Isabella Rule in English houses was facilitated by the fact that the first nuns settling them came from Longchamp.[37] In the license granted to Denise de Munchensey for the establishment of Waterbeach we read of the Minoresses of the order of St Clare, whom she is bringing there "from beyond the seas," and Joan de Nevers, fifth Abbess of Longchamp, became the first abbess there.[38] Blanche of Navarre (whose uncle was Louis IX) brought Minoresses from Longchamp to her London foundation in the same year.[39]

Similar arrangements assured compliance with the monastic rules which governed life at the two other contemplative houses upon which this study focuses: Dartford and Syon. In 1346 four experienced Dominican nuns from the French priory of Poissy were the first settlers of Dartford Priory, and when Henry V laid the foundation stone of Syon in 1415, nuns from the Bridgettine mother house of Vadstena, Sweden, were recruited to live there.[40]

As was the case with all Dominican and Bridgettine communities, nuns at Dartford and Syon observed the Rule of St Augustine, complemented by constitutions of their respective orders – a legal means of

35 Field, *Isabelle*, p. 79. For the Rule of St Clare see *Francis and Clare, The Complete Works*, ed. Regis Armstrong and Ignatius Brady (New York: Paulist Press, 1982), pp. 209–225.

36 Quoted in Bourdillon, *Minoresses*, p. 62.

37 Field, *Isabelle*, p. 119.

38 *CPR, 1292–1301*, 63.

39 Bourdillon, *Minoresses*, p. 16.

40 Lee, *Nunneries*, p. 20; *VCH Kent*, vol. 2, pp. 181–190 for an overview; Aungier, *History*, pp. 21–31; Bridget Morris, *St Birgitta of Sweden* (Woodbridge: Boydell Press, 1999), p. 171; *VCH Middlesex*, vol. 1, pp. 182–191 for an overview.

circumventing the Fourth Lateran Council's 1215 ban on new orders.[41] The Augustinian rule set down only very basic regulations for a monastic life, and it is in the constitutions that the peculiar features of the respective orders come to life. The constitutions observed by the nuns of Dartford were those promulgated for all Dominican nunneries by the general chapter of the order in 1259.[42] These constitutions included regulations for maintaining strict active enclosure: Two keys were to be used to lock the outer doors; communion was to be received through a grille; entrance into the cloister was restricted to monarchs, the highest ecclesiastical officials, and founders; and only the prioress, accompanied by "three sisters of respectable age," was allowed to speak with them.

The constitutions of the Bridgettines of Syon were even more detailed in their treatment of enclosure, Bridgettine spirituality being especially molded by the conviction that even the strictest monastic orders had lately succumbed to laxness.[43] Conversations with seculars were permitted on Sundays and great feast days, but then only with the license of the abbess, in company of other sisters, and at the grated windows designated for such visits. These windows might, again with permission, be opened if a nun requested that her relatives be able to see as well as to hear her. Such requests were to be made only after reflection upon the greater reward reaped in the hereafter by resisting the temptation to do so. As at Dartford, the nuns of Syon were to be heard, but not seen, even by their confessors. To ensure that all members of the community knew of these important specifications, the Constitutions, in their entirety, were to be read aloud three times a year.[44]

From this brief overview, it is apparent that when they took their vows of profession English mendicant and Bridgettine novices knew they would be expected to observe strict enclosure. In the case of the Minoresses, the addition of a fourth vow underscored the centrality of cloistering to the Franciscan contemplative ideal. Among Bridgettines and Dominicans, profession formulae were worded to require a candidate's consent to the

41 Lee, *Nunneries*, p. 25–26; Roger Ellis, Viderunt Eam Filie Syon*: The Spirituality of the English House of a Medieval Contemplative Order from Its Beginnings to the Present Day* (Salzburg: Institut für Anglistik und Amerikanistik, 1984). pp. 3, 40.

42 Lee, *Nunneries*, p. 26.

43 Auke Jelsma, "The Appreciation of Bridget of Sweden (1303–1373) in the Fifteenth Century," in *Women and Men in Spiritual Culture XIV–XVII Centuries*, ed. E. Schulte van Kessel (The Hague: Netherlands Government Publications Office, 1986), pp. 163–175, provides a most lucid discussion of the spirit of the founder and her rule. Aungier, *History*, includes the constitutions of the order in his appendix, beginning at p. 249. Ellis, Viderunt Eam, p. 35 highlights those portions emphasizing enclosure.

44 Ellis, Viderunt Eam, p. 3.

obligations enjoined not only by the rule of St Augustine, but also by the constitutions of their respective orders.[45] These nuns, consequently, could never later assert that the cloister rules under which they were expected to live were outside additions "stricter than the ones under which they had been professed." That they would be less likely to want to make that assertion since they had opted to enter an already enclosed order, seems like a reasonable assumption, and one confirmed by our sources.

But no matter how heartfelt the desire to detach themselves from worldly affairs, mendicant and Bridgettine nuns could not have successfully done so without the compliance of their lay supporters. Relatives, friends, and patrons expected a different kind of 'community service' from contemplative nuns than they did from nuns in open monasteries. The primary appeal of the new orders to benefactors lay not in the regular involvement of religious women with the community, but in their ascetic distance from it.[46] That is not to say that all traditional interaction with the laity was nonexistent. It was human nature to want to get closer to the field of sanctity that a house of ascetic women represented; yet, even as regards passive enclosure, expectations were not the same as for open monasteries.

When locals heard mass in the conventual church, they did so separated by a screen from the "pure women who sing with their high and skillful voices."[47] Although licenses allowing noble women to visit for various periods of time are documented, there was nothing like the press of visitors that often descended on traditional nunneries, and those who received such licenses seemed intent on more than a change of scene.[48] The pious Maud of Oxford, for example, chose to visit Bruisyard instead of Campsey Abbey because the latter monastery was too popular among

45 Aungier, *History*, p. 317, reproduces the formulae.

46 Gee, *Women, Art and Patronage*, Chapter 1, discusses motives for patronage of the stricter orders, such as the Cistercians and Minoresses. Winston-Allen, *Convent Chronicles*, p. 87 mentions the popular wisdom that the more devout the religious, the more effective her prayers. Bourdillon, *Minoresses*, p. 50, suggests that any hint of slack practice would jeopardize long-term patronage.

47 Lee, *Nunneries*, pp. 98–99, quoting Christine de Pisan whose daughter was a Dominican nun at Poissy Priory.

48 Bourdillon, *Minoresses*, pp. 62–63, notes that papal permission was applied for in the case of houses of the Minoresses, and that visitors who went to the trouble to secure a costly license were "almost all of high birth." Application for papal licenses is also noted in Karen Stöber, *Late Medieval Monasteries and their Patrons: England and Wales, c. 1300–1540* (Woodbridge: Boydell, 2007), p. 75. Lee, *Nunneries*, pp. 95–96 notes the privilege afforded Dartford nuns to speak with visitors was an exceptional one although schoolgirls and laywomen did board at the house.

well-to-do ladies.[49] With the exception of the Dominican priory of Dartford (perhaps because it represented the female branch of the Friars Preacher) we find no evidence of schools for local children within any of these nunneries.[50] And save for the London community, lay boarders are almost non-existent among the Minoresses.[51]

The rewards that benefactors reaped for their investment in the new houses were less practical, but no less valued, than those provided by traditional communities. When patrons supported contemplative nuns, they nurtured enclaves of virtue in their midst. They could trust that they had secured particularly pious, and therefore particularly potent, prayers on behalf of themselves and their relatives, both alive and dead. By choosing to be buried at one of these houses, a practice especially favored by founders and their kin, they kept contact with these austere religious even in death.[52] Mary of St Pol, for instance, was buried in the choir at Denney, dressed in the habit of a Minoress, and Mary's cousin Elizabeth de Clare was buried at the London Minories.[53] With these and other spiritual returns in mind, benefactors gave these communities what Pope Boniface VIII had correctly seen as the very cornerstone of the cloistered life, but what his diocesan officials had had so much trouble procuring: ample endowments.

It would be redundant to inventory here the property and other assets that supported the monastic seclusion of the six foundations whose legal activities will engage us. Such inventories are provided for the Minoresses in the appendix of Bourdillon's classic treatment of the order in England; Aungier's history of Syon Abbey reproduces important charters and licenses, lists other bequests, and even includes an abstract of a complete survey of monastic possessions with annual income, from 1492; Dartford's extensive holdings, and the income produced by the leasing out of property is conveniently summarized by that monastery's modern historian, Paul Lee.[54] The many-faceted nature of the monastic endowments

49 Oliva, *Convent and Community*, p. 137.

50 Lee, *Nunneries*, pp. 135, 160–63.

51 Bourdillon, *Minoresses*, p. 67. Oliva, *Convent and Community*, p. 126, notes just three temporary or permanent residents at Bruisyard between 1350 and 1540.

52 Gee, *Women, Art and Patronage*, pp. 36, 89 refers to the legal right of women to make independent decisions about where, and under whose auspices, they would be buried. Bourdillon, *Minoresses*, includes a list of nineteen laymen and women who chose to be buried in Minoress houses.

53 *Ibid.*, pp. 19, 37, 77, 107, 150, for building and burial arrangements dictated by these women. Agnes, Countess of Pembroke, also requested burial at the Minories, Stöber, *Late Medieval Monasteries*, p. 114.

54 Bourdillon, *Minoresses*; Aungier, *History*; Lee, *Nunneries*.

sustaining all these houses will become evident when we survey associated litigation – suits for the restitution of tithes or the collection of rents for urban or rural property for instance. Suffice it at present to say only two things about those endowments.

First, they were always substantial, and in some instances, absolutely enormous. Syon Abbey, for instance, received an initial bequest from the Crown of £1,000, and soon had a permanent endowment consisting of extensive and widely scattered lands confiscated from alien priories during the war with France.[55] Estimates of the wealth of the house at the time of its dissolution make it the richest of the all English nunneries, with a net income of £1,731.[56] The London Minories profited throughout the late medieval period from the increasing value of London property and the income from the rents collected there was supplemented by lands and rents in nine different counties.[57] Dartford Priory, one of the wealthiest English nunneries, had an income from land and privileges that allowed it to sustain not only its nuns but also the Dominican friars at King's Langley.[58] Obviously, such wealth made it less necessary for mendicant and Bridgettine nuns, even if pressed to do so, to supplement their resources by offering unlimited hospitality to the laity or schooling for their children.

Second, and of crucial significance for this book, English contemplative nuns were not tempted to violate *active* enclosure in order to protect and preserve their holdings. Unlike their sisters in an earlier era, they could rely on professional lawyers to conduct the litigation about disputed property rights, debt collection, and myriad other issues with which the landed classes generally were forced to contend. Thus, when Claudine Bourdillon documented the three departures of English Minoresses from the confines of their monasteries, she found that none of them involved forays into the courtroom.[59] Repeatedly, as we shall see, memoranda recording the appointment of attorneys by the nuns of Dartford and Syon referred to them as "recluses" and "secluded nuns" for whom a personal court appearance was impossible. Even for routine transactions, such as the attestation

[55] Dunning, *Muniments*, pp. 103–4; *VCH Middlesex*, vol. 1, pp. 182–183; Aungier, *History*, pp. 31.

[56] Power, *Medieval English Nunneries*, p. 2.

[57] Bourdillon, *Minoresses*, p. 29. As a male mendicant house, King's Langley could not actually own property and Edward II devised the scheme of founding a Dominican nunnery to provide for its permanent income.

[58] Lee, *Nunneries*, pp. 15, 25.

[59] Bourdillon, *Minoresses*, p. 68. The "very irregular change of air" was occasioned by indults to join Elizabeth de Burgh, Lady of Clare, at her house for dinner in 1355–1356.

of an indenture or deed, cloistered nuns availed themselves of the services of professional attorneys and proctors.[60]

Although possessing extensive, varied, and valuable resources, these cloistered women were able to successfully conduct the day-to-day administration of their affairs using bailiffs, stewards, and other paid servants.[61] When their holdings were threatened, their rights challenged, or their endowments unjustly depleted, they retained lawyers. In the first instance, they used the agents traditionally available to religious women and others who could not or would not personally take charge of their temporal affairs. In the second instance, they used the legal professionals who had now become available to, and sought after by, all who could pay for their services. How did the use of hired professionals become such a desirable alternative to deputizing an amateur or going to law in person? Who were the new legal professionals responsible for procuring justice, where did they get their training, and how were they recruited and retained by their cloistered clients? These are the questions the next chapter proposes to answer.

60 See Chapter 3. Of all the memoranda I have examined that deal with such routine matters, I have found only one reference to the personal appearance of the head of a strictly cloistered house. This reference, CCR *1339–1341*, mentions that the abbess of the Minories [Katherine de Ingham] "came to London on 26 September [1339] and acknowledged the preceding indenture." It should be noted that Aldgate was not only a suburb of the city but that the abbess was in the company of John de Ingham who was King's Bench counsel in 1320.

61 Lee, *Nunneries*, pp. 36, 102, notes the active role that the Prioress of Dartford played in administering the temporal affairs of the convent by means of her stewards and other agents. See also Warren, *Spiritual Economies*, Chapter 3, for insights into the relationship between servants and nuns in Bridgettine and Franciscan houses. Eileen Power's classic study, *Medieval English Nunneries*, provides excellent examples of those relationships in traditional open monasteries.

2

Legal Professionalism and English Lawyers

Courts, Procedure, and Personnel

By the end of the thirteenth century, professional lawyers were routinely litigating in English ecclesiastical and secular courts. The jurisdictional divisions between common law and church courts, and the distinctive procedural law under which each set of courts operated had also been established by this time. There were, in fact, two legal professions. Romano-canonical lawyers trained in universities and working in the continental tradition known as the *ius commune* had degrees (bachelor, licentiate, doctor) and practiced as proctors and advocates in the ecclesiastical courts in England, in Chancery, and at the Papal Curia. Common law lawyers were trained in Common Pleas and at the Inns of Court, and then practiced as attorneys, pleaders, and serjeants in all the royal common law courts, central and local. Both types of legal professionals were essential to English litigants who might find themselves required to plead in either type of court at home or, by virtue of an appeal, in the Roman curia. In this chapter, I deal with aspects of professionalization of the English legal system that relate to the individuals and cases to be encountered in the second section of this book.

Division of jurisdiction between common law courts and those of the English church arrived at in this period remained essentially constant in the pre-Reformation era.[1] Given the topic of this book, it is especially important to mention the most distinctive if loudly contested feature of ecclesiastical jurisdiction in England: the way in which English tradition seriously limited ecclesiastical competence. The Crown recognized ecclesiastical jurisdiction *ratione personae*, by virtue of the clerical status of a litigant, solely in criminal cases. In civil cases, the only ones with which we are concerned, "clergy were almost as fully subject to the royal courts as the laity."[2] In addition, a cleric might be sued in a secular court by

1 Helmholz, *Canon Law*, pp. 206, 231.

2 *Ibid.*, p. 509; also, pp. 211, 315, 508. In the 1370s the Roman Rota addressed itself to the English restriction of clerical privilege and found it invalid under the canon law. The finding did nothing to alter that custom.

virtue of the recognized legal maxim: *Actor forum rei sequitur*, the suit must be in the forum of the defendant. So when a cleric sued a layman, the cleric would need to appear in the temporal court to do so.

What all of this meant in practice was that cloistered nuns, along with all other English litigants, brought their cases concerning debts, landed property, rents, and other matters affecting their material welfare to secular courts. Even when the subject of dispute concerned ecclesiastical appointments, late medieval common law had made considerable jurisdictional inroads. The right of a patron to appoint someone of his or her choice to a living, a privilege canonically known as *ius patronatus* or, in England, advowson, is a case in point. Since the right to nominate the parson of a parish church dated from the days when lay lords who held land from the king built churches on that land and subsequently controlled activities affecting those proprietary churches, the Crown still claimed exclusive competence when the right to an advowson was disputed.[3] Because advowsons and the benefices attached to them were sources of income, these disputes were common and the proceeds from their resolution made a nice addition to royal coffers.

That said, the dividing line between ecclesiastical and temporal jurisdiction was not hard and fast. Boundaries were sometimes ignored and sometimes circumvented. Actions for *laesio fidei*, breach of faith, provide a good example of the latter. "By adding three words to a common contract—'by my faith' or some variant—it became possible to invoke ecclesiastical jurisdiction to enforce a contract that would otherwise belong to temporal cognizance."[4] In this way an action for recovery of a debt, in the guise of an action for breach of faith, became a matter for church courts to decide, in fact if not in theory.[5] More straightforwardly, certain matters referred to as *causae spirituales* were consistently seen by the English Crown as pertaining to the Church and not the State. These matters included litigation about marriage and divorce, testamentary succession (to chattels but *not* to land), defamation, breach of faith or perjury, usury, tithes and other ecclesiastical dues (with exceptions), church property (with exceptions), ecclesiastical pensions, and assaults on clergy.[6]

3 The 1330 dispute between the nuns of Waterbeach and "certain persons scheming to impede their presentation of the abbess and convent," treated here in Chapter 4, is a case in point. See also, Helmholz, *Canon Law*, pp. 477–478.

4 *Ibid.*, p. 231. Chapter 6 expands upon the role of the church courts in this and other matters related to monetary obligations.

5 Richard Wunderli, *London Church Courts on the Eve of the Reformation* (Cambridge, MA: Medieval Academy of America Press, 1981), p. 103.

6 *Ibid.*, p. 229; for probate restrictions, pp. 387–388, 423.

Whether the cases fell into a jurisdictional grey area or clearly involved spiritualities, documentation from the courts of popes, judges delegate, and bishops provide us with some of our most involved, colorful, and instructive cases featuring cloistered nuns. We therefore begin with a look at the ecclesiastical legal system, its venues, procedures, and professional personnel. Details about the workings of specific courts will be added in subsequent chapters as they bear on the specific suits brought before those courts.

The English, like all medieval Christians, had the option of taking their ecclesiastical litigation directly to "everyone's ordinary judge" (*iudex ordinarius omnium*), the pope. The court books show that influential individuals and corporations or their proxies did so often, despite the time and tremendous expense involved.[7] A case of great importance might make its way to the pope's own episcopal court, the Papal Consistory. Average English petitioners and their legal proxies in Rome were more likely, however, to have business in one of three other papal courts: The *Audientia literarum contradictarum*, which set the final form of letters dispatched to judges delegate, the Papal Penitentiary, which absolved those under sentence of reserved excommunication, and the extremely influential *Audientia sacri palatii*, or Roman Rota, before which appeals from English courts were heard.[8]

Papal decision-making authority might sometimes be invoked remotely. The establishment of permanent episcopal courts in England made the role of the judge delegate less crucial than it had been a century earlier but these men still played an important role in the legal system of the church.[9] Papal judges delegate made bringing one's case before the pope a possibility for those who lacked the considerable funds needed to travel to, and then conduct their business in, Rome. Ad hoc appointees were chosen from among the prelates of the area where a case arose, "their letters of appointment outlined the case as alleged by a petitioner and

7 E. F. Jacob, "To and from the Court of Rome in the Early Fifteenth Century," in *Essays in Later Medieval History* (Manchester: Manchester University Press, 1968), pp. 58–78; Margaret Harvey, *The English in Rome 1362–1420* (Cambridge: Cambridge University Press, 1999), Chapter 8. These works contain complementary information about English nationals at work in the papal courts.

8 Helmholz, *Canon Law*, pp. 208–210.

9 Charles Donahue, *The Records of the Medieval Ecclesiastical Courts*, Part II: *England* (Berlin: Duncker & Humblot, 1994), pp. 26–34 at which Jane Sayers discusses the records generated by judges delegate in England; Jane Sayers, *Papal Judges Delegate in the Province of Canterbury, 1198–1254* (Oxford: Oxford University Press, 1971), is an in-depth study of the origins and development of delegated jurisdiction.

directed the judges-delegate to investigate the facts of the situation. On the basis of their finding of fact, the judges were then authorized to give the appropriate remedies, as specified in their letters of appointment, with full papal authority."[10]

Judges delegate excepted, the highest ecclesiastical authorities on English soil were the archbishops of the provinces of Canterbury and York. The busiest and most important of their courts was the Court of Arches, the provincial venue of the Archbishop of Canterbury, which was situated in that hub of commerce and contention, London.[11] The Archbishop of Canterbury's Court of Audience, in which he personally heard important cases, and his Prerogative Court which dealt exclusively with testamentary matters, were also in London. His Consistory Court, which dealt with ordinary diocesan litigation, was held in Canterbury Cathedral. Oftentimes the Archbishops of Canterbury and York were also appointed Lords in Chancery, a royal equity court. Indeed, until the Reformation the Court of Chancery was staffed by prominent clergymen who had attained degrees in canon or civil law.

The average English litigant was unlikely to have had a case heard by the Archbishop of Canterbury or York, in the first instance. More than likely, an initial hearing would take place before a bishop. There was no shortage of them.[12] Late medieval England boasted seventeen bishops and by the mid-thirteenth century each of them had a permanent court for dealing with ordinary diocesan matters. Each of these courts, in turn, was presided over by a professional judge called the official-principal, who was assisted in his duties by record-keepers, summoners or apparitors who served citations, and a staff of in-house lawyers who represented parties in civil matters. Sessions of these courts were held roughly every three weeks, and their meeting place was generally the cathedral church of the diocese although a major parish church might be chosen because of practical advantages. "For example, the consistory court for the diocese of Ely often met in Great St Mary's in Cambridge, where a larger number of lawyers was to be found than in the cathedral city itself."[13]

10 Brundage, *Medieval Origins*, pp. 135–137.

11 Helmholz, *Canon Law*, p. 213; F. Donald Logan, *The Court of Arches* (Woodbridge: Boydell Press, 2005).

12 There were courts of lesser prelates, such as archdeacons and rural deans. As records for these courts have survived in far fewer numbers, and since matters concerning marriage, probate, and secular morals were the chief subject matter of these courts, none of our cases comes from them. Brundage, *Medieval Origins*, 145–149; Helmholz, *Canon Law*, pp. 213–216.

13 Helmholz, *Canon Law*, p. 215.

Some types of disputes, those involving monastic benefices or elections for instance, might be handled by ad hoc commissions and arbitrators outside of the courtroom.[14] Canonical procedure in those instances might be truncated or streamlined in some way, but whenever a suit was brought into any of the higher-level ecclesiastical courts it would progress in discrete stages and according to Roman-canon procedural law. By the thirteenth century this body of law had grown highly formal and elaborate.[15] The procedural phases of a civil suit can be briefly summarized as follows.

First, the pretrial. The plaintiff (*actor*) presented his formal complaint (*libellus*) to the judge who summoned the defendant (*reus*) to court to respond to it. The defendant made his answer to the charge, then the plaintiff made his own formal reply to the answer (*replicatio*), the defendant then enjoyed the privilege of making his rejoinder (*triplicatio*), and then the plaintiff offered his counter-reply (*quadruplicatio*). In this way all extraneous matter was winnowed away, and the exact nature of the disputed issue was, at least in theory, clarified. Once the precise issues emerged, the nature of the evidence that each party would be required to produce to support their claims also became clear and the lawyers employed could get busy. The court appointed counsel at this point if needed, and a trial date was assigned.

Second, the trial proper began. The parties restated their claims in the form of a set of propositions which they aimed to prove (*litis contestatio*); an action similar to what the common law called 'joining issue.' Then plaintiff and defendant gave the judge a list of witnesses they wished to call along with a list of the points they expected each witness to prove (*articuli*) and the questions (*interrogationes*) they wished each witness to answer. The judge then gave the opposing parties copies of these documents. Third came the submission of proof (*probatio*). Witnesses were examined and their depositions submitted to the court. Any documentary evidence was also submitted at this stage. Sentencing (*sententia*) took place in the fourth phase. After reading through and evaluating the evidence, and consulting with colleagues or outside legal experts, the judge delivered his decision orally and in writing. At the judge's discre-

14 *Ibid.*, p. 229.

15 Brundage, *Medieval Origins*, pp. 151–163; Helmholz, *Canon Law*, Chapter 5; Norma Adams and Charles Donahue, *Select Cases from the Ecclesiastical Courts of the Province of Canterbury* c. *1200–1301* (London: Selden Society, 1981), Introduction. All provide detailed descriptions of the process.

tion, costs were charged to the losing party and the appeal process, if any, could begin.

All pleas and actions were in writing, even the oral testimony of witnesses being committed to written form, and each procedural step required a court appearance. Raising objections (exceptions) to the arguments of one's adversary was routine procedure and one type of objection (peremptory) could be lodged by the defendant at any time before sentence was passed. The filing of objections and pleas for postponements often extended the trial process to a year or more, sometimes much more. No doubt the construction of such a procedural labyrinth accounts for the fact that a great number of cases never reached the stage of *litis contestatio*, having been either abandoned or settled by arbitration.[16] The elaborate and arcane procedure certainly explains the need for professional lawyers trained to find a way for a client to penetrate that maze: "Procedural innovations more than any other single factor made the services of trained legal advisers and representatives essential."[17]

Already in the twelfth century this need was recognized by jurists like the anonymous canonist who commented wryly, "If someone is brash enough to presume to rely on his own devices even though he is inexperienced and does not wish to have an advocate, let him do so. Everyone is free to muck up his own case."[18] Given the procedural technicality illustrated above, self-representation was an even more foolhardy course of action by the middle of the thirteenth century. University-trained lawyers became vital representatives of clients litigating in the spiritual forum. By the middle of the fourteenth century, nothing less than the bachelor's degree in canon or civil law was acceptable for those wishing to practice as advocates.[19]

Ecclesiastical lawyers were either advocates or proctors, designations signifying distinctions in levels of formal training and ordinary functioning at the bar.[20] A rough comparison can be made with the barrister and solicitor of common law. Like barristers, advocates belonged to the higher level of practitioner. They were the elite of the profession, legal

16 Helmholz, *Canon Law*, p. 328; Wunderli, *London Church Courts*, Appendix A, and tables throughout the book, document this fact with regard to the disposition of a variety of suits.

17 Brundage, *Medieval Origins*, p. 163.

18 "[Si] quis de se presumens, etiam cum imperitus sit, advocatum habere nolit, suo ingenio relinquatur. Liberum est cuique suam causam negligere." *Ibid.*, p. 152.

19 Brand, *Origins of the Legal Profession*, p. 149.

20 For full details about both in the thirteenth century see Brundage, *Medieval Origins*, Chapter 8.

experts in Roman (civil) and canon law whose job was to expertly advise their clients, frame pleadings, and convincingly argue difficult points of law before the judge. They had various titles such as *advocati*, *narratores* (speakers), and *placitatores* (pleaders). Advocates had law degrees in the *ius commune* or Roman-canon law as taught in the universities, and in the fourteenth century such degrees were costly as well as time-consuming to acquire. A bachelor's degree in canon law from Cambridge, for example, would have required approximately seven years of study while a doctorate in both laws (conferring the title *doctor utriusque iuris*) could mean twenty years in training. It was from the ranks of these highly skilled jurists that judges and lawyers practicing in the church courts in England and Rome were drawn. There were several English auditors of the Rota in the fourteenth century including the famous Thomas Fastolf, who compiled the first known collection of Rota decisions. The Lord Chancellor and the masters of the king's equity Court of Chancery were also members of this select group.[21] Advocates also served as assessors or legal advisers to judges and clients who sought a formal opinion (*consilium*) on the merits of a case.[22]

Proctors (*procuratores*) were legal professionals of a less exalted but more numerous and very useful sort. They were multi-purpose legal agents whose principal function was to appear on behalf of a client in all phases of litigation. Whether appointed by a client in the courtroom or by a sealed letter of proxy (*procuratorium*), they were empowered to do whatever that client might be required to do if he/she were present in person. Clients were thus not required to appear in court unless specifically requested by the opposition, a matter of considerable significance for cloistered nuns. The proctor managing a lawsuit might also hire the advocates who gave legal advice and argued points of law for their clients.[23]

Many had attended university and some held bachelor's degrees in law but for the successful proctor it was not advanced study of the law but intimate familiarity with the practice of the courts that mattered.[24] Within

21 J. H. Baker, *The Legal Profession and the Common Law* (London: Hambledon Press, 1996), p. 80

22 For a brief overview of *consilia* literature and discussion of their importance to decision making at the highest levels of Church and State, including the Bridgettine appeal analyzed later in this book, see Elizabeth Makowski, A *Pernicious Sort of Woman: Quasi-Religious Women and Canon Lawyers in the Later Middle Ages* (Washington, DC: Catholic University of America Press, 2005), pp. 71–75.

23 Brundage, *Medieval Origins*, p. 354.

24 Brand, *Origins of the Legal Profession*, p. 149, states that proctors with university degrees were preferred for practice in the Court of Arches by the fourteenth century, albeit even in that distinguished venue, a degree was still not required.

those courts proctors were ubiquitous. "Professional proctors, unlike advocates, swarm through the pages of church court records from the thirteenth century onward."[25] Not all consistory courts employed advocates but they all engaged proctors.[26] Proctors were also employed to lobby for their clients in obtaining privileges, dispensations, benefices, and the like. This function was particularly appealing to English clients who sought the same from the Papal Curia and the regular retention of proctors in Rome (or Avignon) was one way that institutional clients such as monasteries kept watch on their affairs from a distance. English proctors were thus a fixture at the papal courts, especially the *Audientia literarum contradictarum*. There they cautiously raised objections to the insertion of items in a judge delegate's mandate that might undermine a client's soon-to-be decided case and that could make all the difference in litigation.

The process of professionalization summarily described for the *ius commune* in the ecclesiastical forum had its parallel in the sphere of common law. While it was a nearly coterminous process – common law lawyers achieved full-fledged professional status by the end of Edward I's reign, 1307 – it had distinctive manifestations.[27] In surveying the professionalization of this second legal system in England we will once again proceed by discussing venues, procedure, and personnel.

With the exception of the local London assizes which heard complaints related to city property, of which the Minories held a good share, our cases are drawn from the abundant records of the central courts of the Crown. The superior courts of Common Pleas, King's Bench, Exchequer, and Chancery, proved to be regular venues for litigation involving the material goods and economically important privileges of monasteries in general and of cloistered nuns in particular. All these courts met in Westminster Hall and in very close proximity to one another.

The first, and for our purposes most important, was the Court of Common Pleas, sometimes referred to as Common Bench. During the reign of Edward I it became the premier court dealing with, and eventually limited to, civil litigation at common law. It was an especially popular venue for the resolution of disputes about debt. In Edward III's time, it was the busiest and most impressive of the central courts and "by the middle of the thirteenth century it had become the normal expectation that a

25 Brundage, *Medieval Origins*, p. 353.

26 Helmholz, *Canon Law*, p. 221. Jane E. Sayers, "Proctors Representing British Interests at the Papal Court, 1198–1415," in *Law and Records in Medieval England* (London: Ashgate, 1988), pp. 143–163; Brundage, *Medieval Origins*, pp. 346–347.

27 James A. Brundage, "The Medieval Advocate's Profession," *Law and History Review* 6 no.2 (1988): 448.

litigant in the Common Bench at Westminster, though not necessarily in other royal courts, would have a serjeant speaking on his or her behalf."[28] It should be noted that the professional serjeant at law also became a fixture in the City of London courts at this time since there as well litigants needed someone to speak the increasingly technical language of pleading.[29]

> The Common Pleas was the court which more than any other made the medieval common law. It usually had four or five judges, a select bar of serjeants at law, and a large staff of officers: the *custos brevium* or keeper of the writs, the prothonotaries and filazers (who kept the rolls and files), and numerous underclerks. It was the place where young students huddled in a raised wooden box called the "crib," came to learn their law. What a judge or serjeant said in the Common Pleas he published to the legal world as his opinion on the law, and he might be sure someone would remember it or make a note of it; the yearbooks [law reports] were taken up almost exclusively with the debates in this court, and it was not until the sixteenth century that the work of other courts was regularly reported.[30]

As suggested by its lofty title, the Court of King's Bench heard suits in which the king had a direct legal interest. Its jurisdictional range, although two-fold, was far less broad than that of Common Pleas. The Crown side of the bench had unlimited criminal jurisdiction which extended across the realm. The civil or plea side of the bench heard disputes concerning trespass, appeals of felony, and suits to correct errors in the Common Pleas or borough courts of record. Attorneys practicing in Common Pleas could and did also practice in King's Bench.[31] Because cloistered nuns had grants of land from many sources, interference with the interests of the Crown might sometimes bring them to this royal court, or its earlier incarnation, the General Eyre.[32]

The Court of Exchequer was a court of account which dealt with disputes of a financial nature, principally those concerned with royal revenues. The Barons of Exchequer were the regular justices and the court had about a dozen of its own attorneys.[33] Exchequer business was dominated

28 Brand, "Inside the Courtroom," p. 96.

29 Brand, *Origins of the Legal Profession*, p. 48.

30 J. H. Baker, *An Introduction to English Legal History*. 2nd edn (London: Butterworth, 1979), pp. 35–36. For later developments in this court, as well as in the other courts of the Crown see Baker's magisterial work, *The Oxford History of the Laws of England*, vol. 6, *1483–1558* (Oxford: Oxford University Press, 2003).

31 Baker, *Oxford History*, p. 438.

32 The General Eyre was defunct by the later part of the fourteenth century but one case, featuring the Minories, did come before it. See Chapter 4.

33 Baker, *Oxford History*, p. 161.

by suits for recovery of sums and feudal dues owed to the Crown. Cases could be initiated by 'information' (formal accusation) made either by the attorney general of the court who represented the king as plaintiff, or by a common person. If launched by the latter, it would involve a writ of *quominus* alleging that the plaintiff was unable to pay his debts to the Crown because of the delinquency of his own debtors. Thus, private individuals could collect their own debts in this court, at government expense, in order to pay the king what they owed him.

Exchequer had various non-judicial functions related to the recording of revenues and a judicial as well as a clerical staff. Letters of attorney and transcripts of certain causes adjudicated in other courts might consequently be found in its rolls; we find both in fact referencing the nuns of Syon. After the middle of Henry VIII's reign, when Exchequer 'informations' were used more and more often to enforce penal statutes, the nuns of Dartford became litigants in this court.[34] Like many other religious, the 1529 statute against non-residence and "the taking of farms by spiritual persons" forced them to defend themselves before the newly empowered Chancellor of the Exchequer, Cromwell himself.

The Court of Chancery, also a royal court, was not a common law court. It was the court of conscience, a tribunal which allowed a plaintiff to describe his case in detail and to request that it be considered according to standards inadmissible at common law. There were no original writs, there was no jury and judgment was summarily handed down by the chancellor. By the later Middle Ages, Chancery officials were university-trained canonists and civilians deputized by a chancellor who was himself a doctor of civil or canon law. The clerical personnel and ecclesiastical aura of this court mesh with its unique jurisdictional aim: "making sure that justice was done in cases where shortcomings in the regular procedure, or human failings, rendered its attainment by due process unlikely."[35] Like King's Bench, Chancery had two sides or two jurisdictions. The Latin side (where records were kept in Latin) was largely an extension of the Chancery as an administrative office charged with writing letters patent and close and charters that went out carrying the Great Seal. This side also dealt with inquisitions post-mortem and issues related to the chancellor's own clerk and officials. The English side, however, was a very popular tribunal in which equity pleadings and petitions were made in Anglo-Norman French or, by the fifteenth century, in English.

34 *Ibid.*, p. 164.

35 Baker, *Introduction*, p. 87.

The significance of the Court of Chancery derives from its flexibility, vis-à-vis the common law courts.

> The chancellor was free from the procedural formalities and customs of the regular courts. No original writ was necessary, and so all actions were commenced by informal bill of complaint, usually in English. Process in most actions was begun by subpoena, a simple summons to appear in Chancery or else forfeit a penalty. Pleading was relatively informal, there was no jury, and evidence could be taken by deposition or interrogation, even from the parties themselves.[36]

The court might meet anywhere, even in the chancellor's residence, or by commission of *dedimus potestatem*, in that of a country gentleman. While the laws of evidence might exclude a case from consideration by the common law courts it might still receive a hearing in this extraordinary venue.

Chancery excepted, procedure in the courts of the Crown differed fundamentally from that followed in the ecclesiastical forum in its reliance on jury verdict as opposed to judicial evaluation of evidence.[37] Moreover, common lawsuits were strictly bound by distinctive procedural elements like the use of writs and specialized forms of action and pleading. These elements were especially significant in English law since they "preceded the substantive law as it is now understood. The principles of the common law were never mapped out in the abstract, but grew around the forms by which justice was centralized and administered by the king's courts. There was a law of writs before there was a law of property, or contract, or tort."[38]

Legal proceedings were begun with and circumscribed by the all-important writ. Writs originated as letters from the king granting a petitioner the 'favor' of royal justice as distinct from that he might have in a local, customary, court of law. Whether providing a form of action for vindicating a right or compensating for a wrong the number of writs granting specific remedies had grown so large that by the middle of the thirteenth century new formulae were not sanctioned. For plaintiffs this meant a greater than ever reliance on lawyers. As Baker put it, "The writs exerted their dominion not only over procedure but over the common law mind. If there was no writ, there was no remedy."[39] Royal justice could now be denied him if a plaintiff could not find a registered writ appropriate to his

36 *Ibid.*, p. 88.

37 Helmholz, *Canon Law*, pp. 311–312; Although inquests were sometimes a part of ecclesiastical court practice, the generalization about the probative value of juries still holds, as per pp. 336–338.

38 Baker, *Introduction*, p. 49.

39 Baker, *Oxford History*, p. 323.

case, and selection of the correct writ was crucial to successful litigation once begun; commencing an action with one kind of writ might preclude the use of trial methods available with another. Courts had specified dates for the return of writs once procured and a plaintiff's attorney had to make sure that a return date was not missed since if it were the action would be discontinued.

Judicial pleadings at common law began with the court appearance of the defendant. Pleadings were made orally at the bar and before being committed to the court records at the end of term they were mutable. Counsel for the plaintiff made the count or complaint (*counte*, in French, *narratio* in Latin) and the defendant replied, so 'joining issue' or producing the precise question that the jury would be asked to decide. Pleading became a highly technical game of skill and the terms used to describe the proceedings are suggestive of a chess match. The defendant had to deny all of the facts of the count (a general traverse), deny one of the facts (a special traverse) or admit all of the facts but explain them away with the introduction of new facts (confession and avoidance). Only the first two options produced the issue, since the third called for a reply by the plaintiff. This riposte and parry continued until a fact was denied and the disputed issue arrived at. The jury was then charged and confined until jurors reached a verdict.

Like their ecclesiastical counterparts the lawyers who conducted such complex proceedings in the common law courts were of two classes. Pleaders, also called narrators, were akin to the advocates of the ecclesiastical forum and attorneys corresponded to proctors.[40] Roughly akin to the barristers of today, pleaders argued a client's case in court and were the legal experts. It was from this group that a select few, usually only ten in practice at any given time, known as serjeants at law or *narratores* were drawn.[41] Preeminent among the serjeants were the king's serjeants, who argued on his behalf in royal courts, and it is from this exclusive elite that the justices of the bench were drawn. Serjeants at law made up the bar of the Court of Common Pleas while those not 'called to the honor' generally pleaded in the King's Bench, Chancery, and lesser local courts.

The largest group of common lawyers, attorneys, acted for their clients by proxy and bound them by their authorized actions. Those licensed to practice in the Court of Common Pleas were at the top of their profession and could practice in King's Bench, Exchequer and Chancery as well as

40 Baker, *Introduction*, pp. 133–140 presents a concise introduction to the topic.

41 Brand, *Origins of the Legal Profession*, pp. 94–105, discusses the major functions of the serjeant as well as patterns of retention for same; Baker, *Oxford History*, pp. 421–424 for the later medieval and Tudor era.

in local courts if they liked.[42] Attorneys, like modern-day solicitors, were experts in the technicalities of litigation and managed suits in the absence of the parties concerned. Their services required a sound knowledge of the fine points of writ selection and return mentioned above. Attorneys frequently had leave to hire the pleaders required by their clients. By 1300, nearly all clients litigating in the superior courts of the Crown employed attorneys – even if they were quite able to personally oversee their counselors, they knew better than to try to manage their own cases.

Unlike lawyers practicing in the ecclesiastical courts, neither pleaders nor attorneys were regularly educated at university, even in the later Middle Ages.[43] Essentially, they learned their common law by doing. Observation and note-taking in the Westminster courts were the ordinary apprenticeship before the fourteenth century.[44] At that time, the Inns of Chancery and the Inns of Court began to provide additional learning exercises for apprentices in the profession.[45] Unlike the universities of Oxford and Cambridge, the Inns, which were located in the western suburbs of London, evolved through expediency, and served to accommodate as well as to train aspirants. Once ensconced in one of these residences a man would learn his writs and then proceed to learn how to plead in the courts. His education would have included attendance at court, engaging in moots, and hearing lectures. The whole apprenticeship required about six years and what would later be referred to as a 'call to the bar' did not occur before that time.

Identification, Recruitment, and Retention of Lawyers

How can we identify the individual lawyers practicing in the above-mentioned courts? Commenting on how difficult it is to research the careers of pre-Reformation common lawyers, E. W. Ives wrote: "clients record the results of litigation, not the names of their advisers, and the courts are interested in cases, not the advocate who conducts them."[46] It is all too true that in calendared entries complaints are recorded as having

42 Baker, *Oxford History*, p. 438.

43 *Ibid.*, p. 447.

44 Brand, *Origins of the Legal Profession*, Chapter 7, deals with developments in professional legal training during the reign of Edward I.

45 Baker, *Introduction*, pp. 137–139. For more detail about the inns and earlier modes of professional education see Baker, *The Legal Profession*, Chapter 7; Paul Brand, "Courtroom and Schoolroom: The Education of Lawyers in England prior to 1400," *Historical Research* 60 (1987): 147–165.

46 Ives, *Common Lawyers*, p. 93.

been lodged on behalf of an abbess "by her attorney" with vexing regularity. It is also true, however, that when we know the court in which litigation took place it is often possible to identify the lawyers charged to represent disputants. Because under-officers of the court served as in-house attorneys in Chancery proceedings, lists of such office holders can give us an idea of who might have worked with a particular petitioner.[47] Furthermore, from the time of Wolsey's chancellorship (1515–1529) petitions were regularly signed by counsel.[48] Although there is no extant record of the licenses granted to attorneys practicing in the central court of the Crown, we find their names listed elsewhere. In the case of Common Bench, names of all licensed practitioners were recorded on warrants enrolled at the end-of-term plea rolls.[49] Local courts rolls such as those preserved for the London assizes often name attorneys as well.

Additionally, the Close and Patent Rolls record the appointment of attorneys for individuals and institutions. A remarkably good run of these commissions exists for the Dominican Priory of Dartford. They supply us not only with the names of attorneys licensed to act for the house, but also with added evidence of the strictness of its enclosure. Michael Skillyng (1368), Walter Perle (1368), Walter Durant (1370), Thomas Sherdelowe (1375), Nicholas Heryng (1377), John Videleu (1375), John Bretton (1381), William Makenade (1397), and John Martyn (1400) were all licensed Dartford attorneys for periods of one to five years. All were appointed because, in the words of the commissions, the prioress "is a recluse and cannot personally labour about pleas and other matters touching her and her house."[50]

Establishing the identity of lawyers practicing in the king's courts then is usually possible, and it is even easier when the lawyers were canonists or civilians. Most ecclesiastical courts kept registers listing the advocates admitted to practice in them. The so-called *Black Book* of the court of the Bishop of Ely, for instance, included dated lists of active advocates and proctors.[51] When a dispute was formally settled under the auspices

47 Malcolm Richardson, *The Medieval Chancery under Henry V* (Kew: List and Index Society, 1999), p. 29.

48 J. H. Baker, "Lawyers Practising in Chancery 1474–1486," *Journal of Legal History* 4 (1983): 54.

49 Baker, *Oxford History*, p. 438.

50 Lee, *Nunneries*, pp. 36–37. For his career see J. H. Baker, "Townshend, Sir Roger (c. 1430–1493)," in *ODNB*, www.oxforddnb.com/view/article/27632 (accessed July 23, 2010). See Chapter 3 for details about these warrants.

51 James A Brundage, "The Bar of the Ely Consistory Court in the Fourteenth Century: Advocates, Proctors and Others," *Journal of Ecclesiastical History*43, no. 4 (1992):

of a bishop, the record of that settlement names proctors and advocates employed by both sides. Such a final concord survives for a convoluted tithe case involving the nuns of Denney.

Papal letters referring a cause to judges delegate naturally named those judges while outlining the case that required their services. If a suit reached the apex of the ecclesiastical pyramid, the Papal Curia itself, the social prestige of both the complainants and their legal champions increased the likelihood that a record of that litigation would be carefully preserved for posterity. So it was when Syon Abbey's appeal to Rome resulted in the production of expert legal opinions by two of the curia's most prominent jurists: Panormitanus (1386–1445) and the Rota auditor Dominicus de Sancto Geminiano (c. 1375–1436).

Even when the lawyer in question is not as celebrated, more than just his identity can be ascertained if he was among the professional elite. Since by the fourteenth century advocates who practiced regularly in a bishop's court had law degrees, university registers from Oxford and Cambridge serve as supplemental sources.[52] The enrollment books of emerging professional societies are also useful. By the start of the sixteenth century, for example, canonists who practiced in the appellate court of the Archbishop of Canterbury, the Court of Arches, are recorded in the membership lists of their professional society, Doctors' Commons.[53]

Because common law practitioners did not need university degrees, and since the earliest surviving membership lists from the Inns of Court date from 1422, the extent to which an individual was *homo in lege terrae eruditus*, a man learned in the law of the land, is less easy to gauge.[54] Those lawyers who can be identified as serjeants at law, and there are some named in the list of Dartford Priory lawyers, were plainly at the top of their profession. Admittedly, the caliber of independent common lawyers who were not particularly prominent and who belong "in the large grey area which then existed between the more experienced attorneys and the serjeants at law" is nearly impossible to ascertain.[55] Some idea of the social standing of these lesser men, if not the extent of their legal training, can nevertheless be pieced together.

541–560. This study uses the *Act Book* of the court, along with this source to profile Ely consistory court practitioners in the late fourteenth century.

52 Helmholz, *Canon Law*, p. 349.

53 F. Donald Logan, "Doctors' Commons in the Early Sixteenth Century: A Society of Many Talents," *Historical Research*, vol. 61, no. 145 (1988): 151–165.

54 Brundage, "Medieval Advocate's Profession," p. 447; Baker, *Introduction*, pp. 138–139.

55 Penelope Tucker, *Law Courts and Lawyers in the City of London, 1300–1550* (Cambridge: Cambridge University Press, 2007), p. 304.

For example, when the abbess and nuns of the Minories sued one Gilbert de Asshendone in the London Assize of Nuisance in 1306, they appeared by a certain John de Colecestre, identified only as "their attorney."[56] In September, 1318, however, John de Colecestre is again listed in London records. This time his status as "a citizen of the more powerful and better class" is certified by the king's command that he provide a fully equipped soldier for his army.[57]

So too, Robert fitzRobert, attorney for the Minories, was not a regular practitioner in the London courts so we learn nothing more about him from those records. The Close Rolls, however, record fitzRobert's appointment to a number of commissions of the peace and one of his corporate clients, the grocers of the city (he was a London grocer's son), referred to him as a "man of law."[58] His client base tells us something as well. He had been given a one-year appointment as the Earl of Ormond's attorney in 1420, and in 1428 he was nominated to act in England for a year as the attorney of Richard Rede, who was then "about to proceed to Ireland with the king's license."[59]

Once a lawyer working for any house of cloistered nuns is identified, his level of practical competence can often be gauged by discovering his other clients. Take the example of Master Robert Kent, who was named "proctor in all suits" for Syon Abbey in 1455. While he held only a bachelor's degree in canon law, his legal acumen must have been considerable since papal registers show him practicing in the Court of Arches.[60] While there, he worked for some noteworthy clients. From 1459 until his appointment as proctor general in 1466, he represented John Paston in the tortuous litigation surrounding the last will and testament of John Fastolf.[61] In the same vein, Dartford attorney Michael Skillyng had been appointed attorney for the Constable of France, "for one year in all pleas and plaints for or against him in whatsoever court in England," a fact which would inspire some confidence in his abilities.[62]

By using a combination of methods and sources then, most of the professional lawyers featured in this study have been identified. A fair amount of biographical detail even exists for a number of them. One is found

56 Misc. Roll DD, #80.

57 *Ibid.*, #102.

58 Tucker, *Law Courts*, pp. 288–289.

59 *CPR 1416–1422*, p. 261; *CPR 1422–1429*, vol. 1, p. 471.

60 *BRUO*, p. 1037.

61 *The Paston Letters: A Selection in Modern Spelling*, ed. Norman Davis (Oxford: Oxford University Press, 1963), p. 53.

62 *CCR 1346*, p. 92.

in the company of a prominent London merchant, another is glimpsed as he prepares to sail to France under instruction from the Crown, and yet another as he endows his alma mater. But where did the prospective clients of these men, clients who were clearly not at liberty to move in these circles, ever encounter them? How did cloistered nuns acquaint themselves with the lawyers to whom they would entrust matters affecting their very livelihood? Several answers present themselves.

Monastic stewards and bailiffs could help secure legal counsel for the communities they served. Stewards, the grandest of these officials, were sometimes very highly placed men who were accustomed to delegating their duties of oversight – Thomas Cromwell himself had been steward of Syon and Andrew Lord Windsor, steward of the Minories.[63] A well-connected steward, possibly Philip Fitzlewes of the Minories, contracted for the services of the distinguished serjeant at law and Chief Justice of Common Pleas, Sir Thomas Frowyk (d. 1506).[64] Some stewards were themselves esteemed lawyers. Inner Temple lawyer and counselor to Henry VII Sir Richard Sutton (1460–1524) was appointed the steward of Syon Abbey in 1513, and so performed a dual function for the nuns.[65] Roger Higham, under-steward of the Minories, was nominated attorney by Abbess Dorothy Cumberford in 1531.[66]

Franciscan and Dominican friars who provided spiritual care to nuns belonging to mendicant communities were sometimes qualified to act as proctors or attorneys.[67] The same holds true for the brethren of Syon. Friar Walter Durant, "perhaps in residence" at the Dominican Priory of Dartford, was one of those attorneys appointed to represent the house again and again in the years between 1370 and 1401.[68] And the senior friar chaplain of Denney, Richard Brynkeley was proctor for the nuns in a complicated appropriation case dated 1512. But normally friars seem to have made better confessors than counselors and after they were barred by the canon law from legal practice save in the interests of their own houses, monks would be unable to act for most nunneries. Friars were still of use to their mendicant sisters in search of a competent lawyer however, since, like lay stewards, they could secure the services of those professionals on behalf of the nuns.

63 Power, *Medieval English Nunneries*, p. 146.

64 Catherine Paxton, "The Nunneries of London and Its Environs in the Later Middle Ages" (D.Phil. thesis, Oxford University, 1992), p. 79; *DNB* vol. 7, p. 733.

65 *DNB* vol. 53, p. 401.

66 Paxton, *Nunneries*, p. 80, p. 134.

67 Bourdillon, *Minoresses*, pp. 8, 57.

68 Lee, *Nunneries*, p. 36.

One notable example referenced above and treated in detail in a later chapter is that of Syon confessor general Thomas Fishbourne, who hired two renowned Italian advocates to write *consilia* on behalf of his community. On several occasions the priors of King's Langley, or the abbots of Lesnes (in Kent) are mentioned as receiving "by writ" the attorneys designated by Dartford nuns. King's Langley priors John Woderowe and William Syward did so in 1368 and 1379 respectively.

Cloistered nuns recruited the largest number of their lawyers from their families and friends. In hiring lawyers, as in generating bequests, family ties played an even more important role than institutional or spiritual ones. All of the houses in this study attracted women of some social distinction, and those entrants who were related by blood or marriage to prominent lawyers capitalized on their useful connections for the good of their communities. As Catherine Paxton has shown, London houses generally recruited lawyers from the families of nuns.[69] And two abbesses of Aldgate were related to some of the top legal talent of the day. Katherine Ingham, abbess in 1355, was the widow of King's Bench lawyer, John Ingham.[70] Eleanor Scrope, abbess of the same house *c.*1386, was the widow of Geoffrey Scrope of Masham and kinswoman of King's Bench justice Henry Scrope.[71] Outside of London, Elizabeth Cressener, prioress of Dartford, was the granddaughter of king's serjeant and justice of Common Pleas (as well as the first law reporter), Sir Roger Townshend.[72]

Widows with unfinished legal business might bring both that business, and the lawyers retained to conduct it, into the monastic orbit when they became nuns. In these instances, the legal talent might be considerable. Such was the case with Cambin Fulbert, "merchant of Florence" and "citizen of London." A valued legal representative for Italian merchants at the height of the English Crown's dependence on the Frescobaldi, Fulbert was the agent in countless debt acknowledgments recorded in the Close Rolls, and he acted as the attorney for Florentine merchants prosecuting a recognizance.[73] In 1309, Fulbert appeared as attorney for "Constantia [Bonaventura], one of the executors of the will of Guido Bonaventura," who was prosecuting for debts owed the estate.[74] When the widowed Constantia entered the cloister, Fulbert continued to serve her. In 1313 he was acting as the attorney for "Alice de Shersted, abbess of the new

69 Paxton, *Nunneries*, pp. 84–87.

70 CCR 1339–1341, p. 267.

71 Bourdillon, *Minoresses*, p. 52; *SS*, p. 104.

72 Lee, *Nunneries*, p. 39.

73 *CCR 1323–1327*, p. 316.

74 *CCR 1307–1313*, p. 222.

abbey without Aldgate [the Minories]" as well as Constantia who had now become a nun in that house.[75]

Shared regional identity was almost as important a factor as blood relations when it came to establishing or creating bonds between nuns and their lawyers. Regional proximity naturally encouraged contacts between lawyers and clients generally, as Paul Brand has pointed out: "It seems to have been quite common for agreements between litigants and their attorneys for service in the Westminster (or York) courts to be made not at Westminster or York but in the country and normally in the litigant's own county" or, we might add, parish.[76] When lawyers and nuns were fellow parishioners the former might naturally tender their services to their cloistered neighbors. For instance, John Martin [Martyn], Chief Justice of Common Pleas (Common Bench) was among Dartford parish gentry.[77] In 1400, he was licensed to plead for the nuns of Dartford and his connection to the house did not end there. In 1436 he bequeathed a considerable tract of land to the priory and in 1437 he held the offices of overseer and receiver-general.[78]

No matter how they were recruited, lawyers had to be paid, and with this irrefutable fact in mind we proceed to perhaps the most fundamental feature of legal professionalization in late medieval England. When a wealthy lawyer like John Martin, who could easily have counseled his cloistered clients for free, charged them his accustomed fee instead, it was not just a question of need or greed. Pleading *gratis* was not considered ethical. In a profession where men were pledged to serve one client as impartially as another, standard remuneration helped ensure equitable treatment.[79] Exception was made for paupers, of course, but there is no evidence that the nuns in this study benefited from the designation. Cloistered nuns, therefore, like all other clients, had to pay for the services of their legal professionals. That is not to say that what and how they paid them are easily determined.

We know from an entry in the Close Rolls that for the nearly twenty-year-long litigation between the nuns of Denney and Thomas Burgoyne the nuns paid a total of £200 in legal fees; but such statistics are very

75 *Ibid.*, p. 529.

76 Brand, *Origins of the Legal Profession*, p. 94.

77 Lee, *Nunneries*, p. 10. Although Lee places him in King's Bench, see *Select Cases in the Court of King's Bench*, vol. 82.

78 *VCH Kent*, vol. 2, pp. 181–190.

79 Ramsey, "Retained Legal Counsel," p. 106.

seldom provided by the public record.[80] Clients paying legal retainers could be expected to record the amounts tendered, but as noted previously, financial records for English Franciscan, Dominican, and Bridgettine nuns have survived in piecemeal fashion outside of any cartulary. Extant account books for the mendicant houses and Syon contain information about wages paid to household staff and stewards as well as cash outlays for corrodians but they provide no unimpeachable evidence about legal fees paid out to lawyers. Even that exhaustive valuation of monastic income and expenditures made at the time of the Dissolution, the *Valor Ecclesiasticus*, is unhelpful since Henry VIII forbade the inclusion of legal expenses incurred by any save a few (men's) colleges and monasteries.[81] Still, the historian is not without resources for making determinations about fees charged by lawyers for their services and the arrangements made by cloistered nuns to pay for those services.

As with any class of professionals, levels of legal accomplishment were reflected in pay scales, and different types of common lawyers commanded different fees. If and when that level of achievement is determined for an individual, his fees can be estimated with reasonable certainty. For example, in the fourteenth century, the regular salary for the king's serjeants was £20 a year.[82] In the mid-fifteenth century, 40d. appears to have been a minimum fee payable to a serjeant of the Common Bench for his one-time services, if no other agreement had been arrived at in advance.[83] Late in that century the fixed fee for a serjeant at law to plead on a one-time basis was 3s. 4d.[84] The City of London courts had established pay scales for lawyers enrolled to practice there as well and we find the names of some men who had been retained by cloistered nuns on the lists. Abbess Margery de Honylane's attorney, Robert de Waltyngton, was one such regular practitioner in the city, as was Nicholas de Cranle, attorney for the Minories in 1328.[85]

Advocates and proctors in ecclesiastical courts were similarly paid according to a scale, with remarkable constancy over time. In the Consistory Court of York, advocates' maximum fees "remained virtu-

80 *VCH Cambridge*, vol. 2, p. 299; see also Bourdillon, *Minoresses*, p. 30; Lee, *Nunneries*, p. 37; Bell, *What Nuns Read*, pp. 9–10.

81 Ives, *Common Lawyers*, pp. 131–132.

82 G. O. Sayles, ed. *Select Cases in the Court of King's Bench* (London: Bernard Quaritch, 1971), p. xxx.

83 Brand, *Origins of the Legal Profession*, p. 105.

84 Baker, *The Legal Profession*, p. 105.

85 "Misc. Roll DD November 1319–August 1328," #296. See the list in Tucker, *Law Courts*, Appendix 8.2.

ally unchanged for nearly three hundred and fifty years after Archbishop Greenfield established a fee schedule in 1311."[86] Such fee schedules might be based on payment per appearance in court, or they might specify fees per annum. Per-case maximum fees for practitioners in the fourteenth-century Consistory Court of York were set at 50s. for advocates and 10s. for proctors.[87] In the fifteenth century the Consistory Court of Canterbury had a schedule which set proctor's fees at 6d. per court appearance.[88] In the same century an advocate could expect to receive 20s. for a year's service in that court, and a proctor, 1 mark or 13s. 4d.[89]

Dishonest lawyers were popularly satirized in the Middle Ages, but clients too could defraud.[90] Suits filed either by disaffected clients or by lawyers whose clients had defaulted on promised fees provide additional information about salaries. We learn from a suit filed in 1312, for instance, that an attorney might be retained to act in Common Bench and elsewhere for a lifetime retainer of 20s. and a robe, and that a five-year period of service in that same court might command an annual retainer of 5 marks.[91] Finally, although cloistered houses lack them, the cartularies and account books of traditional monasteries abound. Because they include meticulous records of legal fees, cartularies of open nunneries and monasteries have considerable comparative value. For the year 1439, for example, the Durham Priory cartulary recorded the annual outlay for the priory's permanent advocate and proctor retained in the York Consistory Court as 26s. 8d., and 6s. 8d., respectively.[92]

As the case of Denney *vs.* Burgoyne suggests, legal fees must at times have consumed a very significant percentage of a cloistered nunnery's revenue. To put the financial outlay in this case into perspective, Denney's annual net worth at the time of the Dissolution was only £174.[93] Exorbitant legal fees sometimes seriously compromised the finances of open nunneries as well. The Augustinian nuns of Goring pleaded in 1517 that they were unable to repair convent buildings due to the excessive

86 James A. Brundage, "The Profits of the Law: Legal Fees of University-Trained Advocates," *American Journal of Legal History*32 (1988): 13.

87 Brand, *Origins of the Legal Profession*, p. 153.

88 Brundage, *Medieval Origins*, p. 364.

89 Adams and Donahue, *Select Cases*, p. 25.

90 Brundage, *Medieval Origins*, pp. 334–336.

91 Brand, *Origins of the Legal Profession*, p. 91. Subsequent pages contain more evidence gleaned from litigation between clients and their lawyers.

92 Dobson, *Durham Priory*, p. 137.

93 *VE*, iii, 499.

expenses of a lawsuit.[94] Even when nunneries were cash poor, however, they need not have gone without retained counsel. Fees in the form of annual livery of robes, dinners, and other commodities were not uncommonly bestowed upon lawyers by their lay litigants, and religious houses followed suit. They also used a form of remuneration already common in most communities to secure the lifetime services of counsel, the annuity (corrody) or pension.[95]

Between 1360 and 1370 for instance, Durham Cathedral Priory provided about £20 a year in pensions to common lawyers and by 1410 the priory spent between £50 and £60 on annual pensions awarded to practitioners in both canon and common law.[96] During the rule of Walter de Wenlok (1283–1307), Westminster Abbey had numerous annuitants who were being rewarded for services rendered as proctors, justices at King's Bench and Common Pleas, attorneys, and consultants.[97] We can say with certainty that at least two of the cloistered houses whose causes we are about to investigate paid their lawyers in the same way. Foreseeing that the Dissolution was in sight, Prioress Jane Vane of Dartford (1537–1539) began to provide for the friends and faithful officials of the priory in 1538. Of the eleven annuities that she is recorded as granting, three were made to men who had served as counsel to the monastery.[98] Thomas Golde, gentleman, received 53s. 4d. yearly, William Waller of Gray's Inn, and John Wyseman of London, were paid 40s. each. The noted lawyer Sir Richard Sutton was numbered among Syon's annuitants in the sixteenth century and the existence of pensioners at the Minories strongly suggest that similar arrangements were also made there.[99]

One way or another nuns paid for the services of their professional lawyers. But what if a lawyer failed to perform those services or did so badly? It was known to happen. In 1256 the sisters of Nuneaton Priory were obliged to honor a debt of 200 marks amassed by a man claiming to be their proctor at the Papal Curia.[100] There is a hint that something of the sort might have occurred with Dartford attorney Walter Durant, as we shall see in the next chapter. Peculations and misadventures involving lawyers must

94 Power, *Medieval English Nunneries*, p. 202.

95 Baker, *The Legal Profession*, p. 101; Brand, *Origins of the Legal Profession*, p. 100.

96 Ramsey, "Retained Legal Counsel," p. 104.

97 Harvey, *Obedientiaries*, pp. 31–33.

98 C. F. R. Palmer, "History of the Priory of Dartford," *Archaeological Journal* 36 (1879): 266.

99 *DNB*, vol. 53, p. 401; see as well, *VCH Middlesex*, vol. 1, pp. 182–191.

100 Bernice Kerr, *Religious Life for Women from the Twelfth to the Middle of the Fourteenth Century with Special Reference to the English Foundations of the Order of Fontevraud* (Oxford: Oxford University Press, 1995), p. 130.

have occurred as they had done with the stewards and bailiffs upon whom nunneries had traditionally relied to conduct their business affairs; there is no reason to assume that lawyers were made of finer stuff.[101] But there *is* an important distinction that needs to be drawn between these traditional monastic officials and retained, newly professional, legal counsel.

Relied upon as rent-collectors, receivers, and general farm supervisors, lower-level stewards and bailiffs worked for salaries. They were often employed along with their wives and had lodgings or corrodies adjacent to the cloister. Such employees might be especially attentive to the nuns they served because a daughter or niece had become one of their number. Conversely, a familiar, almost domestic, relationship with their employers might tempt them to laxness, encouraging them to use their positions to aggrandize themselves and their kin. In other words, traditional monastic agents and officials were good, or bad, or middling employees, but they were *not* professionals.

The new professional status of men who saw to the legal business of late medieval cloistered nuns set them apart from traditional monastic employees who attended to other temporal business. Professional legal status denoted ethical as well as technical standards, as a comparison of twelfth- and thirteenth-century practice illustrates.

> Twelfth-century legal practitioners were not professionals in any sense of the term that they would have recognized because courts did not require them to make a "profession," to observe a special set of ethical standards as a necessary condition for representing clients before a judge. On this understanding of "profession," twelfth-century lawyers may more accurately be described as proto-professionals. These distinctions are not trivial or a mere semantic nicety. They involve two divergent concepts of what professionalism is all about. In the loose sense of the term, any occupation that requires special knowledge or skill and whose members are rewarded for the exercise of that knowledge or skill may be called a profession. The strict sense of the term adds to this the further qualification that profession necessarily involves an ethical commitment. "Profession" in this view means a skilled occupation in which practitioners agree to observe specific ethical standards in carrying out their work as a condition of entrance into practice. When they swore the admissions oath, medieval advocates and proctors accepted both a legal and a moral obligation. Once they had made that commitment, observance of the stipulated behavioral standards became mandatory and failure to do so was punishable at law.[102]

By the mid-thirteenth century, English common lawyers, like the advocates and proctors referenced above, had achieved professional status in the strict sense of the term. The Statute of Westminster I (1275) first

101 Power, *Medieval English Nunneries*, pp. 147–149.

102 Brundage, *Medieval Origins*, p. 491.

prescribed standards of professional conduct for those practicing in the royal courts.[103] For instance, any serjeant "convicted of deception or collusion or being a party to such – whether the intention was to deceive a litigant or the king's justices – was to go to prison for a year and a day and be disbarred from further practice as serjeant."[104] Oaths of admission to the bar specified further standards of service to clients, and once sworn in, court lawyers were subject to the disciplinary measure of that court. When taking these oaths, lawyers swore to avoid practices such as 'ambidexterity' (receiving money from a client's opponent), 'champerty' (rendering legal service contingent on a share of whatever was at stake in the case), and unauthorized resignation before the conclusion of litigation.[105] The duty of the serjeant at law to serve his client loyally and to rigorously uphold his interests was well established by the start of the fourteenth century and it was a duty extended to professional attorneys practicing in the king's courts and the courts of the City of London as well.[106]

What did the establishment of such clear ethical standards for professional lawyers mean to their cloistered clients? Monastic clients might still recruit their lawyers from among family, friends, and patrons, but the creation of professional norms and standards and the establishment of legal mechanisms to correct departures from those norms meant that bonds of kinship, and the degree of a practitioner's spiritual fervor (or the lack thereof) became less important to the job at hand. The services that hired legal professionals rendered were of a uniform and identifiable quality, and there was no longer any need for a close or continuing personal relationship to be maintained between client and counsel to ensure loyalty. Naturally, like stewards, bailiffs, and other traditional monastic agents, professional lawyers did not always act ethically, but they had pledged to do so in a court of law and they could be, and were, sanctioned by the courts for their failures.

In late medieval England, professional lawyers had the technical expertise essential to master the newly complex and, to the amateur, unfathomable thing that the law had become. They also subscribed to a set of ethical norms. These things mattered most to clients who were themselves bound to abide by the rules of the cloister. Much of this book will

103 Brand, *Origins of the Legal Profession*, Chapter 8, deals with the ethical regulation of common law practitioners, in theory and practice; see also Brundage, "The Medieval Advocate's Profession," p. 448 and n. 59.

104 Brand, *Origins of the Legal Profession*, p. 43.

105 *Ibid.*, pp. 121–123.

106 Baker, *Oxford History*, pp. 438–489 for an example of one of the earliest surviving attorney's oaths.

be devoted to providing examples of the work that professional lawyers performed for clients whose vows denied them the opportunity to enter a courtroom and so exert the subtle influence on judges and opponents that personal appearance in a court of law commanded. Before we enter the courts however, we must deal with some of the varied, often tedious, but always essential routine business for which professional lawyers were also retained.

3

Letters of Appointment and Routine Business

The age of legal professionalization in England was an age of written records, the numbers of which are astounding. Rolls from the courts of the itinerant justices from one century alone, the thirteenth, fill 27,500 membranes.[1] From the testimony of witnesses to the debates of the serjeants at law, legal activities were documented as never before. Nevertheless, it remained possible throughout the period for a client to hire a professional lawyer without drawing up a contract to do so. Courts as well as individuals used parole or verbal agreements to engage the services of lawyers for clients. The central courts of the Crown had their own licensed practitioners who might be appointed for routine matters and even the elite serjeant at law could be approached in the halls of Westminster and hired for consultation on the spot. Lawyers who represented clients in the ecclesiastical courts were likewise retained by verbal agreements which the Church used moral constraints to enforce.[2] Contractual agreements *apud acta*, whereby a proctor was appointed for a litigant in front of the judge, were common methods by which clients retained advocates and proctors.[3]

When a lawyer was hired verbally or appointed in the courtroom, evidence of a contractual agreement for professional services, routine or otherwise, might never surface. Chancery petitions, Year Book accounts, and other records of actual litigation sometimes name the lawyers representing their clients, but often do not. Then as now, of course, it was risky to rely solely on verbal exchanges to cement a contract as there was always the chance that one party would not live up to his obligations. If that situation occurred, a lawsuit generating its attendant sheaf of records and naming names of client and lawyer alike would result.[4] In the absence

1 Ruth Kittel, "Women under the Law in Medieval England, 1066–1485," in *The Women of England from Anglo-Saxon Times to the Present*. ed. Barbara Kanner (Hamden, CT: Archon, 1979), pp. 124–137 at p. 133.

2 Baker, *The Legal Profession*, pp. 101–109; Brundage, *Medieval Origins*, pp. 333–336.

3 Norma Adams and Charles Donahue, *Select Cases from the Ecclesiastical Courts of the Province of Canterbury* c. *1200–1301* (London: Selden Society, 1981), pp. 24, 291, 305.

4 Ives, *Common Lawyers*, p. 139 and Brundage, *Medieval Origins*, pp. 333–336.

of any litigious confrontation between them, however, most evidence of a lawyer–client association begun by parole contract is indirect.

For example, personal books of account and public records of institutional expenditures contain evidence of payment for legal services to named individuals. As we have already seen, methods of payment varied greatly and ranged from cash and annuities to robes and dinners, so these outlays are not always immediately recognizable as fees paid to individuals in return for legal service.[5] An entry in the Close Rolls of Henry IV, dated July 16, 1402, for instance, notes that Margaret, abbess, and the sisters of Aldgate made a lifelong grant to Henry Maupas. Maupas is referred to simply as 'clerk' and the grant is for yearly rent of £20 "of all their tenements and possessions spiritual and temporal," together with a yearly rent of 50 marks "of their house."[6] But only if one knows that Henry Maupas, who died in 1415, was a Chancery attorney and clerk does it become reasonable to assume that this large annuity was payment for routine legal services that he had rendered to the nuns.[7]

From a number of entries in the Patent Rolls, we learn that attorneys commonly performed two non-litigious functions for cloistered nuns. One of these was the exemplification of documents and the other was the collection of court-imposed fines and damages. Exemplification was essentially a safety precaution. When a difficult case had finally been adjudicated in a court other than that of the Crown, it was circumspect for the victorious party to get royal affirmation of the settlement. Attorneys submitted a request in Common Pleas for an exemplification, an officially witnessed and sealed statement of the terms of the final sentence in the case. Two such exemplifications were requested by the abbesses of Syon and Denney respectively, as we shall see in the next chapter. Both asked the king to endorse final decrees in disputes which had been highly resistant to resolution.[8]

The collection of fines levied for non-appearance in a pending suit constituted another bit of routine legal business that any competent lawyer in the relevant court could perform. For instance, William Mopetyet, "gentilman" of Suffolk, was cited for not appearing before the justices of the Bench to answer the Prioress of Dartford regarding an alleged debt of

5 As mentioned in Chapter 2. For many examples, see Ramsey, "Retained Legal Counsel," pp. 95–112.

6 *CCR 1399–1402*, p. 589.

7 Richardson, *Medieval Chancery*, pp. 94–95.

8 *CPR 1467–1477*, p. 238, kings and Syon; *CPR 1476–1485*, p. 304, Denney and John Burgoyn.

£100.[9] If not pardoned, his lapse of memory, or will, would result in the charge of outlawry. It is likely then that Mopetyet eventually purchased such a pardon, just as Stephen Bresynden had done when cited for non-appearance in a trespass case involving Syon Abbey.[10] By securing his pardon a defendant satisfied the court but he was usually forced to tender damages to the plaintiff as well. This is what happened in 1480 in another trespass case involving Syon.

> Pardon to William Wolff, late of Thruley *alias* Threwley *alias* Throweley, co. Kent, "gentilman" of his outlawries in the counties of Kent and Middlesex for not appearing before the justices of the Bench to satisfy the king of his ransom for a trespass committed again Robert Hadde [and] Elizabeth, abbess of Syon, of £10. 16s. 3½d. which she recovered against him and 40s. damages, and William Brygam and William Gasegyll of £4. 6s. 8d. which they recovered against him and 13s. 4d. damages; he having surrendered to the Flete prison, as Thomas Bryan, knight, chief justice of the Bench, has certified.[11]

Non-appearance of a defendant was a common occurrence, and since the amount of money awarded in damages could be considerable, plaintiffs did well to have an attorney who could convey that court award to them.

Appointment of lawyers *apud acta* and by parole agreements continued, then, to be common practice in late medieval England. However, written warrants appointing legal counsel do tend to become more common in this period since the absence of such a warrant could have serious consequences for a lawyer. A case in point is that of John of Chester. In 1347, after an examination "of the rolls of attorneys of the court" John was found to have been acting as attorney for his clients in King's Bench without a warrant to do so.[12] Convicted of "falsity and deceit" John was given the statutory penalty of imprisonment for a year and a day; nor was he ever to be allowed to work again in the king's courts.

Letters in which clients officially appointed their attorneys and proctors took various forms. General warrants commencing with the formulaic"For us and in our name …" placed a lawyer or lawyers at a client's disposal if and when need should arise. This type of letter was frequently employed by monasteries, and the nuns of Dartford appear to have been particularly fond of it. From 1368 to 1415 the Patent Rolls reveal that the Crown regularly licensed attorneys upon receipt of these letters. The names of the attorneys designated by the prioress, and the terms of the appointments,

9 *CPR 1416–1422*, p. 159.

10 *CPR 1476–1485*, p. 31.

11 *Ibid.*, p. 199.

12 G. O. Sayles, *Select Cases in the Court of King's Bench* (London: Bernard Quaritch, 1965), p. 62.

usually one to five years, are specified. Some references even mention that a fellow religious, such as the Dominican prior of King's Langley (John Woderove or William Syward [Siwarde]) or the Abbot of Lesnes, a house of Austin canons located in Kent, personally acknowledged receipt of a license at Westminster. The language of these memoranda is instructive because of the repeated mention of claustration. Although formulaic, the memos also illustrate some interesting variations over time and may be contrasted with other, similar, warrants.

> 1368 Grant that Michael Skillyng and Walter Perle, whom Maud prioress of the house of the order of Preachers, Dertford, pursuant to a power granted her by the king has appointed as her attorneys before him, may make other attorneys at their will. Brother John Woderove received the attorneys by writ.[13]
>
> 1370 Maud, prioress of the house of the order of Preachers, Dertford, who is a recluse and cannot personally labour about the pleas and other matters touching her and her house, has letters nominating Brother Walter Durrant as her attorney in England for one year; and the king, at the instance of the said prioress, has granted that the said Walter may make other attorneys in his place. Brother John Woderove received the attorney by writ. The same prioress has other letters nominating Michael Skillyng and Roger Digg as her attorneys as above.[14]
>
> 1371 Because Maud, prioress of the house of the order of Preachers Dertford, is a recluse and cannot personally labor about pleas and other matters touching her and her house, she had, by the king's licence, attorned before the king in her place Nicholas Heryng and friar Walter Durant to act for her in all pleas in any courts of England for one year. The king has also granted, at the instance of the prioress, that the said attorneys may make other attorneys to act in their place. The prioress had other letters nominating Michael Skillyngy and John Videleu as her attorneys as above.[15]
>
> 1374 Because Maud, etc ... the king has granted her that she may appoint general attorneys in her place; and she had attorned before him friar William [*sic*] Durant and John Videleu at act for her in all pleas in England; and at her instance, the king has granted that her said attorneys may make other attorneys in their place; for two years. John Woderove received the attorneys by writ. She has like letters nominating Michael Skillyng and Thomas Sherdelowe as her attorneys as above.[16]
>
> 1377 The king having granted license to Joan prioress of the house of the order of Preachers, Derteford, of the foundation of the late king, to make her own general attorneys, and she having appointed brother Walter Durant and

13 *CPR 1367–1370*, p. 161. Woderove [Woderowe] was the king's confessor and prior of King's Langley.

14 *Ibid.*, p. 357.

15 *CPR 1370–1374*, p. 75.

16 *CPR 1374–1377*, p. 42.

Nicholas Heryng her attorneys, they at her instance may make attorneys for her for two years. Brother William Siwarde received the attorneys by writ.[17]

1379 Letters for Joan, prioress of the house of the order of Preachers, Dertford, unable personally to attend pleas and other business affecting her house, nominating Michael Skillyng and Walter Duraunt her attorneys for three years. The abbot of Lesnes received the attorneys by writ.[18]

1384 Grant for three year that as Joan, prioress etc. is a recluse, she may make general attorneys, and she having attorned friar Walter Durant, and John Bretton in all courts, at her instance the king grants that they or whichever of them happens to be present, may make attorneys or attorney in her place in the King's Bench. The abbot of Lesnes received the attorneys by writ.[19]

1387 License for Joan etc. as she is a recluse, to make her own general attorneys and for friar Walter Durant and William Makenade, whom she has appointed her attorney, to make attorneys for her for three years. Robert de Faryngton, clerk, received the attorneys.[20]

1391 The king having granted license to Joan, etc. she having appointed brother Walter Durant and William Makenade her attorneys, they at her instance may make attorneys for her for three years. The abbot of Lesnes received the attorneys by writ.[21]

1397 Joan prioress etc. licence to make attorneys general, and at her instance, for William Makenade and friar Walter Duraunt, who she has made her attorney, to make attorneys in her stead for a year. Rober de Faryngton, clerk, received the attorneys by her letter.[22]

1400 Grant to Joan etc. of John Martyn and brother Walter Durant as her attorneys for one year. John Wakeryng, clerk, received the attorneys.[23]

1415 Grant for three years to the prioress of the house of the order of Preachers of Derteford, which is of the foundation of Edward III and of the king's patronage, as she is a recluse and so cannot labour in person about pleas and other businesses touching herself and her house, that she may appoint general attorneys for this purpose and that Robert Kendale and William Gonorby, clerk, whom she has attorned, may appoint attorneys in her place. The abbot of Lesnes received the attorneys by writ.[24]

17 *CPR 1377–1381*, p. 73. Brother Siward [Syward] was prior of King's Langley.

18 *Ibid.*, p. 402.

19 *CPR 1381–1385*, p. 370.

20 *CPR 1385–1389*, p. 377.

21 *CPR 1388–1392*, p. 371.

22 *CPR 1396–1399*, p. 69.

23 *CPR 1399–1401*, p. 398. Richardson, *Medieval Chancery*, p. 73, states that John Wakeryng, d. 1425, "was the most successful and widely-known Chancery clerk of the early Lancastrian period."

24 *CPR 1413–1416*, p. 302.

Aside from these references to Dartford, the Patent Rolls contain only two other mentions of receipt of general letters of attorney from cloistered nuns. In both instances, the letters were received by the Crown from Joan, the Abbess of Waterbeach. Attorneys Thomas de Redeswelle and Hugh le Taillur were licensed to serve her for a term of five years in 1298 and Stephen de Clopton and Robert Barnard were retained for five years in 1305.[25]

What do we know about these men hired by warrant to be the regular legal representatives of the nuns of Dartford and Waterbeach? For most, little more than their names remain behind. But three emerge as fuller figures and bear mention here; two because of their legal eminence, and one because of his infamy.

The active and oft-reappointed attorney for Dartford Priory, Michael Skillyng, served as King's Attorney in the Court of Common Pleas from 1361 to 1377.[26] He is mentioned in the Close and Patent Rolls countless times as suing for the king in complicated cases involving lands and privileges at the highest reaches of English society.[27] Along with Dartford attorney Nicholas Heryng, Skillyng helped the nuns of Dartford to consolidate their numerous holdings and include them under one royal grant in December of 1371.[28] He was also attorney for important officials, such as Robert de Fienles, Constable of France "abiding beyond the sea," and entrusted to sue in their names in any court in England.[29] During his term as King's Attorney, he was appointed steward and surveyor of all priory lands, an appointment that one imagines was made with confidence.[30]

John Martyn exceeded even Skillyng in prominence. In 1418, Martyn was created a serjeant at law and in 1420 he was named a justice of Common Pleas, a position that he held until his death in 1437.[31] While his elevation to the Bench precluded any further involvement as legal counsel for the nuns, Martyn continued to be a friend to the community. He had made a landed bequest to the priory in 1407 and in 1436 he and

25 *CPR 1292–1301*, p. 345; *CPR 1301–1307*, p. 315.

26 Sayles, *Select Cases*, vol. 82, pp. lxxxiv–lxxxv.

27 *CCR 1364–1368*, p. 392; *CCR 1377–1381*, pp. 274–75; pp. 383–83 to cite representative memoranda.

28 Palmer, "History of the Priory of Dartford," p. 250.

29 *CCR 1364–1368*, p. 92.

30 *CPR 1361–1364*, p. 494.

31 J. H. Baker, *The Order of Serjeants at Law: A Chronicle of Creations, with Related Texts and Historical Introduction* (London: Selden Society, 1984), p. 525.

two associates donated an additional 17½ acres of wood and land.[32] In the year of his death, Martyn was still serving the nuns as their receiver general.[33]

Co-counsel with John Martyn in 1400 was Brother Walter Durant. Appointed and reappointed since 1368, Durant was peculiar in virtually all respects. He was one of a handful of Dominican friars resident at Dartford Priory.[34] Given the canonical prohibitions against the study and practice of the law by regular clergy, his repeated attornment must have been the consequence of applying what even moral rigorists recognized as inevitable, the exception to the rule. If a monk, canon, or friar practiced law at the behest of his religious superior, and if he did so for the benefit of his community, he acted legitimately.[35] Durant's residence at Dartford coupled with the fact that his religious superior, Prior John Woderove, had employed him as his attorney in this 1367 case, would seem to have accorded him that legitimacy.

> Friar John Woderove, Warden of the House of Derteford, recently founded by the King, presented a bill by his attorney, Friar Walter Durant, complaining that he had lent to John Chynle, mercer, and his partner Ralph Knyghton the sum of £55 belonging to the House, to be repaid last Michaelmas. The borrowers had traded and profited with the money, which they now refused to pay. He prayed that the said Ralph be summoned to answer. The defendant appeared on summons and denied that he was a partner either at the time of the loan or afterwards. Thereupon with the consent of the plaintiff's attorney he made his law to that effect with his single hand [*cum sola manu propria*]. Judgment that the plaintiff take nothing by his bill and be in mercy and that the said Ralph go quit.[36]

The ever greater technicalities of the common law in this period meant that Walter Durant would have needed more than just a canonical exemption to practice successfully, or even, as his performance for Prior Woderove would suggest, with limited success. And practice he did, as further evidence from the plea rolls demonstrates.

> The sum of 20 marks, paid into court by John Vyne, draper, on 4 Aug. as damages for waste committed by him in a house in Cordwainer Street formerly

32 "Friaries: The Dominican Nuns of Dartford," in *A History of the County of Kent*, vol. 2 (1926), pp. 181–190. Online at www.british-history.ac.uk/report.aspx?compid=38217 (accessed June 4, 2009).

33 *Ibid.*

34 Lee, *Nunneries*, p. 224.

35 Brundage, *Medieval Origins*, pp. 469–470.

36 "Roll A 13: 1367–68," in *Calendar of the Plea and Memoranda Rolls of the City of London*, vol. 2: *1364–1381* (1929), pp. 84–95. Online at www.british-history.ac.uk/report.aspx?compid=36677&strquery=walter durant (accessed June 3, 2009).

> held by James Andreu, Alderman, for life, which tenement having reverted to the King was granted by him to the Prioress and Sisters of the Order of St Augustine at Dartford, was paid over to Friar Walter Durant, attorney of the Prioress, in accordance with a writ under the Privy Seal dated at Westminster 26 Nov. 1375.[37]

He appears again on November 11, 1376, in Chancery, when one Sir John Dannteseye acknowledged his huge debt of 1,000 marks owed to the Prioress of Dartford. In partial payment, Dannteseye released to the prioress and to the friars of King's Langley some inherited property worth 300 marks. The prior of King's, Thomas Walsh, collected his share of 100 marks, and Walter Durant collected the 200 marks due to the nuns.[38] And since Walter Durant and John Bretton were both general counsel for Dartford in 1384, one of them was doubtless the unnamed attorney licensed in another debt collection or repossession case. Counsel for the nuns was to deliver to "the prioress and convent of sisters preachers at Derford," two messuages (dwelling houses together with outbuildings and adjacent land assigned to their use) and three shops in London because the tenants had defaulted on their rent.[39]

How Friar Durant had acquired legal training sufficient to navigate the procedural shoals of the common law courts and Chancery, and where he learned his law, remain mysteries. Mysterious too are the circumstances which, in 1390, led to his need to be pardoned by the Crown "at the supplication of the king's confessor, Alexander Bache, of the order of Friars Preachers ... for all felonies and trespasses whereof he is indicted, and of any consequent outlawry."[40] Then there is the ultimate mystery of his final years working as the Dartford Priory attorney.

Although we have the above memorandum licensing him along with John Martyn as a Dartford attorney in 1400, a petition for Durant's arrest as an apostate was issued on 8 November, 1399.[41] The petition was for the writ *de apostata capiendo*, that is, one which requests the aid of secular authorities to seize and return a religious runaway.[42] It was sued by the provincial prior of the London Dominicans, William Pickworth, and

37 From "Roll A 21: 1375–76," in *ibid*., pp. 206–230.

38 Palmer, "History of the Priory of Dartford," p. 252.

39 *CCR 1381–1385*, pp. 483–484.

40 *CPR 1388–1392*, p. 234. The pardon mentions John Fyfhyde, master of theology, first, and includes Durant, Durant's servant, Thomas, and William Cave, who was a benefactor to Dartford.

41 F. Donald Logan, *Runaway Religious in Medieval England*, c. *1240–1540* (Cambridge: Cambridge University Press), p. 242.

42 C 81/1792/8. For in-depth treatment of the mechanisms for return of apostate religious in England see Logan, *Runaway Religious*.

addressed to the Lord Chancellor John Scarle (1399–1401).[43] In it, Prior Pickworth asked for the forcible return of Brother Walter Durant who, having taken off his religious habit, and left his London house without the permission of his superiors, wandered alone around the city of London and elsewhere as an apostate, *having already been an excommunicate for more than a year.*

A disconcerting picture of Dartford co-counsel, both licensed in 1400, emerges. One man John Martyn, was a distinguished serjeant at law on his way to becoming a justice of Common Pleas, the other, Walter Durant, was a recent excommunicate and apostate. This picture becomes slightly less disconcerting if we note that Durant's record of misconduct was not strikingly different from that of another fourteenth-century lawyer, Master Hugh Candlesby. Candlesby was a notary, proctor, and a flagrant abuser of the legal process in which he was embedded. He was a member of the bar of the Bishop of Ely's consistory, and had been excommunicated, and absolved, twice, after which he continued to offend, without retribution, for most of his life because of his powerful social connections.[44] Invariably, weak men like Durant and Candlesby foundered because the penalties for succumbing to the temptations of office were minimized by the connections one formed while holding it.

General warrants appointing attorneys, like those cited here earlier, were always exceedingly cryptic. Whether they licensed specialists in canon, common, or civil law, general instruments of proxy were required to specify only two things: the name of the appointee and the period of time for which he was to be of service. But despite their brevity, they appear almost without exception to have allowed cloistered nuns to plead through their attorneys without legal challenge.[45] The formulaic reference to the abbess of a cloistered house as "a recluse unable personally to labor about pleas" was used in many general licenses, and it even appears in the law reports as a sort of shorthand for excused absence from court. In 1455, when a justice of Common Pleas debated the legitimacy of a defendant's non-appearance in court because of illness, his excuse was compared to that of "a recluse [who] cannot personally labour about the pleas and other matters touching her and her house."[46]

43 Walter Grumbley, "Provincial Priors and Vicars of the English Dominicans, 1221–1916." *EHR* 33 (April, 1918): 246.

44 James A. Brundage, *The Profession and Practice of Medieval Canon Law* (Burlington, VT: Ashgate, 2004), pp. 551–554. This segment of an article on the bar of the Bishop of Ely's consistory court details the career of Master Hugh Candlesby

45 I have found only one challenge to the use of the general license and it will be treated in the next chapter.

46 Seipp #1455.023, accessed July 19, 2010.

Multipurpose document that it was, a general letter of appointment still had its limitations. The lawyer whom a nunnery retained for routine transactions might not have the expertise to deal with a particularly technical matter, and when such legal business needed doing it was advisable to draw up specialized letters of appointment. Unlike the general letter, specialized warrants do not usually mention a term of service but by their very nature they provide more information about the job to be done by the appointee. The formal acknowledgement of an indemnification or debt, and the receipt or delivery of seisin (possession of property), were two of the most common non-litigious functions for which cloistered nuns issued specific letters of appointment. The case of Cambin Fulbert, already alluded to in Chapter 2, provides a good example of the former.

In 1309 Fulbert (Cambinus Fulberti), designated attorney of Constance Bonaventure, acknowledged payment of a debt due to the estate of Guy Bonaventure.[47] Constance was the widow of Guy, and one of the executors of his last will and testament, but she had subsequently become a Minoress under Abbess Alice de Sherstede of Aldgate. She and the abbess put Cambin in their place to sue for, and indemnify receipt of, all debts due to Guy – a task for which he had ample experience. Cited alternately as a "merchant of Florence" and "citizen of London," Fulbert had sued for many debts owed the Italian merchants, especially the Frescobaldi, upon whom the Crown was so dependent at the time; he even became "tutor curator administer" of the children of one of those merchants.[48] Despite this expertise, however, Fulbert obviously had trouble with his commission for the widow turned nun, although she retained enough confidence in his skills to reappoint him. In 1331, over twenty years after his initial appointment as her attorney, Constance was still struggling to redeem all of her late husband's debts. Surprisingly, she still remained confident that Fulbert could assist her: "Constance Bonaventure, executrix of the will of Guy Bonaventure, her late husband, puts in her place Cambinus Fulberti, citizen of London, to prosecute the execution of all debts due to Guy."[49]

It was a debt again, but this time in the form of unpaid tithes, that prompted Abbess Elizabeth Muston of Syon to license William Lardner

47 CCR *1307–1313*, p. 222 and p. 569 identifying Constantia as a Minoress at Aldgate.

48 *Ibid.* p 129 and CCR *1296–1302*, pp. 139, 296 for other examples of his activities. In 1324, two merchants of Florence attorned him to prosecute for a recognisance due them from the Abbot of Bruern, CCR *1323–1327*, p. 316. See also "Folios ccxxxi – ccxl: October. 1332–," in *Calendar of Letter-Books of the City of London: E: 1314–1337* (1903), pp. 271–288. Online at www.british-history.ac.uk/report.aspx?compid=33118 (accessed June 8, 2009).

49 CCR *1330–1333*, p. 279.

as her proctor in 1496.[50] Lardner was commissioned to appear before Richard Walleff, newly appointed vicar of the parish church of Axmouth (a Syon possession since 1415) "about the tithes within the parish of Axmouth, Devon."[51] Two years earlier, Walleff's predecessor John Capell had granted the parish tithes to Abbess Muston "to hold until the said abbess shall have received the sum of six pounds."[52]

Perhaps it was a stipulation which the new vicar, Richard, had not wanted to honor. In the event, it would be Lardner's job to sort out the affair.

Brief mention of the appointment of attorneys to take possession of property sometimes occurs in the Close Roles. In 1459, for example, John White was appointed attorney for Prioress Margaret Beaumont of Dartford. He was to deliver seisin of a messuage in London.[53] Public records of account, especially those of the Exchequer, often provide more detailed information about the appointment of attorneys to take seisin of property.

Minories abbess Dorothy Cumberford is recorded as appointing Roger Higham as her attorney on 26 June, 1531, for the specific purpose of confiscating a tenement in Hunt's Alley, London, from the Crutched Friars.[54] Those friars had been willed the tenement with conditions, such as upkeep of the property and payment of an annual stipend to the Minoresses and they had apparently failed to fulfill those conditions. In this instance, we know something more than the name of the man licensed to repossess the property for the abbess. Augmentation Office records note that Roger Higham had given the nuns "true faithful and diligent service of a long time hertofore … in soliciting all matters and causes of the law," and that by 1538 he had held the offices of Under Steward and Receiver. For these services he was paid a yearly fee of £8 plus a corrody of meat and drink worth another £4.[55] Higham was clearly an asset to the Minoresses of Aldgate since he also had a furnished house in the monastery precincts and at the time of the Dissolution was pensioned off at £4. 4s. 10d.[56]

In addition to memoranda mentioning them, a few complete letters of appointment survive. The two dealt with here both designate men to

50 E 326/271.

51 "Alien Houses: The Priory of Loders," in *A History of the County of Dorset*, vol. 2 (1908), pp. 116–118. Online at www.british-history.ac.uk/report.aspx?compid=40168&strquery=Loders (accessed June 8, 2009).

52 E 326/272.

53 *CCR 1454–1461*, p. 393.

54 Paxton, *Nunneries*, p. 134, fn 171, records this case.

55 Bourdillon, *The Order of Minoresses*, pp. 33–34.

56 Tomlinson, *History of the Minories*, p. 64.

receive seisin on behalf of cloistered nuns. The 1424 authorization of two attorneys to receive seisin of the manor of Grauncortes for Syon abbess Joan North is a fine example of a clearly executed and specific letter of attorney.[57]

> To all faithful Christians, to those present here, the abbess and convent of the monastery of St Savior and Sts Mary Virgin and Brigitte of Syon of the order of St Augustine, known as St Savior, send greetings in the eternal Lord. We have ordained and put in our place, our beloved in Christ Richard Skot, cleric, and John Seton, to be sent out and to receive for us in our name full and peaceful seisin of and in the manor of Grauncortes with all pertaining to it in the county of Essex, one messuage one cracate [approx. 120 acres] and two virgates [30 acres] of land, twenty-four acres of meadow, four acres of wood, twenty acres of pasture, eighteen shillings rent, and pasture for one hundred sheep in Istelworth, Twyknham, Worton, and Heston in the county of Middlesex with all appertaining according to the same form and offering made to us in a charter by Thomas, bishop of Durham, John Stafford, treasurer of England, late keeper of the privy seal of Lord Henry [V] king of England, father of our lord king [Henry VI], Master William Sevenok, former mayor of London, and Henry of Chadirton, thereupon the aforesaid Richard and John or another whom they grant permission to act in our name, will inhabit it truly, rightly and freely. In present testimony of which thing we cause the seal of our community to be attached. Dated in the chapter house of the monastery this, the third day of November in the year of the reign of King Henry VI, after the third term [1424].

As was true of the general warrants issued for Dartford, Joan North's license countenances the possibility that her appointed attorneys might themselves designate others to act for the nuns if need arose. This stipulation must have saved time and parchment in the event that one or both of the lawyers appointed could not personally appear in court on a given day or time. And in the case of Grauncortes manor, saving time might have been the order of the day for the nuns of Syon since they had already waited for years to take possession of it. In his confirmation of Syon possessions, also dated 1424, King Henry VI mentioned that his father's wish to convey Grauncortes and appurtenances had yet to be carried out since Henry V's trustees had not obtained royal license to do so.[58]

The delays surrounding the Grauncortes transfer were certainly not novel. Gifts in mortmain, of which this was one, were never easily made nor effortlessly secured. Because property bequeathed in mortmain was

57 E 326/3871. Description of this letter can also be found at "Deeds: B.3871–B.3900," in *A Descriptive Catalogue of Ancient Deeds*, vol. 3 (1900), pp. 268–271. Online at www.british-history.ac.uk/report.aspx?compid=64341&strquery="Richard Skot" (accessed June 9, 2009). The catalogue contains numerous other letters of attorney, enrolled by a cross section of society.

58 Aungier, *History*, p. 46.

made 'to a dead hand,' that is, to a monastic corporation deemed immortal, neither the Crown nor potential heirs could profit further from it. Kings were loath to countenance the perpetual loss of revenues in the form of inheritance dues and taxes and prospective heirs (as we shall observe in the next case) might baulk at pious generosity at their expense. Those who made bequests in mortmain without the requisite royal license were fined for trespass; so too, were religious who received such unlicensed grants – as the Minoresses of Aldgate found out on more than one occasion.[59]

After the appointment of attorneys Skot and Seton (although it is not clear how long after) Grauncorte and appurtenances finally did convey to Syon. One of the few surviving surveys of Syon possessions, taken in 1492, lists an annual income from "the manors of Felsted and Grauntcourt" of £95.[60] Nor was it lost to the nuns until very late in the day. Abbess Agnes Jordan alienated Grauncorte manor, along with other property, to the chancellor of the Court of Augmentation in 1537.[61]

The licensing of proctors, appointed when legal dealings involved ecclesiastical right, was also done by specific warrant. This letter on behalf of the Minoresses of Aldgate is typical of the genre.

> Let it be known by this to all that Katherina [de Ingham] abbess, and the convent, house, or monastery of the Minoresses outside of Algate London, of the order or rule of St Clare, ordain, make and constitute our beloved cleric Master Thomas Atteponde, cleric of the same London diocese, and house and monastery aforesaid ... give and concede the same general power and a special mandate to apprehend for us in the name of this house or monastery aforesaid and to bring to our use the parish church of Kessyngland [Kessingland], in the diocese of Norwich, already vacated to us and to our successors, canonically appropriated and conceded to our use and perpetual possession, and to this same person we grant the right to take possession, to enter onto the same and to protect and defend against all and any force and effect this appropriation ... The seal of the monastery is appended and our words are attested to by Robert, cleric and notary whose name is subscribed hereunder and this done publically before us all and dated this day 12 January, 1358, in our aforesaid monastery. And I Robert Spyng cleric of God in the diocese of York, public notary, attest this to all and each this 12th day of January 1358.[62]

The straightforward and unremarkable language of the warrant masks the fact that in this instance Master Thomas Atteponde had his work cut out

59 CCR *1317–1321*, p. 589; CCR *1377–1381*, p. 432. Tomlinson, *History of the Minories*, p. 34, pp. 39–40.

60 Aungier, *History*. p. 77.

61 *Ibid.*, p. 82.

62 LR 14/1175.

for him.[63] Queen Isabella had indeed given the advowson of the Church of Kessingland to the nuns fully two years previously, in June, 1346.[64] The letter of appointment quite correctly commissioned Master Atteponde "to bring to our use the parish church of Kessyngland [Kessingland], in the diocese of Norwich, *already vacated to us and to our successors, canonically appropriated and conceded to our use and perpetual possession* …" The words "perpetual possession," of course, refer to the fact that the gift was made in mortmain, and this was the source of all the difficulty.

Queen Isabella had acquired Kessingland from one Robert de Mohant, knight, but since she had then 'regifted' it, in mortmain, it could no longer descend in normal course; Robert de Mohant's heirs would now never profit from the advowson. William de Mountagu, Earl of Salisbury, was one of those heirs and he had been contesting Robert's power to deny him his due. Enter Master Thomas Atteponde. A year after his appointment to act in the matter, on October 17, 1359, the Earl of Salisbury finally relented and filed a formal renunciation of his inheritance rights. The nuns of Aldgate could now claim their gift, but taking possession of Kessingland had certainly not been a mere formality.[65]

As Atteponde's case demonstrates, legal wrangling often preceded the appointment of an attorney to carry out an apparently routine transaction. In those cases the lawyer's appointment was something like the final round of the game. But the opposite might also be true. The appointment of an attorney to execute a routine legal task might trigger further litigation. Unless his client had eliminated the possibility by restrictive wording in the original instrument of proxy, an attorney who thought he had been hired to oversee a drawing-room deal might find himself enmeshed in a full-fledged courtroom battle instead.

Regardless of how they got there, lawyers representing cloistered English nuns often found themselves in the lists. Intent on maintaining their lands, rights, and revenues, the nuns were named as litigants in nearly every court in England, and several in Rome. The scope of their landed and proprietary interests, and the variety of judicial means employed to secure those interests, emerge from an examination of the records of the courts.

63 Referred to as "Master" Thomas Atteponde, this friar apparently had a university degree but unless he is Master Thomas atte Ponde de Kireling, the Cambridge graduate who thirty years later is listed as an excommunicate (*BRUC*, p. 22) his identity is unknown.

64 *CPR 1346–48*, p. 125.

65 Tomlinson, *History of the Minories*, pp. 34–35; *CCR 1354–1360*, p. 689.

II

SELECT CASES

4

Proceedings at Common Law

We generally picture monasteries as rural retreats, economically dependent on the proceeds from pasture, field, and grange. A glance at the listed real property held by the Aldgate Minoresses dispels that image immediately. Founded on a plot of land in the parish of St Botolph, just outside the walls of London, the economic health of this community rested soundly on the possession of urban real estate. Holdings included residential units, dozens of shops, and even a wharf.[1] As landlords of considerable rental property, the nuns of Aldgate were frequent litigants in the assize courts of London. Centuries of accumulated urban privileges had given London courts a flavor unique to that city, but like other assizes across England, they remained circuit courts ordinarily overseen by superior court justices.

The London Assize of Nuisance was the court that dealt with property disputes between neighbors in the crowded metropolis. 'Nuisance' was a legal category that encompassed any disturbing or annoying conduct without direct physical harm.[2] When a tenant's enjoyment of his or her property was disturbed, but there had been no forcible trespass or ouster involved, the case would come before such an assize. An aggrieved party had a limited right of self-help, which meant that he could try to stop the disturbance or carry on his business in spite of it, but he would have to take the matter to court in order to be awarded damages and to have the nuisance completely cleared up by the offending neighbor. Recognitors, investigators sent by the court to the site of the alleged disturbance, ruled for either plaintiff or defendant.

At what point did the annoying actions of one's neighbor become illegal actions? The law of nuisance developed to "strike a balance between a man's freedom to do as he liked with and upon his own property and his

1 Bourdillon, *Minoresses*, Appendix II, p. 94.

2 Baker, *Introduction*, p. 351 and the whole of chapter 20 as it deals with nuisance in depth. Tucker, *Law Courts*, p. 86 notes the possibility that some nuisance cases might have been heard instead in the distinctive city courts of London. On these metropolitan courts at the end of the fifteenth and beginning of the sixteenth centuries see John Baker, *Oxford History*, Chapter 15.

duty not to injure his neighbor."[3] In an era of few public health regulations, butchers, tanners, dyers, and glovers were accused of causing a nuisance by polluting air or drinking water; so were private householders who failed to repair their leaking latrines. Actions were also brought against those who built additions to their houses that blocked a neighbor's windows, or whose failure to repair a bridge or ditch resulted in the flooding of an adjoining property.

Calendared court rolls from the London Assize of Nuisance for the years 1430 and 1431 are replete with examples of the types of conduct which might be thought to infringe on one's use or enjoyment of property in a teeming city. Attorneys were permitted to litigants in any of the main city courts by around 1300, and even a cursory look at the assize rolls shows that regardless of social standing or gender, people availed themselves of that privilege.[4] Whether abbots or rectors, mercers or scriveners, drapers, priors, or goldsmiths, Londoners employed attorneys. These professional practitioners began to be so popular, in fact, that they were specially licensed to plead in a particular court.

Attorneys representing the Minoresses are sometimes named even when the particulars of a dispute are not. For example, Peter de Shordich was appointed by the abbess in her 1303 suit (details not forthcoming) against one Peter Berneval and his wife, Maud.[5] And Nicholas de Cranle acted as essoiner (a stand-in when both litigant and attorney had to be absent) for the abbess in a suit of an unspecified nature against James Beauflour in 1328.[6] And although Peter de Shordich is not named as one of the attorneys licensed to practice in the city of London courts, Nicholas de Cranle is.[7]

A suit from the early fourteenth century provides us with slightly more information about both the dispute and the attorney involved. In 1305, Minories' abbess Juliana and her nuns brought an action against one Gilbert de Asshendone, and the mayor was asked to send the alderman to her to receive her attorney "since she was enclosed."[8] Just a year later, perhaps not coincidentally, it was Asshendone who brought suit against

3 Baker, *Introduction*, p. 357.

4 Tucker, *Law Courts*, p. 292.

5 "Misc. Roll DD: 10 Feb. 1301–2 Aug. 1303 (nos 1–50)," *London Assize of Nuisance 1301–1431: A Calendar* (1973), pp. 1–10. Online at www.british-history.ac.uk/report.aspx?compid=35969 (accessed July 20, 2009), #45.

6 "Misc. Roll DD: 16 Nov. 1319–5 Aug. 1328 (nos 252–298)," *ibid.*, pp. 54–69. Online at www.british-history.ac.uk/report.aspx?compid=35974 (accessed July 20, 2009), #296.

7 Tucker, *Law Courts*, Appendix 8.2.

8 "Misc. Roll DD: 6 Sept. 1303–19 Aug. 1306 (nos 51–99)," *London Assize of Nuisance*

the nuns. Asshendone complained about a privy in a tenement owned by the Minoresses that adjoined his stone wall.[9] Attorney for the nuns, John de Colechester, managed to save the day for the Minoresses. He argued that although the nuns owned the tenement in question, they had leased it for life to a certain Henry de Stokes. Asshendone's assize complaint had failed to name Stokes and this omission, a procedural gaffe which the plaintiff could not deny, caused the suit to be dismissed.

Detail becomes even more plentiful in the case which Roger de Hortone handled for the London Minoresses in 1314. Hortone brought suit against one John Hardel, complaining that he had caused the repair of Abbess Alice de Sherstede's house in the parish of St Martin Vintry to be stopped.[10] Hardel defended himself by stating that his house adjoined that of the plaintiff and that she had placed the lumber intended for the building repairs onto his land, with certain timber actually "affixed to his wall." When the mayor and alderman went to view the property and building work of the abbess, they found "that her old timber lay upon part of the wall in question, of which she is therefore seised, and that her posts and timber used in her new building do not encroach on the land." They ruled, therefore, that the abbess could continue with her repairs and building undisturbed, and that Hardel was not to demolish that portion of his own wall which had long been used as a structural support for the old section (old timber) of her house.

This judgment might seem odd, unless we know that common law regarded the building of additions and enlargements to existing property as distinct from new building on an unoccupied site. With reference to a householder's right to natural light, for instance, it was argued as late as the seventeenth century that "one who has an old house may build as high as he pleases, even though he thereby stops up his neighbour's lights; but no one is allowed to erect a new house in a vacant space where there was none before, to the damage of neighbours in their lights."[11] Alice de Sherstede's existing property, the "old timber" of which she was already seised, was similarly allowed to compromise her neighbor's property rights whereas the new building material would not have been.

The possessory assizes provided another venue for litigation in the city

1301–1431, pp. 10–22. Online at www.british-history.ac.uk/report.aspx?compid=35970 (accessed July 20, 2009), #80.

9 "Misc. Roll DD: 2 Sept.. 1306–10 Apr. 1310 (nos 100–149)," *ibid.*, pp. 22–32. Online at www.british-history.ac.uk/report.aspx?compid=35971 (accessed July 20, 2009), #102.

10 "Misc. Roll DD: 1 Mar. 1314–1 Dec. 1318 (nos 201–251)," *ibid.*, pp. 41–54. Online at www.british-history.ac.uk/report.aspx?compid=35973 (accessed July 28, 2010), #211.

11 Baker, *Introduction*, p. 355.

of London. These courts were equivalent to the national assizes of Novel Disseisin and Mort d'Ancestor.[12] They were important courts for London property owners, as they dealt with the question of restoring occupancy to tenants who had been ousted, that is, 'disseised,' from homes or businesses. London's possessory assize calendars reveal that here too the Aldgate Minoresses were active litigants, and that they featured as both defendants and plaintiffs.

In November of 1382, for example, the abbess (probably Eleanor Scrope) and convent, along with a timbermonger, John Bythewod, and a vintner, John Michell, were charged by one Juliana Stokesby with having deprived her of a house in the parish of St Michael Paternostercherch.[13] The calendared record is a model of precision in this instance, specifying the name of the defendants' attorney (James Lovet), the jurors who rendered the final decision, and even the dimensions of the 'house' in question: 17 x 11 feet. The jury found that the defendants John Bythewod and John Michell were culpable, and fined them 13s. 4d. in damages. They decided that the abbess, however, had been unjustly implicated in the matter. Consequently, Juliana Stokesby was fined for lodging a false complaint against her. Although the attorney for the Minoresses, James Lovet, has left no trace in the London registry, it is noteworthy that his clients in this suit included two London merchants, as well as cloistered nuns.

The next possessory complaint was brought by the Minories' abbess, Isabel de Gloucester, through her attorney John Stafford. Stafford is not listed among the lawyers licensed to practice in London, but he was no stranger to the assizes, having successfully represented both the rector of St Mary Abbechirche (1423) and the prior of St Mary Suthewerk (1430) in these courts.[14] Given the complications that attached to proprietorship in medieval London, Stafford earned his fees. In this 1423 case, for instance, the abbess lodged a complaint against four individuals whom she accused of collectively dispossessing her of a fractional interest in the proceeds from two shops.

> Isabel, abbess of St Clare without Aldgate, complains that on Thurs. 4 Nov. 1423 Walter Langrigge and Margaret his wife, Thomas Haccher and John Lumbard disseised her of the fourth part of a messuage in the parish of All

12 Tucker, *Law Courts*, p. 86.

13 "Calendar of Assize Rolls: Roll BB," *London Possessory Assizes: A Calendar* (1965), pp. 46–72. Online at www.british-history.ac.uk/report.aspx?compid=64182 (accessed July 20, 2009), #168.

14 *Ibid.*, pp. 100–115. Online at www.british-history.ac.uk/report.aspx?compid=64185 (accessed July 23, 2009), #227, #241.

> Hallows at Hay. The plaintiff appears by John Stafford her attorney. The defendants make default. The assize comes by John Brikelys, William T[ ], Robert Smyth, John Harry, Peter Wymondham, John Sadeler, John Blomvill, Thomas Wyche, Robert Pelycan, Robert Rosse, Thomas Thuresle and Robert Whaplode. The jurors say that Adam Rous, citizen, in his will devised the fourth part of the messuage in view under the name of two shops to Juliana his wife for life, with remainder to Eleanor Nevill then abbess of the minoresses to hold to her and her successors in perpetuity. The abbess Eleanor, by an indenture produced in court, granted the reversion of the premises after Juliana's death to John Chartesay for life. On the death of John Chartesay she entered and was seised of the two shops until the defendants disseised the plaintiff, her successor. Damages 26s. 4d. Defs. in mercy.[15]

As we see, Abbess Isabel's claim was made not for the income of two shops, but for *a fourth of an interest* in that income. Furthermore, that fractional interest had been a testamentary gift to the nuns, on condition that the testator's wife, Juliana, retain a life interest in it. Once Juliana was no longer alive to enjoy the revenues, and the gift to the nuns had been effected, Abbess Eleanor Nevill immediately farmed it out to John Chartesay for life.[16] Only after Chartesay's death did the plaintiff, Abbess Isabel, lay claim to the actual shop revenues—her fourth interest in them that is—until the defendants tried to defraud her of same. However contorted the negotiations for this bit of income property had been, the abbesses of Aldgate had wisely documented them at every turning. Their evidence convinced the jury. It summarily awarded 26s. 4d. in damages to the plaintiff.

Just about a hundred years earlier, the Abbess of the London Minoresses (Alice de Sherstede) had appeared by attorney in yet another type of London court, the London General Eyre. This circuit court would not feature much longer in the city's history since by the close of the fourteenth century the court of King's Bench had made it redundant. Few Londoners seemed to mourn its passing. The General Eyre was staffed by broadly commissioned royal justices who were concerned with insuring that the interests of the Crown were not being jeopardized by local attempts to evade taxes, tariffs, and common law procedure.[17] It was to answer questions about such possible evasion that two *quo warranto* proceedings were

15 *Ibid.*, #230.

16 Eleanor Nevill does not appear in any of the lists of Minories abbesses that I have consulted. Bourdillon, *Minoresses*, p. 38, mentions a 1386 annuity left to one Elizabeth Neville, a London Minoress, but contains no further information about the Nevill named in this assize.

17 Baker, *Oxford History*, p. 255. Maureen Mulholland, "Eyre," in *The Oxford Companion to British History*, ed. John Cannon (Oxford: Oxford University Press, 2009). *Oxford Reference Online*. Oxford University Press. Texas State University–San Marcos. July

begun in 1321 against the nuns of Aldgate. They were to have two very different outcomes.

In the first proceeding,

> the abbess of the house of St Mary Grace of the order of Saint Clare outside the walls of London was summoned to answer to the King in the plea by what warrant she claims to have this liberty: that she and her successors be quit forever of all summons before the Justices Itinerant of the King and his heirs, alike for common pleas and for pleas of the forest in all the counties of the King's realm.

Attorney (unnamed) for the abbess provided letters patent stating that

> the lord Edward, father of the King who now is, on the twentieth day of August in the twenty-second year of his reign, at the instance of his dearest brother Edmund, granted for himself and his heirs to his beloved in Christ, the abbess aforesaid of the aforesaid house of St Mary Grace which is of the foundation of his said brother, that the abbess herself and her successors, the abbesses of that place should be quit for ever more of all summons before Justices of the lord King and his heirs itinerant, alike for common pleas and for pleas of the forest, in all counties of the King's realm.[18]

By presenting letters patent issued by Edward I, "father of the king who is now," the Abbess of Aldgate was allowed to "go hence without day, saving the rights of the lord King." The letters served as proof that the Minoresses were exempt from being summoned to certain of the king's courts and the abbess was spared any further complications.[19] In the second *quo warranto* proceeding, held the same year, things did not run as smoothly. As in the first case, the attorney for the Minoresses produced letters patent as evidence of their royal exemption. This time, however, a distinction was made between the interests of the Crown and the interests of the man who wore it. Edward II, "the king who now is," had issued the letters in this instance and he was not the unfettered agent that his father had been.

Summoned "to answer to the lord King in the plea by what warrant she claims that she and her successors be forever quit of paying tallage by reason of their lands, tenements and rents that are in the city of London," attorney (unnamed) for the Abbess of Aldgate produced letters from Edward II dated "the twentieth day of April in the ninth year of his reign."

31, 2009 www.oxfordreference.com/views/ENTRY.html?subview=Main&entry=t110.e1605

18 Helen Cam, *Year Books of Edward II*, vol. 26, pt 2: *The Eyre of London, 14 Edward II (1321)* (London: Bernard Quaritch, 1969), pp. 163–164.

19 See *CPR 1292–1301*, p. 86. As Cam noted, a dating discrepancy (August 28 versus August 22) which did not seem to have troubled the Crown's counsel, Geoffrey le Scrop.

They proved, he said, that "the Sisters Minoresses of that house and their successors, sisters of that house, should forever be quit of paying tallage to the use of the lord King and his heirs by reason of their lands, tenements, and rents that are in London." But Geoffrey le Scrope, who sued for the Crown, demurred. Edward II's letters, he noted, "were granted to the said abbess subsequently to the Ordinances made by the prelates, earls and barons concerning the not giving of gifts and granting of liberties, as is manifestly clear by the date of those letters, which is the twentieth day of April in the ninth year of the king who now is." Consequently, Scrope asked that "the Justices take counsel on the matter."[20]

Geoffrey le Scrope was referring of course to the Ordinances of 1311. An additional comment of his, added at the end of the court record, makes this reference even clearer: "The Ordinances say that the King may grant nothing that may be to his impoverishment except in parliament, and the charter [charter meaning here the letters patent which the attorney for the abbess had presented as proof of her claim] does not say this, therefore we pray that the franchise be seized."

Edward II had been compelled to sign the Ordinances of 1311 by a committee of prelates, earls, and barons. The document had been compiled mainly to prevent "evil counselors" such as Piers Gaveston from influencing royal policy, but some of the forty-one separate stipulations that it contained specifically addressed the deplorable fiscal situation of the realm. Ordinance number seven, for example, the one referenced by Geoffrey le Scrope, speaks of the kind of privilege which Edward II had given the nuns of Aldgate, the kind of privilege that had contributed to the Crown's insolvency:

> And besides, since the Crown has been so abased and ruined by numerous grants, we ordain that all grants made to the damage of the king and the impoverishment of the Crown since the commission was given to us … shall be annulled; and we do annul them entirely, so that they shall not be given back to the same persons without the common assent in parliament."[21]

Clearly then, the 1321 General Eyre before which the London Minoresses had been called was no ordinary eyre, and this was no routine *quo warranto* proceeding. Like many other individuals and corporations across England, the Aldgate nuns had been called into court to defend privileges granted them by an incumbent whom the peers of the realm had sought

20 Cam, *Year Books of Edward II*, pp. 164–165.

21 Carl Stephenson and Frederick George Marcham, eds, *Sources of English Constitutional History* (New York: Harper and Row, 1937), p. 193. Online at www. constitution.org/sech/sech_.htm.

to bridle. As history tells us, the attempts of the peerage to do so were ultimately unsuccessful, and we get a hint of what was to come when we return to the case at hand. Geoffrey le Scrope had made his recommendation about the tax exemption granted to nuns of Aldgate; he had called for its annulment. That was not a recommendation that Edward II wanted to hear and the king quickly expressed himself accordingly.

> And thereupon the lord King sent commands to his Justices here under his privy seal in these words: Edward by the grace of God, King of England, Lord of Ireland and Duke of Aquitaine to you, or dear and trusty Hervey of Stanton and his companions, or Justices in Eyre at the Tower of London, greeting. We command you that concerning the matters touching our beloved in God, the Prioress and Convent of the Minoresses of London (that have been raised) before you at our suit in the said Eyre, as of tenements purchased without license from our ancestors, or us, [hence without tallage] you shall do nothing until you have special commands from us, for we have reserved the same matters to ourselves.
>
> Given under our privy seal at Fulmere, the eight day of March the 14th year of our reign.
>
> Therefore the said abbess goes without day in this matter for the present, saving the king's right etc.[22]

Because the king had personally intervened in the *quo warranto* proceeding against the nuns of Aldgate, commanding his justices in eyre to "do nothing until you have special commands from us," the investigation into their exemption had been delayed. The delay lasted just long enough to ensure that it would never take place. By 1322, one year after the action against the Minoresses had been shelved "for the present," Edward II had succeeded in having the Ordinances of 1311 repealed and Thomas of Lancaster, the leader of the committee who had put them together, executed.

With the next case, we move from the circuit courts to the central courts of the Crown housed at Westminster. In Trinity term, 1402, Henry Manpas [Maupas], identified as clerk, sued a writ for the collection of debt before the justices of Common Pleas.[23] He claimed that Margaret Helmystede, Abbess of the Minoresses of Aldgate, had granted him a lifetime annuity of 50 marks, which was to be paid to him or to his attorney in four equal installments. The funds were to be delivered to St Paul's Cathedral, London, but the abbess had stopped payment a year before. Henry sought damages to the total of £20, and to that end displayed his

22 Cam, *Year Books of Edward II*, p. 165.

23 "CP40/566: Trinity term 1402," *Court of Common Pleas: The National Archives, CP40: 1399–1500* (2010). Online at www.british-history.ac.uk/report. aspx?compid=118042 &strquery=minoresses (accessed September 23, 2010).

copy of the grant bearing the seal of the Abbess of Aldgate. The evidence appears to have convinced the defendant to concede victory. Indeed, readers might recall having come across that evidence themselves since the plaintiff was the same Henry Maupas, Chancery attorney, to whom Abbess Margaret had granted a yearly rent of £20 "of all their tenements and possessions" and one of 50 marks "of their house."[24] Had the 'stop payment' to Maupas been an oversight? Had the Minories been short of cash? We shall never know. Appearing through her attorney, William Aunger, Abbess Margaret simply pled no contest and Manpas was awarded arrears totaling £41 13s. 4d. as well as damages of 6s. d.[25]

Common Pleas was the venue for a less straightforward case involving the abbess and convent of Waterbeach in December of 1330. Because this dispute involves the exercise of a privilege with implications for ecclesiastical as well as secular authorities, it provides a good illustration of the working relationship established between the two legal systems. When issues were jurisdictionally mixed, the Crown actively asserted its rights but just as actively cooperated with clergymen circumspect enough to recognize and uphold those rights. Bishop of Lincoln Henry Burghersh (1320–1340), ordinary of the monastery of Waterbeach, was definitely one of those circumspect clerics.[26]

As summarized in a Close Roll memorandum, the nuns of Waterbeach complained that Bishop Burghersh was keeping them from the enjoyment of an advowson.[27] Notwithstanding the fact that he had previously given them permission to present their candidate to the parsonage of their recently acquired church in Wydenham, the bishop had rescinded that permission. He had done so because "certain persons scheming to impede the presentation of the abbess and convent" had suggested that the Wydenham advowson actually belonged to the Crown and not to the nuns of Waterbeach. They had put forward their own candidate for the parsonage in Wydenham, "one William Shereman, clerk, to be presented to the church *by the king*." They then "procured the king's writ of prohibition to be directed to the bishop [Burghersh] that a person should not be

24 See Chapter 3 for that grant.

25 While he was licensed to practice in Common Pleas, I have not found any biographical details regarding William Aunger.

26 "Bishops," in *Fasti Ecclesiae Anglicanae 1300–1541*, vol. 1: *Lincoln Diocese* (1962), pp. 1–3. Online at www.british-history.ac.uk/report.aspx?compid=32590 (accessed August 10, 2009). His tumultuous relations with the Crown need not concern us here but are admirably documented in Nicholas Bennett, "Burghersh, Henry (c. 1290–1340)," in *ODNB*. Online at www.oxforddnb.com/view/article/4007 (accessed August 10, 2009).

27 *CCR 1330–1333*, p. 83.

admitted to the church until it should be determined in the king's court whether the advowson pertained to him or to the abbess and convent."

As soon as he received that writ of prohibition a scrupulous Henry Burghersh stopped in his tracks, or rather, he took two paces backward. Not willing to risk interference with a Crown right, the bishop withdrew his earlier permission to the Minoress and staunchly "refused to admit the [right of] presentation of the abbess and convent to the church." Having lost the support of their local ordinary, the nuns had no option but to petition the king for redress; this he gave them, but not without meticulous preliminary investigation into the matter.

First, he ascertained that there was "not any plea before John de Stonore and his fellows, justices of the Bench, between him and the abbess and convent concerning the aforesaid church," and he ordered the justice to search the court rolls and certify to that fact.[28] Then Edward III's lawyers made sure that "Alexander de Hadenham, who sues for the king, had not prosecuted any plea for the king against the aforesaid abbess and convent concerning the aforesaid church and that he did not know of any plea prosecuted by the king against them concerning them."

Only after making sure that Crown interests were not (as William Shereman's supporters had claimed) being jeopardized did Edward order Henry Burghersh "to do further at the presentation of the abbess and convent what pertains to his office, nothwithstanding the king's presentation or prohibition aforesaid." This royal command was enough to convince the bishop that it was now politic to proceed. The scruples of their ordinary may have cost the Waterbeach nuns some time, but it gained them the exercise of a more secure right.

Names of lawyers like that of John de Stonore, Chief Justice in the foregoing case, and Alexander de Hadenham, "who sued for the Crown," remind us that the Court of Common Pleas was more than just the premier venue for civil suits. It was in Common Pleas that the most distinguished of the common lawyers, the serjeants at law, spoke for litigants. Logically then, law reporters recorded debates in this court to the near exclusion of those framed by lesser lawyers in other courts.[29] The law reports, collectively known as the Year Books, are useful supplements to court rolls and calendars for Common Pleas since they often name presiding justices,

28 Baker, *Order of Serjeants at Law*, p. 539. Stonore was created a serjeant in 1311 and had served as king's counsel until appointed as justice in Common Pleas in 1320. He served there and in King's Bench for several terms.

29 Baker, *Introduction*, p. 36. Note that in the case just dealt with from the London Eyre, it was the argument of a serjeant that was highlighted by the reporter.

serjeants at law, and even attorneys. But the Year Book reports have some peculiarities.[30]

Court records on the rolls were drawn up to preserve an account of proceedings that could serve as proof that a particular matter had been adjudicated. The rolls consequently included essential identifying details such as the names of the litigants and the location of contested property. Year Book reports left out such detail. A particular case was "reported solely because it contained, or was supposed to contain matter of general use. For this reason, the names of the parties and of places were frequently omitted or represented by letters chosen at hazard, or, if given, most inaccurately. They were not the facts which the lawyer wished to know."[31]

Written by lawyers for lawyers, law reports served not as public record, but as pedagogic tool. Reporters provided guides to successful pleading by recapitulating the arguments of the serjeants at law, men who knew how to deploy that arcane knowledge that had become the hallmark of the legal professional. Because they record the legerdemain of *narratores* within the framework of formal procedure, the Year Books are filled with what F. W. Maitland once called "a whole scheme of actions with repulsive names."[32] It is fitting then that the element essential to the initiation of any one of those actions, the writ, should be the centerpiece of our first case culled from the Year Books.

The inflexibility of the writ system has already been remarked upon, and this rigidity is superbly illustrated by the 1365 Common Pleas case of John of Baa versus the Prioress (Matilda) and nuns of Dartford.[33] As recorded in the Year Books of Edward III, arguments were presented for the plaintiff by serjeant Sir John de Cavendish and for the defendants by Sir Robert Belknap and Edmund Chelre, also serjeants.[34] Sir Robert Belknap must

[30] J. H. Baker, *Judicial Records, Law Reports, and the Growth of Case Law* (Berlin: Duncker & Humblot, 1989), pp. 15–46 distinguishes between the record and the report as well as examining the origins of the year-book form in some detail.

[31] L. Owen Pike, "An Action at Law in the Reign of Edward III: The Report and the Record." *Harvard Law Review* 7 no. 5 (1893): 266–280. Also see the witty and useful Thomas Lund, "The Modern Mind of the Medieval Lawyer." *Texas Law Review* (April, 1986): 1–22.

[32] Maitland, "Why the History of English Law Is Not Written," p. 486.

[33] Seipp #1365.098.

[34] Herbert Eiden, "Cavendish, Sir John (*d.* 1381)," in *ODNB*, www.oxforddnb.com/view/article/4938 (accessed August 12, 2009). John L. Leland, "Bealknap, Sir Robert (*d.* 1401)," in *ODNB*, www.oxforddnb.com/view/article/1809 (accessed August 10, 2009); Baker, *Order of Serjeants at Law*, pp. 499 and 504. The dramatic events in Belknap's career which included a narrow escape from a death sentence, exile, and restoration, are nowhere evident in that of Chelre. He was created king's serjeant in 1354 was a justice in King's Bench by 1371, and died a year later.

have been a particular asset to the nuns of Dartford, Kent, having been a Justice of the Peace for the county since 1362. But all of these *narratores* were seasoned lawyers; they would all eventually be appointed justices of the bench as well. Sir Robert de Thorpe was the presiding justice in this instance.[35]

The writ subscribed by the plaintiff in the case was one of *formedon in the descender*. This writ was designed for use by an heir who claimed entailed property against the tenant in possession of that curtailed estate (fee). A curtailed/entailed fee was one which had been given to the recipient and his heirs, with limitations. The 'form of the gift' (*formedon*), the exact wording of the grant designating title of descent, was therefore extremely important. A grant limited to a married couple and their biological children, for example, reverted to the donor if the pair never had children. The Prioress and nuns of Dartford were being sued in this case by writ of *formedon in the descender* since they were in possession of a curtailed property to which the plaintiff /heir (John of Baa) said they had no legal right, 'according to the form of the gift.'[36]

Having said all this, it was the form of John of Baa's *writ*, rather than the form of the gift with which counsel for the nuns first found fault. Belknap and Chelre's logic was clear: If the writ which initiated the suit were found to be defective, the case would be summarily dismissed. Defense therefore argued that the plaintiff's writ was invalid because it contained inconsistencies. John's name appeared in it in two places, and in two different ways; once he was styled John *of* Baa, reference to the manor of Baa, or Bay farm, and once he was referred to as John Baa, 'Baa' being his surname.[37]

Plaintiff's counsel immediately challenged this argument. He claimed that any confusion involving the different forms of address was mitigated by the use, in the same writ, of the word 'aforementioned.' John of Baa and 'John Baa aforementioned', were by implication one and the same person. Justice Thorpe appeared to be convinced by the response, since the writ was not immediately nullified (abated).

35 W. M. Ormrod, "Thorpe, Sir Robert (*d.* 1372)," in *ODNB*, www.oxforddnb.com/view/article/27383 (accessed August 13, 2009).

36 If there were a tenant in possession of a curtailed fee at the time when it theoretically reverted, that tenant might try to bar its reversion to the donor, suing a writ called *formedon in the reverter*. It is unclear whether the nuns had sued that writ previous to this action.

37 "Parishes: Ickham," in *The History and Topographical Survey of the County of Kent*, vol. 9 (1800), pp. 167–179. Online at www.british-history.ac.uk/report.aspx?compid=63553 (accessed August 10, 2009).

Counsel for the nuns next demanded 'the view.' This request for a formal inspection or land survey of the tenements in question was challenged by Cavendish. On a previous occasion, Cavendish said, John Baa "had brought a similar writ against the Prioress of Newark [New Work] of Dartford." At that time the prioress "had had the view and had won the case because she had produced charters of the king as evidence of her right, and because there was "too much in the first writ." Consequently, now that John Baa "had brought a good writ for the same tenements" the prioress was prohibited from having a second formal survey of the property.

Once again, plaintiff's counsel Cavendish had a sound argument. According to statute, if a litigant had been granted the view in a lawsuit and had won that suit (because of a technical fault in his adversary's writ as here) he/she would not be allowed to exercise that option a second time, if and when a good writ was submitted. Belknap and Chelre, however, took exception. The argument *would be* a sound one they contended, if only the prioress in this case were the same prioress as in the first! Baa's original writ "was brought against the Prioress *of New Work* of Dartford and this writ was brought against the Prioress of Dartford, who could not be understood to be the same prioress."

Emboldened by this parsing of names, Cavendish retorted with an insider's joke: If a writ were brought against Robert, son of *William* Thorp, and the writ abated for misnomer, and afterwards the person conceived another writ against him [Robert] by his true name, the defendant would still not be entitled to have the view. The attempt at levity might have fallen short, but it could not have been lost on presiding justice Robert Thorpe. Thorpe was the son of *Robert* Thorpe of Orton, but a relative of his, William Thorpe, was also a chief justice.

Justice Thorpe (Robert, son of Robert, that is) concluded by saying that if two prioresses of Dartford actually existed in fact (according to record), that fact might be alleged by the defendant as grounds for obtaining 'the view' a second time. But since the Second Statute of Westminster, Chapter 44, denied a second view after a revived writ "for misnomer of the vill [age] and abatement of the writ after the view, and things of like kind," it could not be so alleged. Thorpe obviously felt that the present circumstance was covered by those catch-all words "and things of like kind." In the end, the "defendant passed over the view and prayed aid of the king." As used here, 'aid' refers to a legal right exercised by the nuns to petition the Crown for further help in establishing their defense. Thorpe granted their request, but we do not know if sarjeants Belknap and Chelre won the case for their clients as a result.

Win or lose, serjeants at law were always prepared to return to the contest another day. As professionals who placed their skills at the disposal of any client with the necessary fees, that could easily involve pleading against the interests of a former client. In 1369, four years after the conclusion of the John Baa case, we find Edmund Chelre doing just that.[38] Characteristically, the law report omits the name of the plaintiff, Chelre's client, and the attorneys representing Dartford this time are referred to only by the initials M. and W. However, since Michael Skilling and Walter Perle had been licensed by the Crown as Dartford attorneys in 1368, this detail at least can be filled in.[39]

Proceedings in this instance were initiated by a writ *per quae servitia*, a writ which required that a tenant show cause why he should not be attorned, that is, 'turned over' to a new lord.[40] While the writ has a decidedly archaic flavor to it, in this late fourteenth-century suit transfer of homage and service would have involved merely a commuted cash payment. The case is of special interest because the arguments engendered by the ancient warrant used to initiate it touch on the right of cloistered nuns to routinely act through designated attorneys. There were still a few instances in civil litigation in which the court could order defendants to appear in person. Counsel for the plaintiff in the present case demanded such an appearance from the nuns of Dartford, saying that the writ by which they had been summoned demanded it.

Serjeant at law Cherle began by recounting the particulars: Dartford attorneys Skilling and Perle had come to court saying that the Prioress of Dartford "was confined, so that she could not come, and that she had made her attorneys, the said M and W jointly and severally to do that which they should do, in the name of the prioress, and if they could not attend, that they could make attorneys, such as they wanted, to prosecute and defend in the manner that they should" – a fairly straightforward general letter of proxy. But Chelre noted that "the Court saw plainly how this was a writ [the writ *per quae servitia*] in which they demanded an attornment and the one who should attorn could not be present [legally represented] by attorney." He concluded that since the abbess had not come personally to court she should now lose her case.

Chief Justice Robert Thorpe did not concur. He declared that "it was not right reason when there was a special cause in the writ [mention by Skilling and Perle of their general letter of proxy] which proved that she could not come upon this because she was confined." Chelre, however,

38 Seipp #1369.090.

39 See Chapter 3, p. 000.

40 Frederick Pollock and F. William Maitland, *The History of English Law*, vol. 1, 2nd edn (Cambridge: Cambridge University Press, 1968), pp. 348–349.

retorted that this was not quite good enough for the case in question: "It has been seen in this court [Common Pleas], that a woman had been received by attorney to defend her right by a writ made in the Chancery, and the reason was because it was recited in the writ the whole matter, how and for what reason she had to be received to defend her right." With this precedent in mind, Chelre argued that "as it was here, she [the Abbess of Dartford] should have a writ reciting the cause in this special case."

Chief Justice Thorpe agreed this time. He "judged it good enough; therefore he said to answer." By requiring the defendants to reply to the charge, the Chief Justice was responding to Cherle's logical argument. Attorneys Walter Perle and Michael Skilling could not act for the nuns of Dartford in this particular case merely by presenting their general letter of appointment. To satisfy the requirements of an action begun by writ *per quae servicia*, the Abbess of Dartford should have given Skilling and Perle a specific mandate detailing the reasons why she could not come to court to attorn in person. The right of cloistered nuns to sue by proxy had not been undermined; nor had the requirements of an ancient writ.

Not all cases that came before the justices of Common Pleas (or any other court for that matter) were so tidily resolved. Many causes were simply abandoned, and others required plaintiffs to file a second writ in the same, or in another, common law court; some were settled only by the intervention of an arbiter, or by a shift to the ecclesiastical forum. And then there were some, defying resolution, that were still doggedly pursued in various courts and before countless judges. But then some affronts rankle.

In 1442, the Bridgettines of Syon Abbey suffered such an affront. Anxious to enrich his new foundation of the College of St Mary and St Nicholas, better known as King's, Henry VI forced the community to give up a considerable portion of its endowment. Four years later the Minoresses of Denney also lost property to King's College, Cambridge.[41] But whereas Denney's loss would be unremarked and permanent, the Bridgettines remained determined to reassert their claim to what their founder Henry V had meant them to have. They began a decades-long battle, waged by petition and writ, with agents of the Crown and with the fellows of King's College. It was a protracted struggle, and the memory of wounds sustained would endure: as late as 1937, the nuns of Syon still

41 *CPR 1441–1446*, p. 460. They had property required to accommodate the building of Godeshous, Cambridge, which was adjacent to Henry's new college of St Mary and St Nicholas.

omitted Henry VI's name from their prayers "because he took from us what his father gave, in order to found King's."[42]

One of the most important things Henry VI took was the Benedictine monastery of St Michael's Mount in Cornwall. Like so many other estates that went to make up Syon's endowment, this former cell of Mont St Michel in Normandy had been an alien priory.[43] Throughout the early Middle Ages, continental monasteries often profited from having affiliated houses in England which sent their surplus profits to the mother house. English kings had been among those who bequeathed the revenues of these affiliates, the so-called alien priories, to their foreign foundations, but by 1300 attitudes had changed. Kings began to view the alien priories as leeching English coin from the soil on which it had been produced. When at war with France, Edward I, Edward II, and Edward III had all seized the estates of these priories, returning them only with the return of peace. Richard II and Henry IV began a trend of claiming alien priory revenues for the Crown or granting them to favorites even when not at war.[44] Henry V made the decision to permanently dissolve all alien priories that were still fully subordinate to foreign houses – the relationship that characterized that between St Michael's Mount and Mont St Michel. By an act of Parliament, the lands formerly belonging to those priories were bestowed on the Crown. Then, by a charter dated 1417, Henry V gave much of that confiscated land to his new foundation of Syon Abbey.[45]

Far from taking exception to this gift, Henry VI (1422–1461) confirmed his father's grant of alien priory estates to Syon in the second year of his reign. Among those estates which his confirmation charter of 1424 identifies are the vicarage of Felstead in Essex, and the manor of Tyleshyde [Tillishyde] in Essex, both formerly held by the Abbey of the Holy Trinity, Caen, Normandy; St Michael's Mount, Cornwall, formerly belonging to Mont St Michel, Normandy; lands formerly belonging to the Abbey of St Nicholas, Angers, in Spalding, Lincolnshire; all the tithes of the church of Cosham in the county of Wiltshire, former possession of the Abbey of St Wandrille.[46]

But by 1441, Henry VI had changed his mind. In that year he made his own foundation, King's College, Cambridge. His original plan for

42 "Houses of Minoresses: Abbey of Denney," in *A History of the County of Cambridge and the Isle of Ely*, vol. 2 (1948), pp. 295–302. Online at www.british-history.ac.uk/report.aspx?compid=40019 (accessed July 16, 2010).

43 William Dugdale, *Monasticon Anglicanum*, 1693, VI, p. 989.

44 Aungier, *History*, pp. 31–32, fn 5.

45 *Ibid.*, p. 33.

46 *Ibid.*, p. 42.

the college had been modest but it eventually described an institution of grand proportions, large enough to accommodate seventy scholars. As his dream expanded so did his search for funds with which to fulfill it. The wealth of the alien priories, so recently confiscated for the Crown by his father, loomed into view. *Quo warranto* proceedings reminiscent of those brought against the nuns of Aldgate in 1321 were begun to test the validity of titles by which beneficiaries of Henry V's largess held their alien priory estates. Because Syon Abbey had been the principal beneficiary, it followed that it should be the first to be placed under scrutiny. Things moved rapidly from then on. By September 30, 1441, a list of arrears for specific elements of alien priory bequests – namely Syon estates of Corsham, Spalding, St Michael's Mount, Felstead, and Telshead – had been compiled.[47] On March 15, 1442, Henry VI made the following bequest to King's, which might instructively be compared with his 1424 confirmation charter to Syon.

> Grant to the rector and scholars of St Nicholas' College in the University of Cambridge, of the king's foundation, of the priory of Mount St Michael, Cornwall, belonging to the duchy of Cornwall, of the manor of Tyleshyde, sometime parcel of the abbey of Caen, of the manor and rectory of Felstede, co. Essex, sometime parcels of the same abbey, of all the lands and possessions sometime of the abbey of St Nicholas, Angers, in Spaldyng co. Lincoln, and of all fruits of the church of Cosham, co. Wilts, with all their appurtenances (specified).[48]

The first response of the Bridgettines to this dramatic loss was designed to staunch the flow of revenues. In 1443, they secured their title to other lands held in frank almoin by letters patent, and in 1444 they sought to protect themselves against any future charges for arrears from the profits of the lands they had lost to King's and were granted a pardon for any trespasses or other offenses committed by their proctors, officers, servants or ministers on the estates that had been transferred.[49] These defensive actions must have been accomplished with some degree of tact since Henry VI actually began to favor the nuns for the next few years. In 1444, he made them a gift of a manor (a former possession of the Abbey of Caen) which had reverted to the Crown at the death of the Earl of Suffolk, accorded them a comprehensive tax exemption, and fined a debtor for non-appearance in suit brought by the Abbess, Maud.[50] The charter of liberties that he issued to that same abbess in 1447 was so extensive that

47 SYO/3 Arrears.

48 *CPR 1441–1446*, pp. 111–112.

49 *Ibid.*, pp. 234, 256.

50 *Ibid.*, pp. 255, 272, 300. See Chapter 7 for related action on Henry's part.

it virtually exempted her from royal justice and allowed her to take all the profits from courts held on her own estates.[51]

All this largess was compensatory, however, as concluding remarks in his 1447 charter made clear: Parliament had decreed that the estates of the alien priories which Henry V had seized

> should remain to himself and his heirs under a certain form contained in the same Act ... and that in those presents no mention be made of the true value of all and singular the premises or of any parcel of the same, or of the other gifts or grants by us or any of our progenitors to the now abbess and convent aforesaid, and their successors, or to any of their predecessors formerly made.

These remarks reveal that Henry VI had no intention of altering his grant to King's since he regarded the alien priory lands seized by his father as his patrimony. He allowed that his father had wished to give a certain portion of the *value* of those lands to Syon, but in Henry V's time that value had only impressionistically been established. Now that Henry VI had done so with precision, and now that he had added estates and privileges to those granted by his father, he had been required to subtract the excess. This 'excess,' he gave to King's. Indeed, Henry VI began to claim that in so doing he had merely been fulfilling his father's wishes regarding alien priory lands since Henry V had wanted to "to appropriate them *all* to a noble college."[52]

Now the litigious decade began. The sisters and brothers of Syon Abbey meticulously calculated the full extent of their losses, put their case before the justices of the Crown, and endeavored to recoup what the king had alienated. A file of documents "relating to a suit by Syon abbey in the Exchequer touching the payment of taxes" signals the start of proceedings.[53] Another file, preserved in King's College archives and covering the years 1450–1461, contains extracts from these Exchequer rolls, as well as details of the abbey's case and the response of the college.[54] Finally, there is the solemn testimony of Abbess Elizabeth Muston (1456–1497), Confessor General Robert Bell (1428–1460), and a long list of brethren and sisters, given in conjunction with their 1458 Exchequer suit alleging unlawful desseisin of St Michael's Mount, Cornwall, and other holdings by the king.[55] Collectively, these records give us a very good idea of the particulars of the dispute and the manner in which the commu-

51 Aungier, *History*, pp. 60–67.

52 *Ibid.*, pp. 31–32, fn 5.

53 E 135/22/80.

54 SYO/5 Extracts; SYO/4 Dispute.

55 E 211/417.

nity presented its claims in the courts of the king—a king who, as every student of Bracton knew, was supposed to rule by *ius*, not *injuria*.

In his sworn testimony before the Exchequer, Robert Bell deposed that, as priest and brother at Syon for over thirty-eight years, and as one who held the office of Confessor General for thirty of those years, there were not many still alive "who knew and labored against sealing the release [of St Michael's Mount etc.]" more than he. He stated that he was one of the eyewitnesses to the fact that "the bishop of Exeter with other feofees, in the second or third year of the king that now is, released to the abbess and convent the said livelihood that the provost and fellows of the said college occupied now." He insisted that when those lands were subsequently surrendered by the abbess and convent, "the sealing [of the release] was … not of will and freedom as it is pretended." To confirm his statement, Bell referred the judges to the testimony of Robert Huseoyse [Huswyse] "then steward without," who by virtue of the office he held at the time would be able to recount "by what means the abbess and convent were compelled to sign the release."

The Bishop of Exeter and Syon trustee to whom Bell referred was Edmund Lacy. Bishop of Hereford (1417–1420) and then of Exeter (1420–1455), Lacy had been one of the feofees designated by Henry V in his 1417 charter enlarging Syon's endowment, and he was mentioned by name in Henry VI's 1424 confirmation of his father's grant.[56] Since Bishop Lacy was one of Henry V's executors, and known as well for his probity, Bell's account of his agency in the transfer of alien priory lands to Syon is beyond dispute.[57] Unfortunately the corroborating testimony of the other man named in Bell's deposition, the Syon steward Robert Huswyse is not in the dossier. We get a fair idea of what that testimony might have contained, however, from the depositions of other Bridgettines who, like Bell, had belonged to the congregation at the time of their despoiling.[58]

Ellen Eton, professed sister for thirty-eight years and Prioress of Syon in 1458, was one of those deposed. She averred that everything about the

56 "Bishops," in *Fasti Ecclesiae Anglicanae 1300–1541*, vol. 2: *Hereford diocese* (1962), pp. 1–3. Online at www.british-history.ac.uk/report.aspx?compid=32667 (accessed August 11, 2010); "Bishops," in *Fasti Ecclesiae Anglicanae 1300–1541*, vol. 9: *Exeter Diocese* (1964), pp. 1–3. Online at www.british-history.ac.uk/report.aspx?compid=32237 (accessed August 11, 2010).

57 Nicholas Orme, "Lacy, Edmund (c. 1370–1455)," in *ODNB*, www.oxforddnb.com/view/article/15846 (accessed August 13, 2010).

58 Aungier, *History*, pp. 51–52. When he had been elected confessor general in 1428, a list of the brothers and sisters had been drawn up for the bishop of London's register, and a few of the deponents named were on it.

forcible loss of monastic lands as reported by Abbess Elizabeth Muston was true, adding that "god knoweth it full sore against my heart and will, and utterly against my consent." Along with several elder choir nuns, Sisters Margaret John, Margaret Lathe, and Margaret Sukelyng, who were among the first professed nuns of Syon, next affixed their signatures to a general statement upholding that of the prioress. They then made a fuller statement that begins to clarify Robert Bell's reference to a coerced release of their alien priory holdings. Sisters John, Lathe, and Sukelyng swore to the fact that they had witnessed the release of title to St Michael's Mount etc. and "were there present with the said abbess named Maud Muston [1434–1447] and heard all such menacings and utterances of Sir James Fynes [Fiennes] and Master John Langton in the king's name."

Because the notion of 'the king's evil counselors' has become a literary trope, it is sometimes hard to remember that the motif had flesh and blood reality. Royal agents Fiennes and Langton who reportedly threatened the nuns of Syon were certainly real. Sir James Fiennes (1390–1450) was the first Baron of Saye and Sele, and a royal administrator. He had been at Agincourt, participated in Henry V's conquest of Normandy, and been part of nine-year-old Henry VI's coronation entourage. By the 1440s Fiennes had become a member of the king's inner circle, along with William de la Pole, Earl of Suffolk (d. 1450). And then there are further biographical notes of special import for the case at hand.

> He was one of the courtiers involved in the implementation of the two projects that above all else provoked Henry VI to enthusiastic activity, namely the foundation of the colleges of Eton and King's, Cambridge … Purchase and, it was said after his death, intimidation made him the dominant secular landowner in the county. Two territorial blocks in particular were created by 1450. In the neighbourhood of Sevenoaks he acquired the manor of Knole, and also that of Seal – hence his title of Sele – and Kemsing. Jurors before a royal commission in August 1450 charged that in extending the latter, he had forced a prominent landowner to make an unprofitable exchange of property and then had kept both estates. Plaintiffs in a later unsuccessful chancery suit told a similar tale. After purchasing a substantial group of estates in the Romney Marsh area, he had the supposed heir arrested and coerced into sealing a release before a chancery master … Fiennes's accumulation of property and offices in the south-east, when added to those of his brother and their gentry associates, made the Fiennes affinity one of the most formidable in the country. His control of local affairs in Kent would attach his name to the manifold charges of extortion and corruption soon to be made against county and archiepiscopal officers.[59]

Master John Langton (d. 1447), the other crown agent mentioned in the

59 Joseph A. Nigota, "Fiennes, James, first Baron Saye and Sele (c. 1390–1450)," in *ODNB*, www.oxforddnb.com/view/article/9411 (accessed August 13, 2010).

Syon depositions, was neither as prominent nor as infamous a figure as Lord Saye but his expertise as a lawyer might have made him quite as menacing a presence.[60] Langton held a doctorate in civil law and a licentiate in canon law from Cambridge, and his attachment to King's would have been hard to overlook: In May of 1447, Langton was consecrated as Bishop of St David's in the hall of that college.

Another deposition by another Bridgettine elder named Brother Richard Thuxston contains even more detail about the coerced signing of the release. The eighty-two-year-old Thuxston affirmed that

> I never knew to this hour that any sisters or brothers was willing to consent to the sealing of the said release or to leave the said livelihood or any parcel of it. Notwithstanding that some, for great fear and dread to lose much more than that, or all, agreed ... some asking in the matter the righteous judgment of god upon the doers and workers, and see now what ends they had, the Duke of Suffolk [William de la Pole, Earl of Suffolk] the Bishop of Salisbury, [William] Aiscough, Lord Say [James Fiennes], Master John Langton, ... as it hath been said, died in despair as to mans' estimation and Master John Somerset painfully confined and wasted.

Thuxston's testimony adds three more names to the list of royal agents implicated in, and by his account suffering for, defrauding Syon; all three were apparently as suited as James Fiennes to that unsavory job. William Aiscough (1395–1450), administrator and Bishop of Salisbury, was also chaplain and confessor to Henry VI. His Cambridge attachments were strong, since he held both his Master of Arts and doctorate in theology from that university, and in the 1440s he not only loaned the king £1,602 for the twin royal foundations of Eton and King's, but also helped compile the latter's statutes. Finally,

> His membership of the inner circle of royal advisers made him dangerously unpopular ... his climate of hatred seems to have persuaded him to leave London for the apparent safety of his castle in Sherborne. On his way there his baggage was plundered and then, on 29 June, he was captured by a large group of local men while celebrating mass at the church of the Bonshommes, Edington, Wiltshire. He was dragged out onto a hill, hacked to death, and despoiled. In the following days his palace at Salisbury and several episcopal manors were ransacked. The goods taken were valued at 10,000 marks.[61]

60 "Bishops of St Davids," in *Fasti Ecclesiae Anglicanae 1300–1541*, vol. 11: *The Welsh Dioceses (Bangor, Llandaff, St Asaph, St Davids)* (1965), pp. 53–56. Online at www.british-history.ac.uk/report.aspx?compid=32472&strquery=langton, john (accessed August 13, 2010).

61 Margaret Lucille Kekewich, "Aiscough, William (*c*. 1395–1450)," in *ODNB*, www.oxforddnb.com/view/article/954 (accessed August 17, 2010).

Sir William Pole, Duke of Suffolk, has already been noted as an intimate of Fiennes, but what of Thuxston's "painfully confined and wasted" John Somerset (d. 1454)? Doctor of medicine and courtier, he was a Londoner by birth, a fellow of Pembroke College, Cambridge, and physician to Henry VI from 1428 until about 1451.

> Fur-trimmed robes were regularly assigned to Somerset from the royal wardrobe throughout the 1430s and 1440s, marking his arrival at the pinnacle of his profession. He secured gifts of cash and goods, corrodies, an additional fee of £40 a year, and land in Cambridgeshire and Yorkshire. In 1437 part of his pension was exchanged for the manor of Ruislip in Middlesex, prompting him to acquire an additional estate of over 750 acres and a mansion nearby at Osterley, where he lived as a country gentleman when not at his London residence.[62]

Brother Thuxston's comments about Somerset's final years can be explained by the fact that although he had helped to draft the statutes of both King's and Queens' Colleges, Cambridge, his general unpopularity undercut those efforts. There is poetic justice in the fact that King's College succeeded in depriving him of one of his own manors. That affront, coupled with Parliament's demand that he be ousted from Henry's household, seems to have made him melancholic, if not "painfully confined and wasted," for the rest of his life – at least that is the picture that emerges from his final composition, which was a *Queremonia*, or long list of complaints in Latin hexameter.

The remaining two depositions in the Syon Exchequer suit of 1458 were taken from younger brethren whose knowledge about the events of 1442 came from overhearing their elders discuss the matter. Both deponents were quite clear about what exactly that matter was: "the great wrong … and the violent extortion of their livelihood of great value to the king's college Cambridge which occupies the said livelihood against right." Brother Thomas Boulde, professed only twelve years earlier, specifically noted the loss of "Michael's Mount with certain other parcels." He swore that he was familiar as well with all his monastery's attempts to redress the grievance, he himself having "read diverse writings and supplications, some of the abbess, some of the confessor, some of the whole congregation to the king, to lords, and to other diverse now beseeching audience."

Finally, Brother Nichol Paynto added his personal recollection about Master John Langton, the lawyer who, along with Fiennes, coerced the community in the king's name.

62 Carole Rawcliffe, "Somerset, John (*d.* 1454)," in *ODNB*, www.oxforddnb.com/view/article/26012 (accessed August 17, 2010).

> Wherefore one thing cometh to mind as touching Master John Langton which was one of the doers, which thing I shall rehearse the truth of at least in so far as I can remember. It happened that when I was sacristan of Saint Stevens chapel at Westminster I was his [Langton's] confessor and under familiarity of the which we talked of other things out of confession; he asked me upon a time a little before I come hither whether I would go to religion and whether I would be professed in Syon, saying, as me seemed with [relishing?], that they had a marked loss of livelihood than they had to fore, as if he had, or at least helped to, bring that about.

Quality of the depositions notwithstanding, the Exchequer suit of 1458 failed. As we have seen, the opponents of Syon were great (if not good) men in very high places, and the "diverse writings and supplications, some of the abbess, some of the confessor, some of the whole congregation" were of no avail. What is more, the nuns of Syon also found themselves on the other side of the dock in this stormy decade. They appeared as defendants in the Court of Common Pleas on two occasions.[63] In 1456, the plaintiff was the Master of Christ's College, Cambridge, and in 1460, it was the king (represented by King's Serjeant Richard Choke). In both cases, serjeant at law William Laken [Laicon] pleaded for the nuns.[64] Because the writ *quare impedit* originated both suits, the defendants were required to explain why they had hindered plaintiffs attempting to install their candidates to vacant benefices. Most of the relevant locations and names were omitted from the Year Book reports of these suits, but internal evidence still links them to the larger contest over Syon's alien priory revenues.

For example, in the 1456 case, the Master of Christ's College claimed that it was his right to appoint to an advowson that had been "part of a French priory, and so annexed to the Crown [Henry V]." He argued that the advowson had been conveyed to the current king, who had granted it to Christ's College by letters patent. In the 1460 suit featuring that 'current king' as plaintiff, the issue of contested transmission of title was made even more obviously. William Laken argued that Henry V had granted the nuns of Syon title to an advowson which, again, was referred to as "part of a manor formerly belonging to a French abbey." After Laken's fellow serjeants had disputed some technicalities, counsel for Syon ended as he had begun: "Defendants argued again that the advowson remained appendant to the manor and passed by the letters patent to defendant [Syon] abbess." Not surprisingly, Chief Justice Prysot was not convinced: "Prysot said that it did not, and this was the opinion of all the Court."

63 Seipp ##1456.018, 1460.025.

64 Baker, *Order of Serjeants at Law*, p. 522. Laken was created a serjeant in 1453.

So began the thirty-ninth year of the reign of Henry VI. The congregation of Syon had succeeded neither as petitioners, nor as litigants in the courts of the Crown. The brothers and sisters had failed to regain their lands from King's College and had unsuccessfully asserted their rights to advowsons which had also been part of alien priory estates. But these were unstable times politically and by the spring of that same year Syon Abbey, like the house of York, had survived its last serious pummeling.

Having defeated the Lancastrians in March of 1461, Edward Duke of York was acclaimed king by hereditary right. On February 26, in the first year of his reign, Edward IV confirmed a release to Abbess Elizabeth Gibbs (1456–1518) and her successors, of all rights which the provost and scholars of King's College, Cambridge, had claimed to St Michael's Mount in Cornwall, Tilshead manor, Felstead manor and rectory, the lands formerly belonging to the Abbey of St Nicholas of Anjou in Spalding, and the revenues from the church of Cosham—in short, all that Henry VI had taken away in 1442.[65] By the summer of that year, Abbess Gibbs had become confident enough to formally conclude her lawsuit against the proctor and scholars of King's.[66] Even now, however, the saga was not quite finished.

For a few months in 1470–1471 (October 5–April 11), an etiolated Henry VI was returned to the throne and the Parliament which met in November 1470 proceeded to repeal nearly every one of 'the usurper' Edward IV's statutes. Very much alarmed at the prospect of having to face another decade reasserting her right to what Syon had just recovered, Abbess Gibbs petitioned this Parliament in eloquent terms to allow no harm to come to Syon as a consequence of political upheaval.[67] She asked that the November Parliament pass neither statute nor ordinance that would jeopardize the monastery's original endowments, whether these grants were made directly by Henry V or by his "deputees or fefees." She also pleaded that any portion of that endowment that had been granted by Henry VI to the provost and scholars of King's College "be voide and of none effecte." That being done, she promised Henry VI "to tendirly pray God for the gode astate and prospirite of your most noble persone, and of this your noble realme in prosperity long to endure."

Parliament agreed to this petition, and it was duly sealed. Nevertheless, the reassertion of Yorkist rule a few months later must have been a considerable relief to the community. Back on the throne for good, Edward IV proceeded to reconfirm all of the monastery's exemptions, privileges and

65 Aungier, *History*, p. 68.

66 SYO/1 Release.

67 Aungier, *History*, pp. 71–73.

possessions, including those alien priory estates it had lost under Henry VI.[68] This time, the confirmation was not challenged. A survey of 1492 showed the nuns regularly collecting the proceeds from all of their alien priory estates. The abbey derived an annual income of over £27 from a lease of some of the lands of St Michael's Mount; Cosham rectory, Tilshead manor, the lordship of Felstead, and the priory of St Nicholas of Spalding netted the community over £150 more.[69] In an era when the yearly income of a gentleman was between £10 and £20, that was a considerable revenue and the nuns of Syon found it difficult to fulfill Abbess Gibb's promise to "tendirly pray God for the gode astate and prospirite" of the man who had tried to deprive them of it.

Elizabeth Gibbs' successful appeal to Parliament would have no sequel. With the expert and zealous guidance of the Putney blacksmith's son turned royal minister, Thomas Cromwell, Henry VIII had started using Parliament to undermine the juridical and financial independence of the English Church many years before the Dissolution.[70] In 1529, for example, when Cromwell became an MP, Parliament passed what was generally know as the Statute of Farms (21 Henry VIII c. 13) prohibiting pluralism, non-residence, and importantly for our final case, "the taking of farms [fixed annual revenues from leased holdings] by spiritual persons."[71] By enlarging the scope of *praemunire*, the exercising of foreign jurisdiction through ecclesiastical courts, all clerical legislation soon required the king's assent and by 1533 the Act in Restraint of Appeals entirely abolished the medieval church court system in England. From then on, religious men and women would be exempt from neither the criminal nor the civil jurisdiction of the Crown.

Dartford Priory remained in existence throughout the period in which these monumental alterations took place – it would not be dissolved until 1539. And in May 1534, Prioress Elizabeth Cressener (1489–1536) found herself facing the charge of violating the Statute of Farms by holding the lease to "the lordship [term encompassing jurisdiction on said land], manor and parsonage of Dartford."[72] Since the Statute of Farms had been in place since 1529, the late filing of this Exchequer indictment (informa-

68 *Ibid.*, p. 69.

69 *Ibid.*, p. 77.

70 Howard Leithead, "Cromwell, Thomas, Earl of Essex (*b.* in or before 1485, *d.* 1540)," in *ODNB*, www.oxforddnb.com/view/article/6769 (accessed August 22, 2010).

71 *The Statutes of the Realm*, vol. 3 [n.p.], 1810–1828. The Making of the Modern World. Gale 2011. Gale, Cengage Learning. Texas State University at San Marcos. January 20, 2011. Online at http://galenet.galegroup.com/servlet/MOME?af=RN&ae=U3608176862&srchtp=a&ste=14.

72 "Henry VIII: May 1534, 11–15," in *Letters and Papers, Foreign and Domestic, Henry*

tion) might have had something to do with the vulnerability of the lessee in the case, the Bishop of Rochester. At the time of the filing, that man was John Fisher (1469–1535). Soon to be executed for failing to recognize Henry VIII's divorce, second marriage, and status as supreme head of the Church of England, Bishop Fisher had already been confined to the Tower of London and deprived of all his preferments by an April bill of attainder.[73]

As with the timing of the suit, the venue signified. The case was begun in the Court of the Exchequer, and although that court had always been concerned with the recovery of money due to the Crown, it had heard only a small number of cases involving breach of penal statutes before the 1530s. Subsequently, however, "informations upon violation of statutes represent an ever growing proportion of the total business [of the court]" with the 1529 statute occasioning a wave of those accusations.[74] Furthermore, by April, 1533, Thomas Cromwell had become Chancellor of the Exchequer.[75]

In earlier Tudor times, the chancellor had concerned himself with keeping the exchequer seal and overseeing the records of the court; there is no evidence that he sat in judgment with or without the barons. In this, as in so much else, Cromwell went his own way:

> Cromwell had given the chancellor sufficient standing to make him part of the judicial machinery of the exchequer. In fact, the wording of the record suggests that he had reduced the barons to mere assistants in a court presided over by himself ... a chancellor who in other capacities governed as the king's chief minister could not be expected to take an inferior place in the exchequer.[76]

Given the odds against their success in 'Cromwell's Exchequer,' Prioress Cressener and her nuns needed excellent counsel, and in this they were fortunate. The fact that Elizabeth Cressener's maternal grandfather was the distinguished lawyer Sir Roger Townshend (d. 1493) might have helped the priory in its bid for counsel. In the event, Dartford's cause was argued by the senior judge of the central criminal court of London (1526–1535), Recorder John Baker. Baker had been schooled at the Inner Temple, and with his appointment as counsel in the Court of Requests began a lifetime

VIII, vol. 7, *1534* (1883), pp. 247–259. Online at www.british-history.ac.uk/report.aspx?compid=79313 (accessed August 20, 2010).

73 Richard Rex, "Fisher, John [St John Fisher] (*c.* 1469–1535)," in *ODNB*, www.oxforddnb.com.libproxy.txstate.edu/view/article/9498 (accessed January 4, 2011).

74 Baker, *Oxford History*, p. 163–164.

75 G. R. Elton, *The Tudor Revolution in Government* (Cambridge: Cambridge University Press, 1960), p. 99.

76 *Ibid.*, p. 114.

of service in central government; he would, in fact, replace Cromwell as Chancellor of the Exchequer in 1540.[77] The Recorder's own spiritual convictions were conservative, although he proved amazingly able to work with the opposition – his legal expertise was sought by Henry, Edward, *and* Mary. A précis of his arguments in Exchequer, dated May, 1534, illustrates both his religious inclinations and his learning:

> A reply to the arguments of the recorder of London, who had defended the prioress of Dartford in her refusal to surrender the lordship, manor and parsonage of Dartford, as the writer affirmed she was bound to do by the statute of farms, 21 Hen. VIII. The Recorder had asserted that she might lawfully detain the lease, as the lands of the priory were under 800 marks. On this plea she had taken the lease in question of the bishop of Rochester contrary to the meaning of the statute, as the writer contends. At the close of the argument the writer accuses the Recorder of stating in open court that if the matter had not been great he would not have "sticked" upon it; – also that he had said he had evil luck in the court in two matters, of which this was one; – that he went to the prioress and induced her to agree with the opposite party; – that he acknowledged in Parliament that spiritual persons ought to have no farms, but that the law should not be retrospective; – his whole object being to defeat the King's highness.[78]

The respondent here was Thomas Derby who argued the case for the king, or better, for Cromwell to whom he owed his appointment as master of the Posts and a clerk of the signet.[79] A member of the so-called Reformation Parliament, which had approved the Act in Restraint of Appeals, and destined to become clerk of the newly minted Privy Council, Derby's interests in preserving the rights of the Crown were unreserved.[80] He alleged that Baker had advised the nuns of Dartford to accept their lease, despite the fact that they violated a penal statute by doing so. He also accused counsel for the defense of having a personal distaste for the work that he was obliged to do. Judging from Derby's next communication with Cromwell, dated 30 July, 1534, Baker was not alone in his scruples.

77 J. D. Alsop, "Baker, Sir John (c. 1489–1558)," in *ODNB*, www.oxforddnb.com.libproxy.txstate.edu/view/article/1124 (accessed January 4, 2011).

78 "Henry VIII: May 1534, 11–15," in *Letters and Papers*, vol. 7, pp. 247–259.

79 Elton, *The Tudor Revolution*, p. 124. "Henry VIII: March 1533, 26–31," in *Letters and Papers, Foreign and Domestic, Henry VIII*, vol. 6: *1533* (1882), #299, pp. 121–144. Online at www.british-history.ac.uk/report.aspx?compid=77544&strquery=derby (accessed August 18, 2010); "Henry VIII: August 1535, 11–20," in *Letters and Papers, Foreign and Domestic, Henry VIII:* vol. 9, *August–December 1535* (1886), #142; pp. 19–40. Online at www.british-history.ac.uk/report.aspx?compid=75663&strquery="mr derby" (accessed August 18, 2010).

80 Baker, *Oxford History*, p. 201; Elton, *The Tudor Revolution*, p. 335. See also note 70 above.

> Thomas Derby [Darby] to Cromwell. Your warning for the delay of justice is likely to be frustrate without your further aid, and judgment will be deferred in the matter of the prioress of Dartford. There are those who ought to be diligent for the King and be present in court, that do now, when the matter is at this point and the counsel against the King can make no reasons for his client, still allege the same frivolous allegations, and others refuse to go into the Exchequer to call upon the matter. The recorder goes about from one to the other, "rounding in their ears." When the Lord Chief Baron proposed Monday next, another on the bench spoke against it, and I shall never get the King's council together to determine this cause. The importance of the cause, especially for the common weal, is twentyfold greater than the matter itself. It is not fit that the Act of Parliament should be deluded. The Prioress alleges the matter is great, but if it is great for her it is a hundred times greater for the commonwealth. The King's subjects about Dartford allege they can get no hay or pasturage for their cattle, by reason of my Lady's housewifery. Some calling themselves my friends think that I act against my honesty, and that I ought not to have done as I have done for all the money in demand. I hope to see the day when the contrary opinion shall be held amongst the common sort, and the lawyers especially.
>
> London, this Sunday.[81]

Derby was obviously having difficulty winning support for his cause and his bitterness toward those who impeded it is clear. Had his reference to "my Lady's housewifery" been designed to spur the Chancellor of the Exchequer into action on behalf of the King's poor subjects? As the case was still unresolved in October, the tactic does not appear to have succeeded. Furthermore, when it is next alluded to, Elizabeth Cressener is the one styled a "poor subject."

> [John] Hylsey to Cromwell. The prioress of Dartford, my poor subject, for whom I spake to you the last term, is still sore troubled with the same suit, which she is too poor to defend without your favor. She would agree with Mr Darby, but he will not consent under 100£, which is more than she can bear. I am threatened with the loss of the offices in which you have put me, this term without your support; for the provincial that was my predecessor has prevailed upon my lord of Oxford and my dowager lady of Oxford, and my lord of Essex and Mrs Marshall, mistress to the Queen's gentlewomen, and the prior of London, my predecessor, to labor for him; and he has made divers friends to come to it again, as Sir Will. Kingston, and one Mr More of Wyer and others. The provincial of the Austin Friars takes upon him the office of master-general of our religion, to which you appointed me, and has broken certain assignations made by our general chapter, saying he is our master-general and we shall do nothing but under him.[82]

81 "Henry VIII: Appendix, 1533–1534," in *Letters and Papers*, vol. 7, #34, pp. 628–642. Online at www.british-history.ac.uk/report.aspx?compid=79360&strquery=dartford (accessed August 03, 2010.

82 "Henry VIII: October 1534, 16–20," in *Letters and Papers*, vol. 7, #1265, pp. 487–493.

Prioress Cressener's new ally was the Dominican friar John Hilsey who, not surprisingly, had problems of his own.[83] Hilsey had administered the oath of obedience to the king as supreme head of the Church of England in all Dominican priories; he had done so at Dartford on May 14, 1534. Consequently, Henry VIII had appointed him Master General of the Dominican order in England.[84] As is apparent from his recitation of woes to Cromwell, objection to Hilsey's appointment as English Master General was made at the highest levels; he was never confirmed by the Master General of the order and is not named in the official list of provincial priors and vicars of the English Dominicans.[85] These circumstances notwithstanding, Hilsey argued for Cressener and her nuns, saying that Derby now refused to take anything below £100 as a fine for her transgression of the statute.

With the benefit of hindsight, it seems surprising that the Dartford cause was still being argued in 1535, but a cryptic mention of the dispute surfaces in the calendars that year.

> Objections taken to an information filed against the prioress of Dartford for occupying in farm the manor of Dartford, by lease from the late bishop of Rochester for 40 months, in contravention of the statute 21 Hen. VIII.; claiming for her the benefit of the Act 7 Hen. VIII., requiring such information to be made within a year, and of statute 22 Hen. VIII. c. 14 [*sic*], pardoning all abbesses, prioresses, &c. for matters before 10 March 22 Hen. VIII.[86]

If the unidentified lawyer who made these objections was not John Baker, counsel for the defense was someone equally well versed in the common law and equally keen to deploy it in the interest of the nuns. Citing statute 7 Henry VIII c. 3, 1515, which mandated a time limit for suing informations upon a penal statute, the anonymous advocate hit home.[87] As noted above, the indictment in the Dartford manor case had been sued fully five years after the passage of the penal Statute of Farms. Equally compelling was counsel's reference to statute 22 Henry VIII c. 15, 1530–1531.[88] This statute registered actions taken by the Crown in December, 1530. As

Online at www.british-history.ac.uk/report.aspx?compid=79344 (accessed August 3, 2010.

83 S. Thompson, "Hilsey, John (*d.* 1539)," in *ODNB*, www.oxforddnb.com/view/article/13325 (accessed January 20, 2011).

84 Lee, *Nunneries*, p. 39.

85 Gumbley, *Provincial Priors*, p. 248.

86 "Henry VIII: Miscellaneous, 1535," in *Letters and Papers*, vol. 9, pp. 367–402. Online at www.british-history.ac.uk/report.aspx?compid=75684 (accessed August 18, 2010).

87 *The Statutes of the Realm*, vol. 3. Online at http://galenet.galegroup.com/servlet/MOME?af=RN&ae=U3608176747&srchtp=a&ste=14 (accessed January 20, 2011).

88 *Ibid.* Online at http://galenet.galegroup.com/servlet/MOME?af=RN&ae=U3608176904&srchtp=a&ste=14 (accessed January 20, 2011).

recompense for the subsidy of £100,000 bestowed upon him by the clergy of Canterbury, the king had granted to religious of that province a general pardon for all offenses against the statutes of *praemunire* committed before 10 March, the twenty-second year of his reign. Presumably, the Dartford manor lease had been signed a few months before March, 1530, and its possession challenged only near its expiration date in 1534. However late in the day these legal objections were made, they seem to have been persuasive. At the time of its dissolution, Dartford Priory holdings included Dartford manor, which, in 1548, was granted to Anne of Cleves, along with the priory itself.[89]

[89] "Friaries: The Dominican Nuns of Dartford."

5

Chancery Suits

As stated previously, the Court of Chancery, although a royal court, was not a common law court. It was the court of conscience, where a plaintiff was allowed to describe his case in detail and to request that it be considered according to standards inadmissible at common law. The following example shows that this aim was taken seriously.

> In 1468, a subpoena was sued in the Chancery for the breach of a parol [verbal] promise. The defendant argued that the plaintiff's only remedy lay in the Church courts. The Chancellor [the Bishop of Bath and Wells, Robert Stillington] was short with him. "You say that for breach of faith he must sue by the Canon Law; but in this case, because he is damaged by the non-performance of the promise, he shall have a remedy here." The defendant persisted that, had the plaintiff taken the trouble to obtain the defendant's promise under seal, he could have sued in Covenant [by writ in a common law court], and that it was "his folly not to have a deed." But the Chancellor dismissed the suggestion with the beneficent, if uncomplimentary maxim, *Deus est procurator fatuorum.*[1]

An uncomplimentary maxim to be sure, but not quite the scathing indictment that it might seem. Robert Stillington, chancellor from 1467 to 1470, held a doctorate in civil law from Oxford, and unlike some of his predecessors he took a real interest in procedural law. Therefore, by both training and inclination, he was acutely aware of the challenges facing *every* fifteenth-century litigant in the courts of the Crown.[2]

He knew, for example, that notarial registers bulged with exemplars of writs from which one was obliged to choose in order to commence an action. "If there was no writ, there was no remedy. And the forms had been frozen in an earlier period ... A writ which departed from the proper form was considered to be void and unamendable."[3] If, like the plaintiff in

1 "God is the fools' lawyer." For commentary and paraphrase of this case, Seipp #1468.018, refer to: www.bu.edu/phpbin/lawyearbooks/display.php?id=19979 (accessed January 12, 2009).

2 *ODNB*, vol. 52, pp. 798–800.

3 Baker, *Oxford History*, pp. 323–324. See also Chapter 2.

Robert Stillington's court, a litigant had failed to secure written evidence of a promise, he would find no writ at all designed to remedy its subsequent breach; if he chose his original writ badly, his suit would be thrown out of court.[4]

Separate from writ selection, there were myriad procedural technicalities. If a litigant, or one should say his lawyer, failed to meet a submission date, ignored a technicality in pleading, or hesitated to jump some other procedural hurdle, his case could be seriously jeopardized. In these circumstances more than one 'foolish' plaintiff found his or her way to that 'court of conscience,' the English side of the Chancery. In this chapter I examine the circumstances that led cloistered religious women to this court. Whenever possible I identify their *procuratores* as well, those human agents upon whom the nuns depended for their fair share of 'God's justice.'

There were many kinds of petitions made to the Chancery but they all fall into one of two broad categories: those for which the king's courts provided no remedy, or no further remedy, and those for which a common law remedy theoretically existed.[5] A variety of alleged injustices could not be vetted in the courts of common law because of evidentiary lacunae. Breach of promise when that promise was undocumented, and fraud occasioned by the failure of a litigant to secure written evidence for a transaction such as the repayment of a debt, are issues of this sort. Since breach of promise or fraud often involved dower rights, women as well as men became regular suitors in Chancery.[6] A petition involving the feoffment to use, an arrangement of particular value to wives but particularly susceptible to pettifoggery, illustrates this point.

The practice among late medieval landowners of making living trusts called feoffments to use was responsible for a dramatic increase in Chancery business. Designed to spare heirs and especially widows the necessity of paying feudal incidents on landed property, these collusive agreements

4 *Ibid.*, p. 814 for specific reference to contract enforcement when lacking a deed.

5 William Baildon, ed., *Select Cases in Chancery* (London: Bernard Quaritch, 1896), pp. xxi–xxiv surveys these reasons; Margaret Avery, "The History of the Equitable Jurisdiction of Chancery before 1460," *Bulletin of the Institute of Historical Research* 42, no. 106 (November, 1969): 129–144, provides a lucid overview of some of the most common complaints addressed to Chancery.

6 See for example, Michele Seiler, "'She hath no remedy by the common law': English Women and the Medieval Court of Chancery." Unpublished master's thesis, Texas State University San Marcos, 2010. By the fourteenth century, English widows could expect to inherit one third of their husband's property, so the temptation to hinder the process was not easily resisted.

depended completely upon the reliability of the trustees (feofees) to honor a verbal compact.[7] The 1453 case of Joan Lyngen documents the difficulties that could arise from such arrangements.[8] Joan's husband, Rauf Lyngen, had thought to provide her with a life interest in his manor of Sutton, free of death dues, by enfeoffing his friend, John Barre. Barre, Joan alleged, had grudgingly followed Rauf's wishes, but her son, John Lyngen had not. Joan's petition asks the chancellor to redress the actions of her own son who, "not dredying God the kyng nor his lawes," had with a group of forty men "arrayed in mane [manner] of werre [war]," invaded and despoiled what Rauf had intended for her use.

Without documented evidence of a promise broken or a deal gone wrong, would-be litigants could not secure a writ to sue in the king's courts. But some cases that ended up in Chancery had actually begun in the common law courts where they had foundered on a point of principle or procedure. For instance, a plaintiff who secured a viable writ to sue at common law, but then abandoned his suit for some reason (however significant), would find his case summarily abated. Crown remedy had been exhausted. But if in his petition to Chancery the plaintiff could claim a compelling reason for having abandoned his suit and then argue for the existence of a consequent lingering injustice, he had reason to hope that the matter would be reopened and resolved in this court of equity. A plea lodged by William Togode and his wife Alianore provides a classic example of such a suit.

Alianore's deceased father, Thomas, had made testamentary bequests to charity and to his daughters, Agnes and Alianore. All of those bequests, however, had been contingent on the repayment of a debt of £100 owed to him by a certain Richard Brakynburgh. At the time of Thomas' demise, Brakynburgh still owed him that debt. Thomas' widow, Elizabeth, remarried and her new husband William Adams launched a suit for non-payment of debt against Brakynburgh in the Court of Common Pleas. But Brakynburgh was then outlawed and while he was still classed as such Adams died; William Adams' suit against Richard Brakynburgh was conveniently abated, with bad results for Alinore and her family.

> William Adams, late husband of the said Elizabeth, sued an action of debt against the said Richard [Brakynburgh] before the King's judges of the Common Pleas at Westminster, and the process continued at great cost to him up to the

7 Baker, *Introduction*, pp. 211–213; Avery, "History of Equitable Jurisdiction," pp. 134–137.

8 *Calendars of the Proceedings in Chancery in the Reign of Queen Elizabeth*, vol. 1, pp. xlviii–xlx.

> time that Richard [Brakynburgh] was outlawed and while he was so outlawed, the said William Adams died, by whose death the said Richard [Brakynburgh] had the said process of the said action and also that suit abated. Then Richard, one of the said executors, fell our of his mind and another of the said executors, Agnes, became a professed nun under Alice Fizlewes, abbess of the Minoresses without Aldgate of London and so willed the said xl *li.* to remain to the use of your said beseechers, and that not withstanding, they can have no action by the common law against the said Richard [Brakynburgh].[9]

The Chancery petition of the "said beseechers" William Togode and his wife Alianore stressed that, as a consequence of an abated common lawsuit, Thomas' testamentary bequests remained unfulfilled. It underscored the fact that some of those bequests were charitable grants, and it argued that there was some urgency about resolving the matter since the number of persons still alive and legally able to execute Thomas' last wishes was steadily diminishing – madness and the monastery having already claimed two of them. It was a strong case and one that we suppose succeeded because of the tenacity of Thomas' heirs.

While inequitable judgments and inelastic procedure in the courts of the Crown accounted for much Chancery business, a number of petitions to the chancellor involved disputes for which there *were* common law remedies. In these instances, petitioners alleged that fear prevented them from seeking out those remedies. Intimidation of a plaintiff by more powerful and well-connected members of society sometimes manifested itself violently, with litigants claiming that they did not dare to sue at common law for fear of death or the destruction of their property; it could also take subtler forms. In all such cases, however, petitioners stated that they were unable to bring common law to bear against an individual whose influential connections provided him with immunity from the ordinary machinery of local justice. It should be noted that those influential adversaries might be lay or religious, male or female, and that their victims were not confined to the lower classes.

No less a personage than the Abbot of Burton, for example, petitioned the chancellor to redress a wrong of some twenty years' standing which had been perpetrated by the formidable Prioress of Kings Mead, Derby, Isabel Stanley. A gentlewoman related to the most prestigious knightly families in the region, she had not only turned a deaf ear to the abbot's annual requests for the rent due him from her house, but also had met the

9 C 1/168/41. The petition states that Agnes entered the abbey under the Abbess Alice Fitz Lewes, which means she would have entered the abbey after 1501 (the year Alice became abbess). This means the case can be dated to 1504–1515. I have modernized grammar and spelling for readability.

bailiff sent to distrain for it saying that he and his men would be "nailed with arrows" if they tried to do so again.[10] And lest we think that cloistered nuns were any less confident of their powers of persuasion there is this Chancery petition of Robert Wilde, proctor of the much disputed church of Wrestlingworth.[11]

> To the right reverend father in god the bishop of Lincoln and chancellor of England.
>
> Robert Wilde, clerk and parson of the church of Wrestlingworth in the county of Bedford, shows and complains to your good lordship that a cause concerning the right of the certain tithes hangs before the right reverend father in god the Archbishop of Canterbury in a dissension between Johanna Barton, abbess of the monastery of the order of Saint Clare without Aldgate of London of the one part, and your complainant on the other part for the which cause your said complainant upon the xi day of September last past came to London to commune with such persons as were of his learned counsel in the spiritual law, and one William Baker then being servant to the said abbess therefore having knowledge and the same, by subtle means contrary to good conscience intending to make the said complainant wary to sue in the said cause hanging before your right reverend father in god the archbishop of Canterbury, and to impoverish your complainant so that he should be of no power to sue in the said cause, caused the said abbess to affirm a complaint of trespass against your said complainant before one of the sheriffs of London and by force of the same caused him to be arrested and kept in prison, and that the same abbess contrary to truth and good conscience has declared that your said complainant the xi day of September last past in the parish of Saint Boltoff [Botolph] without Aldgate of London with force of arms made assault upon the said William Baker then being her servant and him had wounded and mistreated so that he should be in despair of his life, and furthermore that because of this [attack] the same William Baker her servant dares not go about his occupation, whereas in very truth your complainant was not guilty as god knows and yet by such means of surmise and for lack of acquaintance without the city of London your complainant is likely to be undone, and such persons as shall try the said matter be tenants and of special acquaintance and assigns of the said abbess and they have expressly said that they will pass against your said complainant and will not hear nor take any regard to true obedience given to them for the profit of your said complainant and upon their untruth there lies no attaint nor other remedy by common law, therefore that it may please your gracious lordship in the way of charity tenderly to consider the premises and to grant a charter to be sent to the Sheriff of London commanding him by the same to certify the

10 *Calendars of the Proceedings in Chancery in the Reign of Queen Elizabeth*, vol. 1, pp xxiii–xxxiv. This case is also mentioned briefly in Power, *Medieval English Nunneries*, p. 4.

11 C 1/67/163. The case which occasioned his petition is dealt with in Chapter 7.

> said causes before the king in his chambers there to be examined according to conscience for the love of god and in the way of charity.[12]

Arrested and imprisoned for allegedly assaulting the servant of Johana Barton, Abbess of the Minories, Wilde had thrown himself on the mercy of the Chancellor because the chances of clearing himself of criminal charges by going before a jury composed almost entirely of Abbess Barton's "tenants and special acquaintances" were impossibly slim. He also claimed that the assault charges themselves were the result of collusive and illegal action: Barton had accused him of the assault in order "to impoverish your said complainant wherefore he should be of no power to sue" in a cause between them pending in another court. Wilde's claims against a social superior with means and method resonate in our first case involving cloistered nuns as plaintiffs in Chancery.

In 1470, the Abbess of Denney petitioned the chancellor, Robert Stillington, to take action against the executors of Thomas Burgoyn, erstwhile Justice of the Peace and lord of the manor of Impington. The decedent's property lay next to their own manor of Histon, and the nuns alleged that for over twenty years (since September of 1452 to be exact), Thomas Burgoyn had misused his powers, both those that naturally flowed from his local personal prominence and those conferred upon him as a representative of the king's justice, to visit a series of injuries upon them. Their petition stated:

> that the said Thomas Burgoyn robbed and wrongfully vexed by writs of trespass and otherwise the tenants and servants [of Histon manor] to the number of forty ... and also caused them to be indicted before himself, being Justice of the Peace and keeper of the books within said County Cambridge. And when writs of *certiorari* [writs issuing from a superior court upon the complaint of a party that he had not received justice in an inferior court, or could not have an impartial trial] were sued for the removing of the same the same Thomas returned that there were no such records, how be it that the said servant and tenants were put in arrest and paid great sum for their deliverance ... by the space of seven years to the great cost and damage of your said poor oratrices in defence of the same to the sum of £200.[13]

Nor did their neighbor's gross subversion of local justice constitute his only wrong. The nuns maintained that Thomas had also forbidden their tenants and servants from attending their manorial courts, had impeded their officials from taking strays that wandered onto their fields, and had

12 Note that according to common law there was no writ of attaint which would have run against a dishonest jury when the verdict had been given in a city of London court.

13 C 1/40/30. This particular segment is also transcribed in Bourdillon, *Minoresses*, p. 31.

occupied some of the fens owned by the convent, all actions which over the course of many years had cost the convent a calculated £883.

Thomas Burgoyn's particular power and influence help to explain why the nuns of Denney delayed their suit until after the death of their nemesis. Yet even then, and even with undisputed evidence that Thomas had ordered his executors to pay his debts, their victory was not assured. Burgoyn's executors, Alice and John Burgoyn, answered the petition of the nuns by stating that Thomas' last will and testament instructed them to pay his debts, but that it did not mandate that restitution be made for the injuries and wrongs specified by the nuns. The nuns in turn countered that they would be prepared to support their claims for damages by having those claims examined by the court, and that they were "neither satisfied nor content" with the limited recompense offered by Alice and John.[14]

Before 1500, judgments of the Court of Chancery are seldom recorded, but in this instance we can be guardedly optimistic about the outcome of the case. Robert Stillington may not have been a model of clerical virtue but, as noted at the outset of this chapter, he seems to have taken his duties as chancellor quite seriously.[15] Furthermore, if the nuns of Denney had not recouped their losses in 1470 they might have lacked the confidence, not to mention the cash, required to engage in yet another legal battle with the Burgoyns some ten years later.

Their second suit was heard around 1480 by Chancellor Thomas Rotherham (1474–1483), Archbishop of York.[16] Like Stillington, he had a university degree, albeit in theology, and a clear interest in civil and canon law.[17] The nuns and convent in this instance were co-petitioners with the Abbot of Eynsham, who claimed traditional rights identical to those of Denney. They included the right to hold certain leets and lawdays (courts of record held periodically in a hundred, lordship, or manor, before the lord or his steward, and attended by the residents of the district) in Impington, and the right to have livestock owned by their tenants

14 C 1/40/30.

15 H. C. Maxell-Lyte, ed., *The Registers of Robert Stillington*. 1937, Introduction, pp. xiv–xv. After recounting the bishop's pluralism and his political difficulties resulting from the York–Lancaster struggles, the editor notes the likelihood that Stillington was a father several times over.

16 *CCR 1476–85*, pp. 217–218.

17 T. S. Haskett, "The Medieval English Court of Chancery." *Law and History Review* 14, no. 2 (1996): 245–313, Appendix: "Education and Experience of the Chancellors, 1396–1532," p. 312, notes that Rotherham had an MA from Cambridge and that he bequeathed a good number of law books to his alma mater. Also see Rosemary Horrox, "Rotherham, Thomas (1423–1500)," in *ODNB*, www.oxforddnb.com/view/article/24155 (accessed October 24, 2010).

pastured in common with that of the tenants of Histon. The violator of those rights was listed by both the Abbess of Denney and the Abbot of Eynsham as Thomas Burgoyn's son and executor, John.

Apparently John Burgoyn, "gentilman of Impyton," was less inclined than his father to row with his neighbors or else he was simply less able to taint the evidence (which consisted of court rolls) against them. For whatever reason, John capitulated to the time-honored demands of the two petitioners. In a gesture befitting the 'court of conscience' both the abbess and the abbot displayed generosity in the composition they made with Burgoyn. Both agreed that given the dimensions of the common pasture at Impington "they would not overcharge the comyn in the said fields with an outrageous number of beasts, contrary to reason."[18]

We do not learn the names of the lawyers who represented the nuns in either of these suits, although their existence is confirmed by the Close Rolls: "And to avoid further variance between the parties, it was agreed between the abbot and John Burgoyne in person, and the abbess being represented by an attorney."[19] As a substantial number of the lawyers practicing in Chancery from 1474 to 1486 have been identified, the attorney representing the abbess was likely one of these men.[20] We can further surmise that because both suits alleged injuries for which there were remedies provided by the common law, the litigants would have consulted lawyers practicing in Common Pleas or King's Bench. The chancellor and his clerks decided such cases in consultation with common lawyers, usually serjeants at law – Richard Pygot, John Catesby and William Husy, for instance, were serjeants who sat in judgment with Thomas Rotheram.[21]

The case of Dorothy Cumberford, last Abbess of the Minories, vs. William Atkyns illustrates another category of Chancery suit. It involved what would come to be termed an equitable matter, one for which there was no suitable remedy at common law. The case came before Thomas Wolsey, who was chancellor from 1515 to 1529.[22] With no training in the canon or civil law (he had studied theology at Oxford), Wolsey was apparently skillful and astute enough as a judge. His court drew great numbers

18 *CCR 1476–1485*, p. 218.

19 *Ibid.*, p. 217.

20 Baker, "Lawyers Practising in Chancery," pp. 54–76.

21 *CCR 1476–1485*, p. 217.

22 Haskett, "Medieval English Court of Chancery" p. 313 observes that although Wolsey's titles and honors were many "he remains a figure not usually associated with great or subtle learning." He had an MA from Oxford. For a very full treatment of his career see Sybil M. Jack, "Wolsey, Thomas (1470/71–1530)," in *ODNB*, www.oxforddnb.com/view/article/29854 (accessed May 27, 2009).

of litigants to it and his successor, the consummate lawyer Sir Thomas More, praised his conduct in office.

Dorothy Cumberford's case may best be approached by first laying out the original petition, with my annotations in brackets.

Chancery bill of Dorothy Cumberfford, abbess of Minoresses of London, v. William Atkyns, vicar of Potton, county of Bedford, 1518–29.

To the most reverend father in god my lord legate cardinal archbishop of York and chancellor of England meekly beseecth your good lordship your oratrice [petitioner] Dorothe Cumberfford abbess of the house and monastery of the minoresses without Algate of London, that whereas the parsonage of Potton in the county of Bedfford by many years past was appropriated unto the said monastery [This was done in 1394 by the prior and convent of St Andrew, Northampton and it was done without expense to the abbey under the auspices of Thomas de Woodstock, Duke of Gloucester] after which appropriation was had and a vicar ordained to be vicar of Potton aforesaid, a composition was had and made between the predecessors of your said daughter [Alice Fitz Lewes, mentioned, 1501] and the convent of the monastery on the one part and William Rychman vicar of Potton aforesaid on the other part, upon which composition a sufficient endowment was then made and appointed to the said vicar and to his successors as by the same composition it may appear, with which the vicars there [at Potton] have been content and pleased, and that not withstanding, one Sir William Atkyns, now vicar of the said parish of Potton pretendeth to have and by rigor [force] takes yearly from your said oratrice all the mortuaries due to your said oratrice within the said parish of Potton and also by rigor takes from your said oratrice the tithes of hay due to your said oratrice within the said parish and by rigor hath distrained the tenants of your said oratrice for Xls. yearly to be had of them which mortuaries, tithes of hay and Xls. of yearly rent is not comprised in the said composition for the said vicar to have, and of it, his gracious lord the said Sir William Atkyns detains and keeps diverse evidences, descriptions, writings and muniments concerning the right and title of your said oratrice and of her said monastery of and in the said parsonage, certain of which evidences, descriptions writings, and muniments being to your said oratrice unknown, and [he] will make no delivery thereof to your said oratrice wherefore she can maintain no action for them against the said Sir William Atkyns by course of the common law. In consideration whereof that it may please your said lordship to grant a writ of subpoena to be directed to the foresaid Sir William Atkyns commanding him by the same to appear before the king in his chancery at a certain day upon a pain to answer to the premises and to take such further direction therein as shall be according to right and good conscience, and thus at the reverence of god and in way of charity.

Pledges for the prosecution [if plaintiff failed to prove allegations and was charged for costs] John Orenge, John Johnson, of London, yeoman
Thomas Done of the same, yeoman
John Marten [attorney][23]

23 C 1/534/1.

The situation was complex, but far from unique among the landed classes of late medieval England whose claims and counterclaims seldom rested upon recent transactions. Dorothy Cumberford based her petition upon the fact of an appropriation which had taken place at least a century and a quarter earlier. Under the terms of an appropriation, a benefice and its revenues would be held by an impropriator or patron. In this case, the benefice was the parsonage of Potton and the patron the monastery of the Minories. Patrons were to set aside revenues for the maintenance of a priest or vicar who would fulfill the spiritual obligations attendant upon the benefice; another portion of tithes and associated fees deriving from the benefice might be reserved for the patron's own use. According to her petition, such an arrangement (composition) had been made by the Minoresses of Aldgate with the vicar of Potton "many years past" and had endured without challenge until the arrival of the current vicar William Atkyns. Atkyns was obviously not happy with his share of the revenues and allegedly withheld an assortment of tithes from the nuns, the proprietors of Potton.

Dorothy Cumberford filed suit in Chancery because, along with her revenues, the vicar withheld "certain evidences, descriptions [land surveys] writings and muniments." These records were essential to establishing her claims about the original appropriation settlement. She could not sue at common law because she lacked the written evidence that law required to prove her case against the vicar of Potton. With this Chancery suit she aimed not to reclaim the tithes and fees due her monastery, but to force William Atkyns to tender that evidence that she alleged would support that claim. That she would have then proceeded to file suit in an ecclesiastical court, or in certain circumstances the Court of Common Pleas, seems likely. Unfortunately we know neither the outcome of this action nor anything more than the name of the man, John Marten, who served as Dorothy Cumberford's attorney.

The case of Syon Abbey vs. the executors of the will of Giles Lovell, last Prior of Lancaster, also found its way into the Court of Chancery because the plaintiffs lacked the documentation required to sue by writ.[24] As with Dorothy Cumberford's suit, the goal of the nuns of Syon was not to reclaim debts more appropriately sued for in a church court – in this case *post mortem* debts contracted by a cleric – but to get back the evidence that those debts were actually owed them. Subsequent contests, and there were several, which involved the advowson and/or tithes of the

24 PL 6/1/22.

church of Lancaster would be heard in ecclesiastical courts specifically those of papal judges delegate, preserving the interests of the Crown.[25]

Because their suit concerned the Lancaster Priory, the plaintiffs petitioned not the chancellor in Westminster, but the chancellor of the Palatinate of Lancaster. By long-held privilege of the Crown, the palatinate courts were independent from those of the rest of the country although they administered a justice consistent with that of the rest of the realm.

The identity of the chancellor before whom the nuns brought this case is unknown because the petition is not dated internally. We know only that it was presented to the chancellor of the Palatinate and Duchy of Lancaster during the reign of Henry VI (1422–1461).[26] Four men all well schooled in, and well rewarded for, crown service held that office during the time: William Troutbecke (1424–1431), Walter Sherington (1431–1442), William Tresham (1442–1449), and John Say (1449–1462). While nobility rather than legal training seems to have been the chief requisite for this office, William Tresham was a prominent common lawyer and John Say, the consummate administrator.[27]

According to the plaintiffs, King Henry V had stipulated that the Priory of Lancaster was to be given to Syon in frankalmoin (free alms, requiring only a return of spiritual services, such as prayers for the soul of the departed) upon the death of the incumbent prior, Giles Lovell. Lovell had died, leaving a priory worth £200, but his executors, William Haryngton and John Morley, refused to concede to the nuns certain mortuary dues and other income owed them. The sisters also alleged that Haryngton and Morley were impeding their claims by withholding certain priory muniments that would have confirmed these debts. In the absence of written proof of precisely what it was that they were owed, the abbess and convent petitioned Chancery for justice, adding the reminder that, as recluses living far from the said priory lands, their need to have the dispute resolved was especially acute.

How well do the facts of the case as presented by the petitioners mesh with the facts as independently documented? That King Henry V intended the Priory of Lancaster to become part of Syon's endowment is indisputable. In 1417, the king supplemented his foundation charter by setting up

25 Chapter 7 contains details of three such conflicts.

26 Giles Lovell did not die until 1428 however, so the case cannot have reached the court earlier.

27 Henry Summerson, "Tresham, William (*d.* 1450)," in *ODNB*, www.oxforddnb.com/view/article/27713 (accessed May 21, 2009); L. Kirby, "Say, Sir John (*d.* 1478)," in *ODNB*, www.oxforddnb.com/view/article/24764 (accessed May 21, 2009).

a trust for the convent consisting of much land and revenue, including a specific grant of "£110 yearly from the farm of the Priory of Lancaster, at the feasts of Michaelmas and Easter, to be paid by the hands of the now prior of the said Priory of Lancaster [Giles Lovell] during the life of the same prior; also the Priory of Lancaster, with appurtenances, after the death of the aforesaid prior."[28] In 1424, the abbess and convent asked Henry VI to confirm his father's grant, which he did.[29] The wording of this 1424 confirmation makes it clear that Henry V's wishes had not yet been carried out: "in like manner we have given special licence, because the aforesaid licenses of our aforesaid father in his life-time were in no wise executed, or the statute of lands and tenements not bestowed at mortmain published, or any other statute, grant, gift, matter or cause whatsoever to the contrary made notwithstanding."[30]

Giles Lovell died in 1428 and the nuns of Syon probably began to ask for back payments from Lovell's executors shortly thereafter. Their Chancery petition does not specify the grounds for Harrington and Morley's refusal to hand over "certain mortuary dues and income" so we do not know their motives for demurring. They could have been acting out of a desire to defraud the rich recluses of Syon. But given the Byzantine history of the Lancaster priory farm, they could well have believed their actions were justified.

As noted in Chapter 4, when a monarch faced a costly war, or needed extra property to endow a favorite foundation, all or some portion of the wealth of the alien priories would be seized.[31] Henry V had made crown seizure of all fully dependent alien priories, of which Lancaster Priory was one, permanent. That seizure of property in turn accounted for his 1417 grant of "£110 yearly from the farm of the Priory of Lancaster" to the nuns of Syon. But it seems that Henry V had already given that gift, and in perpetuity! The renting out or farming of the alien priories had been going on for years before their final seizure by the Crown and in 1415 Henry V had granted to "the king's uncle Thomas, earl of Dorset, Henry Fitz Hugh, chevalier, John Rodenale, chevalier, and Robert Morton, esquire, their heirs and assigns £110 from the farm of the alien priory of Lancastre."[32] If the same amount were to have been delivered annually to the nuns of

28 Aungier, *History*, p. 33. Aungier reproduces the entire charter, pp. 31–35.

29 *Ibid.*, p. 40. Once again, the whole charter is transcribed.

30 *Ibid.*, p. 50.

31 *Ibid.*, pp. 31–32 fn 5.

32 *CPR 1413–1416*, p. 358.

Syon, the priory's net worth would have had to have been considerably more than the £200 mentioned in their chancery petition.

All of these issues muddied the waters with reference to Henry V's grant of Lancaster priory to Syon, and they clearly affected the disposition of Giles Lovell's estate; a fact which will become obvious when we look at the subsequent struggles over the tithes of the church of Lancaster. But even if the chancellor of the Palatinate sympathized with the defendants, he would not have approved of the self-help methods Haryngton and Morley used to deflect the demands of the Abbess of Syon; sequestering title deeds and muniments was not really cricket. That abbess in turn, seems to have been well aware that Chancery was a court in which her demands for justice could be asserted even without benefit of written evidence.

Did the abbess in our next case also lack documented proof of her claim? Since we have only the defendant's answer to Abbess Cressener's petition and not the complaint itself we shall probably never know why she chose to sue in Chancery.[33] Her adversary's precisely worded answer does, however, provide considerable ground for informed speculation.

Undated, but with the plaintiff identified as "Elizabeth, prioress of the monastery of Dartford," this case might have come before any of several men who held the office of chancellor during the long tenure of Elizabeth Cressener (1489–1537). But since the defendant is listed as "Thomas, prior of the monastery of Westacre," we may narrow the field slightly.[34] Thomas Clerk appears named as prior of Westacre, Norfolk, in 1503, so it is probable that Cressener's petition was made to Chancellor William Warham (1502–1515), Archbishop of Canterbury.[35] Trained in canon and civil law with a doctorate from Oxford in the former, Archbishop Warham had held positions in the Court of Arches and had been a proctor in Rome.[36] He continued to practice law throughout his career and seemed to find satisfaction in judging disputes about wills and tithes rather than regarding such cases as irksome components of public office. As the sequestering of tithes was clearly an issue in the case at hand, Warham would have been well equipped to deal with it.

Saying that Elizabeth Cressener's complaint "and the matter therein

33 C 4/10/80.

34 Note that National Archive descriptors identify him as "prior of Westage [*sic*]."

35 "Freebridge Hundred: Westacre," in *An Essay towards a Topographical History of the County of Norfolk*, vol. 9 (1808), pp. 158–163. Online at british-history.ac.uk/report.aspx?compid=78517&strquery=westacre (accessed November 2, 2010).

36 J. J. Scarisbrick, "Warham, William (1450?–1532)," in *ODNB*, www.oxforddnb.com/view/article/28741 (accessed November 2, 2010).

contained is insufficient," Prior Thomas Clerk began his answer by making a declaration of the facts as *he* knew them. He alleged that of the four manors in the town of Great Massingham, Norfolk, one of them "always called and known by the name of Ladye Manor also by the name of the manor of Great Massyngham" had long been in the possession of the nuns of Dartford. The abbess, seisined in demesne of this fee, had let it to farm to Prior Thomas' predecessor at Westacre, Richard [Pawe or Palle, his name occurs in 1467] "for a time of forty years not yet expired." She had drawn up an agreement which allowed for Prior Richard to collect certain rents from the manor and permitted him to keep the tithes as well. When Prior Richard died, however, Abbess Cressener had not recognized the right of the newly elected prior, Thomas Clerk, to continue farming Ladye Manor although the lease made to his predecessor had not yet expired. Thomas consequently demanded that his right to continue to farm the manor be recognized. He also asked "that he may be dismissed out of court with his reasonable costs and that by them sustained in his behalf."

By implication, Elizabeth Cressener and her nuns had complained that Prior Thomas was withholding rents and tithes from their manor of Great Massingham. That they legally and fully possessed that manor as well as the right to farm it out, was not disputed. That they had made a forty-year lease with the prior of Westacre was at issue. Perhaps it was the duration of the lease that was contested; perhaps it was the precise wording—a lease specifically to Prior Pawe and extending for forty years or his death in office, whichever came first. Maybe the abbess contended that the lease never existed at all. Although Thomas Clerk appeared confident enough in his answer to ask for court costs as well as a decision in his favor, neither he nor Elizabeth Cressener appears to have had the written evidence to prove their side of the matter in a common law court.

So far, we have dealt exclusively with Chancery cases in which cloistered nuns were the plaintiffs. But oftentimes the economic interests of those nuns might could be affected by petitions of aggrieved third parties. That is the point illustrated by the next two suits, one brought by some debt-bound executors and the other begun by a harried contractor.

Heard in the court of Chancellor Cardinal Thomas Wolsey, the first petition was made some time between 1518 and 1529.[37] In a slightly macabre contest, John Barrett and John Garlond, executors of the last will and testament of John Kirby, made their claim against another set of executors. The defendants, John Roo, serjeant at law, John Smyth, clerk, and John Skewys, were the executors of Edward Courtenay, late Earl of

[37] C 1/471/20.

Devon. Plaintiffs Barrett and Garlond maintained that at the time of his death Kirby was owed money by the Earl of Devon for cloth purchased for the earl's funeral. The purchase had been a timely one since the earl had died before he could repay his debt, which totaled £120.

The plaintiffs petitioned Chancellor Wolsey to force the earl's executors Roo, Smyth, and Skewys to repay the debt, adding that they had repeatedly asked the executors for the £120 to no avail. As a consequence, they continued, they had been unable to fulfill the last wishes of the deceased John Kirby, which they were duty bound to do as his executors. Those wishes included the following expenditures, all to be made from recovered debt funds: £30 "for the building of the Mynores, late burnt"; £20 for the upkeep of Rochester bridge, a cause to which the deceased John Kirby had been particularly attached; and the residue funding poor scholars.

As usual, the outcome of this suit is unknown. Because a portion of the reclaimed debt was to be expended on the rebuilding of the fire damaged Minories, however, the plaintiffs might have felt particularly confident. Chancellor Wolsey's sympathy for the plight of the nuns of Aldgate may be unexpected, given his association with Cromwell (together they had worked to dissolve twenty-nine small monasteries by 1516), but it was a matter of record:

> It must have been shortly after the outbreak of plague [1515] that the convent buildings were destroyed by fire. The mayor, aldermen, and citizens of London contributed 200 marks besides the benefactions of private persons, but at the special request of Cardinal Wolsey to the Court of Common Council, it was decided in 1520 to give 100 marks more to complete the building. The king also gave £200 at this time.[38]

A courtroom victory for John Kirby's executors would certainly have benefitted the Minoresses of Aldgate, and it was the nuns of Syon who stood to gain by another third-party suit, that brought by John Broun against James Hales, stone carver.[39] Broun's case was heard some time between 1493 and 1500 in the court of Chancellor John Morton (1487–1500).[40] Morton held a bachelor's degree in both laws, and a doctorate in civil law, both from Oxford, and had been a practicing lawyer in the

38 "Friaries: The Minoresses without Aldgate," in *A History of the County of London*, vol. 1: *London within the Bars, Westminster and Southwark* (1909), pp. 516–519. Online at www.british-history.ac.uk/report.aspx?compid=35371 (accessed May 27, 2009).

39 C 1/189/5.

40 Haskett, "Medieval English Court of Chancery" pp. 312–313; Christopher Harper-Bill, "Morton, John (*d.* 1500)," in *ODNB*, www.oxforddnb.com/view/article/19363 (accessed May 27, 2009).

Court of Arches, which he eventually headed as dean. Morton was also very active in politics and diplomacy and appropriately enough for the case of Broun vs. Hales, the chancellor is credited with the building or repair of churches and manors throughout England. He is the man responsible for preserving the bishop's palace at Hatfield, Croydon Palace, the gatehouse of Lambeth Palace, and the school of canon law at Oxford, to mention just a few of his projects: a man particularly well suited to assess the alleged pettifoggery of a master stone carver.

Because nearly a third of John Broun's petition is now unreadable, we must be satisfied with a somewhat impressionistic picture of this case. Nevertheless, most of the salient facts emerge as follows. The nuns of Syon had commissioned a new altar table for the altar of Our Lady in their monastery church, and Broun had hired a mason named Robe to construct it. Given the two draft memoranda preserved in the records of the Exchequer detailing a number of projects to be undertaken at Syon, Broun might have been supervising workers on several of them.[41] In any case, the altar as represented in the "exampler" or blueprint was to have ten stories (rows) of images of Our Lady on it, and the prospect of undertaking such an ambitious project daunted Robe. Although he was a stone mason, "Robe was not expert" at carving images.

Broun and Robe therefore agreed that a skilled stone carver named James Hales should undertake the carving of the images. James was promised "£61 in money and mete drynk chamber beddes and otder thyngs necessary for hym and all theym that shuld work upon the altar with hym duryng the tyme of their work." He then agreed to "make all the stories of ymagery that shulde be therin accordyng to the exemplar or better and contynally work upon the imagery until finished."

According to the plaintiff that agreement had not been honored. Broun attested that Hales and his men had eaten and drunk up all the wages paid them by Robe and "yet a grate part of the said stories of ymages is not yet don nor fynysshed and summe of them not yet begonne." This after the passage of two years. The petition went on to state that James not only refused to finish the carving but had lately undertaken a new "full deceitful occupation, to make fustians with works to be like damask, whereby many a person is deceived." All this dubious activity has cost Broun and Robe money "besides the hurt that the said monastery hath." Subpoena was therefore requested for Hales to answer these charges in Chancery. Whether the stone carver-turned-clothier ever did so or not,

41 E 101/683/93. Unfortunately, these memoranda are also virtually unreadable.

one suspects that the images on the marvelous Lady altar of Syon were completed by other hands.

For cloistered nuns as for their lay and clerical countrymen, the Court of Chancery was the only recourse in some disputes. The Chancery petitions we have just examined used the same language and formulae as those employed by the many secular litigants importuning the court of conscience. The reasons why cloistered nuns chose Chancery rather than a court of common law – reasons such as the lack of written evidence or intimidation by the more powerful – were also identical. But cloistered nuns were religious women and for the resolution of ecclesiastical disputes that lay outside the jurisdiction of both the common law and Chancery, religious men and women alike relied on Church authorities to act as arbitrators. We turn next to cases heard by the ecclesiastical official who most commonly judged monastic disputes, the bishop.

6

Episcopal Arbitration

Bishops, archbishops, and their officials were often called upon to settle disputes outside of their courtrooms. By agreeing to abide by the decision of a respected and experienced arbitrator disputants saved both time and money. Justices and serjeants at law strove to effect out-of-court settlements in matters governed by the common law and bishops and their officials did the same in the ecclesiastical forum.[1] Like their secular counterparts, episcopal arbiters executed a final decree or concord in a case after considering the petitions and arguments of the disputants. Of course that decree did not always have the desired effect. Settlements were sometimes only temporary and parties to a dispute might find themselves in a courtroom after all, or at least before another arbiter. This was precisely what happened when a conflict arose between the Minoresses of the newly founded monastery of Waterbeach and the canons of Barnwell Priory.

Founded by Denise de Munchensey in 1293–1294, and completely subsumed into Mary St Pol's new foundation of Denney by 1351, the Abbey of Waterbeach had a short but turbulent history. The serious difficulties attending the merger of the two houses will be treated in the next chapter since the affair was resolved only by active intervention of the papacy via judges delegate. Although the dispute with Barnwell Priory would also involve such a papal petition it more aptly illustrates the role of the local bishop, or, in this case, bishops as arbiters.

The conflict between Waterbeach and Barnwell was regarded by historian Claudine Bourdillon as a sort of diversion ("A quarrel with neighbours is always an excitement") for nuns who might have been bored with the monotony of cloistered life.[2] Yet the duration of the dispute, the amount of effort expended to achieve a lasting compromise, and the potential loss of income and property in the interim made it an exhausting and altogether serious confrontation. It was rooted in the decision of Denise de Munchensey to alienate, in mortmain, her manor house and grounds

1 Joseph Biancalana, "The Legal Framework of Arbitration in Fifteenth-Century England," *American Journal of Legal History* 47 no. 4 (2005), pp. 347–382. Brundage, *Medieval Origins*, pp. 459–63 discusses the process as described by canonists.

2 Bourdillon, *Minoresses*, p. 63.

located in the parish of Waterbeach, Cambridgeshire. In 1281, she received royal permission to grant that manor to unspecified religious.[3] The Minoresses became the designated recipients of her largess and she had the monastery of Waterbeach built for them. But when the first nuns arrived from France to take up residence they quickly learned that their neighbors, the prior and canons of Barnwell, "strenuously opposed the foundation."[4]

Barnwell Priory had been established near the end of the eleventh century. As one of the earliest foundations of Augustinian canons regular in England it was rich in privileges and endowments. One of these endowments was the parish church of Waterbeach, Ridgewell [Radewelle], which the canons had appropriated in 1198.[5] As impropriators they were entitled to collect all the great and small tithes of the parish in return for maintaining religious services there. Since that parish included Waterbeach manor which, thanks to Denise de Munchensey, now belonged to the Minoresses, the canons of Barnwell were justifiably worried. They noted with alarm that the nuns were claiming exemption from the payment of tithes (small, large or all, it is unclear at this point) by virtue of a papal mandate. Having a tax-exempt corporation within their parish diminished priory income without decreasing the amount of money the canons were obligated to spend on religious services for the parishioners of Waterbeach. Conflict was almost inevitable, and it erupted quickly.

The Bishop of Ely (William de Luna/William of Louth, 1290–1298) was called upon to act as arbitrator and a copy of his settlement, dated 1294, has been preserved in the *Liber Memorandorum Ecclesie de Bernnewelle*.[6] Negotiations that resulted in that settlement were overseen by the Bishop of Ely's official, identified only as Gwydo. The first stipulation was that the nuns of Waterbeach were to pay 22s. a year, 11s. at Easter and 11s. on the feast of St Michael, to the vicar of Ridgewell and his successors. This payment was to compensate the canons of Barnwell for the loss of small (sometimes called vicarial) tithes from the manor, including burial

3 *Ibid.*, p. 13.

4 John Willis Clark, ed., *Liber Memorandorum Ecclesie de Bernewelle* (Cambridge: Cambridge University Press, 1907), p. 215.

5 "Houses of Augustinian Canons: Priory of Barnwell," in *A History of the County of Cambridge and the Isle of Ely*, vol. 2 (1948), pp. 234–249. Online at www.british-history.ac.uk/report.aspx?compid=40001&strquery=waterbeach (accessed May 27, 2010).

6 Clark, *Liber Memorandorum*, p. x. This chronicle was composed by a Barnwell canon in 1296 and the final concord is on pp. 214–218. On the career of the bishop see G. H. Martin, "Louth, William of (*c.* 1240–1298)," in *ODNB*, www.oxforddnb.com/view/article/60124 (accessed October 17, 2010).

oblations; the vicar was therefore specifically warned not to seek anything further from the nuns. Second, unless they had been original parishioners of Waterbeach, all lay servants of the Minoresses who lived within monastery gates and were engaged in domestic work, along with one domestic overseer, were exempt from paying their small tithes as well. Indeed, even if some of those domestics *wished* to pay them, they would have to secure the permission of the Abbess of Waterbeach to do so. Third, all of the nuns' servants who lived outside monastery gates and were employed in the fields were to pay all their customary tithes, receive the sacraments in the parish church, and be buried in the parish.

The stipulation which concluded this settlement is noteworthy, considering what would shortly ensue: *Priorem autem Conventum de Bernewelle et eorum monasterium per hanc nostram ordinacionem in nullo ledi volumus, sed in decima garbarum et feni, pasture et alijs, libere et plene percipiant sicut ante.*[7] The settlement then involved only the vicarial tithes and not the greater or predial tithes, that is, the portion of annual crops (garbarum referring to sheaves of grain) which the canons of Barnwell were still entitled to collect "as before." By inserting this concluding provision in his final decree the Bishop of Ely was abiding by what had become standard Church policy: "in practice all monks [and nuns] were expected to take into consideration the interests of the owners of the tithes, to be willing when necessary to make a composition and even to pay tithes, and generally to treat their privileges as a basis for negotiation rather than as a rigid right."[8]

All enmity between the parties seemed to dissipate following this composition which was formally attested to by Simon [de Ascellis], prior of Barnwell, Joan de Nevers, Abbess of Waterbeach, and the vicar of Ridgewell, and witnessed by two knights, two friars, two canons regular, the bishop's chaplain, and "a large multitude of others." But when hostilities began once more they did so with a vengeance. And once again, Denise de Munchensey's charitable bent added fuel to the fire. In June, 1296, she received papal as well as royal approval to grant the advowson of Ridgewell, worth 40 marks annually saving the endowment of a vicarage, to her nuns.[9] This meant that while the canons of Barnwell were proprietors of the church of Waterbeach, the Minoresses of Waterbeach now had the right to decide who the vicar of that church would be. Although relations between nuns and canons must have been further strained by this

7 Clark, *Liber Memorandorum*, p. 217.

8 Giles Constable, *Monastic Tithes* (Cambridge: Cambridge University Press, 1964), p. 304.

9 *CPL*, vol. 1, p. 566. *CPR 1292–1301*, p. 190.

grant, the breaking point did not come until two years later. In December, 1298, the king issued a commission of oyer and terminer to investigate Abbess Joan de Nevers' charge that Prior Benedict of Barnwell, accompanied by seventeen other named individuals, had "carried away her goods at Waterbeche, co. Cambridge."[10]

What had motivated the new Prior of Barnwell, Benedict de Welton (1297–1315), to take such drastic action? It is possible that he was attempting to collect his quota of a clerical subsidy granted to the king. In 1294, the prior and convent of Barnwell had been named as collectors of that subsidy for the diocese of Ely and this appointment "gave him a very presentable excuse for adopting a course of violence."[11] Since the nuns of Waterbeach possessed exemptions from both secular and papal dues by 1296, however, this argument leaves something to be desired.[12] Prior Benedict's acts are more easily explained by the fact that the nuns of Waterbeach had ceased to abide by the final stipulation in Bishop Louth's 1294 settlement. Perhaps emboldened by their receipt of the Ridgewell advowson, the Minoresses had stopped paying the large tithes owed to Barnwell and they were being supported in their contumacy by the now elderly Denise de Munchensey, her granddaughter, and her granddaughter's husband, Sir Hugh de Vere.[13] Logically, this subtraction of revenues was more than the new Prior of Barnwell had been prepared to endure.

But with the Crown commissioners of oyer and terminer set upon him by the abbess, Prior Benedict was forced to admit that his effort at self-help had been futile. He therefore resolved to employ the tactic used by his predecessor, Prior Simon de Ascellis, and put his case before the Bishop of Ely. Yet even in this, the prior was unlucky since when he made his petition the episcopal see of Ely was vacant. Upon the death of William of Louth, March 25, 1298, two rival candidates for the office had emerged. The monks of the cathedral priory of Ely were divided in their preferences between their prior, John Salmon, and John Langton, Treasurer of the Exchequer, and the king's favorite.[14] Both candidates appeared before Boniface VIII (1294–1303) to whom the monks had appealed, and resigned their rights into the pope's hands. Boniface allowed the monks

10 *CPR 1292–1301*, p. 458.

11 Bourdillon, *Minoresses*, p. 64.

12 *Ibid.*, n 3.

13 "Houses of Minoresses: Abbey of Waterbeach," in *A History of the County of Cambridge and the Isle of Ely*, vol. 2 (1948), pp. 292–295. Online at www.british-history.ac.uk/report.aspx?compid=40018 (accessed May 28, 2010).

14 M. C. Buck, "Salmon, John (*d.* 1325)," in *ODNB*, www.oxforddnb.com/view/article/24553 (accessed January 21, 2011).

to elect again, but their proctors could not reach a consensus. Boniface finally resolved the dispute in June, 1299, by translating Ralph Walpole to Ely, and providing Salmon to Norwich. Edward I acquiesced, the temporalities of Ely being restored on October 10.[15]

Prior Benedict made his petition during this period of contention and so it was handled by the Archbishop of Canterbury, Robert Winchelsey, who was overseeing the diocese of Ely for the duration. In March, 1299, Archbishop Winchelsey responded to the prior's petition by sending minatory letters to the redoubtable Denise de Munchensey and to her grandson-in-law, Sir Hugh.[16] While the letter to the former is in law French, and that to Hugh de Vere in Latin, both contain the standard fulminations and the essential details about this, the newest phase in an old struggle. All those who undermined the law of the Church, Winchelsey reminded them, merited excommunication, and their continued support of the Minoresses of Waterbeach in their refusal to pay tithes due to the Prior of Barnwell imperiled their immortal souls. Both were therefore "asked, warned, and admonished" to stop their interference immediately.

Had the recipients been less doughty, or less august, folk they might have been suitably chastened by Winchelsey's admonition. Had the archbishop been more than a place-holder *sede vacante*, he might have treated the unrepentant pair to something stronger than a warning – he was, after all, known for his zeal and his eager defense of ecclesiastical liberties.[17] But by June of 1299, the still unresolved situation was out of Winchelsey's hands. Newly invested Bishop of Ely Ralph Walpole was the one who had to decide what to do next, and he opted to refer the case to Rome. A supporter of Boniface VIII in his struggle over clerical taxation in England, Walpole now pitted the strength of the pope who had challenged Edward I against that of two stubborn aristocrats. He did not live to see the result. The papal decision in the case of Barnwell vs. Waterbeach was delivered in 1304, and the officials of yet another incumbent, Robert Orford (1303–1310), entered it into the Ely diocesan record: the Minoresses of Waterbeach were ordered to pay the disputed tithes to the prior, but they were granted a papal subsidy of 100 marks to help them do so.[18]

15 Dorothy M. Owen, "Walpole, Ralph of (*d.* 1302)," in *ODNB*, www.oxforddnb.com/view/article/28598 (accessed January 27, 2011).

16 *Registrum Winchelsey*, Lambeth MS fol. 263a. See the edited version in *Registrum Roberti Winchelsey Cantuariensis Archiepiscopi* AD *1294–1313*, ed. Rose Graham (Canterbury and York Society, Oxford 1928), pt 82, pp. 323–324.

17 J. H. Denton, "Winchelsey, Robert (c. 1240–1313)," in *ODNB*, www.oxforddnb.com/view/article/29713 (accessed October 17, 2010).

18 EDR A 6/1 ff. as cited in "Waterbeach: Church," in *A History of the County of Cambridge and the Isle of Ely*, vol. 9: *Chesterton, Northstowe, and Papworth Hundreds*

A full papal exemption from both lay and ecclesiastical taxes, granted the nuns in 1317, ultimately obviated the need for that subvention.[19]

The nuns of Waterbeach would be able to enjoy their tax exemption until 1351 when the monastery ceased to exist and its residents were transferred to Denney. As we shall see in the next chapter, that transfer was not easily accomplished and the undignified spectacle of internecine conflict must have provided the canons of Barnwell with some guilty pleasure. Since the Minoresses of Denney inherited all lands and exemptions hitherto enjoyed by the imperious sisters of Waterbeach, however, bad blood continued between the heads of the two adjacent houses – in 1373 the Prior of Barnwell was accused by the Abbess of Denney of stealing cattle that belonged to the Minoresses.[20]

As local ordinary, it had fallen to the Bishop of Ely to arbitrate the dispute involving the nuns of Waterbeach and Barnwell Priory. The Bishop of London was the natural choice when the nuns of Syon sought to settle their quarrel with the proprietors and vicar of the parish church of Isleworth in 1474. Unlike their mendicant sisters, the Bridgettines would have been personally acquainted with their bishops since they were not exempt from episcopal jurisdiction. By the time he was called upon as arbitrator, Bishop Thomas Kempe (1448–1489) might very well have made one or more of his prescribed triennial visits to Syon.[21] Granted, there is no surviving record of his visit, but Syon constitutions actually anticipated that a successful visitation would leave no paper trail. With characteristic precision, those constitutions specified exactly how a visiting bishop should interrogate the nuns about possible infractions of monastic discipline, but they also prescribed how he should act if he found none: "Nevertheless, if so be that it be answered of all to the bishop that all things be well, he ought to joy thereof greatly, and to thank God, and so to bless them all, and go out as he came in."[22]

Whether he was personally acquainted with the nuns or not, Bishop Kempe would undoubtedly have known the abbess named in the deed of composition drawn up under his direction. Lady Elizabeth Gybbs (d. 1518) as she is styled in the abbey's lists, had been head of Syon since

(1989), pp. 257–262. Online at www.british-history.ac.uk/report.aspx?compid=15427 (accessed June 18, 2010).

19 *BF*, vol. 5, p. 125.

20 Bourdillon, *Minoresses*, p. 64, fn. 4.

21 "Bishops of London," in *Fasti Ecclesiae Anglicanae 1300–1541*, vol. 5: *St Paul's, London* (1963), pp. 1–4. Online at www.british-history.ac.uk/report.aspx?compid=32378 (accessed July 1, 2010).

22 Aungier, *History*, p. 280. See also Ellis, Viderunt Eam, p. 59.

1461 and she fit in well among the choir sisters, all of whom hailed from the nobility, gentry, or rich London merchant classes. Her status and that of her nuns is reflected in the quality of legal advice available to them in this instance, beginning with the arbiter himself.

Bishop Kempe knew the law and was concerned about those who practiced it in the church courts. When he died he left a number of books on civil and canon law

> for use of the officials of the Dean and examinators, advocates and proctors of the Court of Canterbury on condition that within a year from the time of my death, place competent is provided for the safe custody and conservation of the foresaid books in the city of London near the Cathedral Church of Saint Paul at which place the Court of the Official of the Dean and Examinators, advocates and proctors and other masters of Canon or Civil [law] doctors or bachilors can conveniently have access at proper times.[23]

And although Kempe's formal education was theological, his London consistory court attracted some notable advocates, one of whom was of particular service to the nuns of Syon.

Richard Lichefeld [Lichfield] held a doctorate in civil law from Oxford by 1458 and was Bishop Kempe's vicar general by 1468. After Kempe's death in 1489, he would serve as official principal of the consistory *sede vacante*.[24] The composition of 1474 resolving the present case would not have gone without the careful scrutiny of Lichefeld who was a member of the bishop's curia at the time; he was also the advocate whose *pro bono* work for the nuns of Syon merited him their prayers as a special benefactor.[25]

The parties in this dispute concerning tithes were the nuns of Syon, and "John, warden, and the fellows and scholars of the college of St Mary Winchester, nigh Winchester, proprietors of the parish church of Isleworth."[26] The warden, fellows and scholars of St Mary Winchester owed their claim to the founder of their college, Bishop William of Wykeham.[27] The bishop founded his school designed to educate poor scholars bound for New College, Oxford, in 1382, but the first students did not enter until 1394 by which time the bishop had acquired a fine endowment for them. The church of Isleworth, obtained from the Abbot of St Valery

23 Thomas Kempe, will of February 4, 1488. Online at www.kentarchaeology.org.uk/Research/Libr/Wills/Bk56/page%2024.htm (accessed July 16, 2010).

24 *BRUO*, vol. 2, pp. 1144–1145.

25 *VCH Middlesex*, vol. 1, p. 185.

26 E 328/48.

27 Peter Partner, "Wykeham, William (*c*. 1324–1404)," in *ODNB*, www.oxforddnb.com/view/article/30127 (accessed July 15, 2010).

in 1391, was part of that endowment. A glance at the London register of Bishop Kempe shows that the wardens and scholars of Winchester College had been exercising their right of appointing the vicar of Isleworth for at least twenty years preceding the present dispute.[28] Judging from the regularity with which they did so, the vicarage appears to have been used to benefit aspiring Winchester scholars.

The interests of the nuns of Syon are easily established since it was within his manor of Isleworth that Henry V founded Syon in 1415. The original site of the monastery was in another parish, that of Twickenham, but in 1431 the community moved to newly constructed, more spacious buildings on their lands in the parish of Isleworth. Conflict with the warden and scholars of Winchester College must have begun with this relocation, and it was triggered by the Bridgettines' claim to be exempt from tithing. Like the Waterbeach Minoresses, the nuns of Syon alleged tax-exempt status within their parish; like the Barnwell canons, the warden and scholars of Winchester College were concerned about the consequences of this claim for their parish church. It was up to Bishop Kempe and his curia to craft a settlement that respected Bridgettine privileges without impoverishing the parish vicarage of Isleworth. The text of the final settlement signed on October 5, 1474, establishes the painstaking precision with which this was done.

First, the legal rights of both parties were established. The Bridgettines claimed their privilege – "the said abbess and convent protesting that by reason of such composition no prejudice should be to their exemption to non-payment of tithes" – and the scholars of Winchester claimed theirs: the right to collect "all the tithes oblations, obventions, and other ecclesiastical rights and emoluments whatsoever in the parish church of Isleworth."[29] There followed the negotiated adjustments to those blanket claims. The proprietors of Iselworth were allowed to collect the tenth part of any *grain* tithes "only from the lands *without and in no wise within the precinct of the said monastery*" and the nuns of Syon agreed to compensate them for their loss of monastic tithes. To arrive at a monetary sum for that composition the boundaries of Syon monastery had to be (and were) scrupulously defined, since a lasting composition hinged upon the words 'without' and 'within' monastery precincts. Then the sources of tithes,

28 Register of Thomas Kempe, bishop of London (1448–1489), fols xxxiii, lxxii, lxxxxi, ccxxi. These pages document the appointment of vicars, due to the death or resignation of incumbents, for the years 1454, 1461, 1464, and 1483 respectively. See: Registers of the Bishops of London 1304–1600. Pt 5 Brighton, Sussex: Harvester Press Microform Publications, 1984.

29 E 328/48; See also the transcription of "the material parts of this deed of composition," in Aungier, *History*, pp. 136–138.

oblations, obventions and ecclesiastical rights within those precincts had to be (and were) determined.

The resulting list of natural and man-made products which might generate tithes from Syon lands is staggering, and accounts for nearly one folio page of the four-page deed. In addition to a variety of grains, it enumerates such things as reeds, bushes, furze, hedges, herbs, brambles; fish of ponds, fens, lakes, pits, marches, ditches, rivulets, watercourses; fruits of orchards and gardens; tenements, farms, mills, mines, piscaries; "all river birds and winged animals, water-fowls of every kind and sort, as well wild and warren fowls as tame, especially swans and bees." In recompense for non-payment of tithes on all these things, the abbess and convent agreed to compensate the vicar and proprietors of the church of Isleworth. Their composition was to be in cash and in kind, with everything once again precisely detailed.

Elizabeth Gybbs and her convent promised to indemnify the warden and proprietors of the church, 20s. with 6s. 8d., designated as a fine to be levied "in case of non-payment." To the vicar, the abbess and convent promised to pay 40s. with another fine of 6s. 8d. to be levied if payment was not timely, that is, annually received at Michaelmas and Christmas. Additionally, the nuns were "to allow the said vicar daily, at the upper table of the hall of the monastery, meat and drink and the like to be allowed to the vicar's servant at the groom's table; and in case the said vicar should from sickness be unable to attend the monastery, he shall be allowed at the rate of 7d. per week for his provisions at home." Each year, the vicar and his successors were to be provided as well with one robe "containing four yards of cloth of the suit," along with livery for his servant.

Finally, one more possible occurrence which might have caused friction at some future date was addressed. If someone in the parish of Isleworth donated lands or tenements currently in their possession to the nuns of Syon and the tithes from those lands and tenements would normally have gone to the parish vicarage, the vicar and his successor retained the right to collect them. All that the Bridgettines asked in return was that "when they should so come to the hands of the said abbess and convent, [the vicar] should first fully give notice thereof to the same abbess and convent by specifying and denominating the same." In this final stipulation, Bishop Kempe drew a distinction that canon law regularly applied in matters of tithing. Even fully tax-exempt regulars such as the Templars and Cistercians were under the obligation to render tithes when they acquired lands from which tithes had previously been paid.[30]

30 Constable, *Monastic Tithes*, p. 306.

All the forethought that went into Bishop Kempe's composition appears not to have been wasted. Syon retained the manor of Isleworth for its entire pre-Reformation existence, and it was a valuable holding – in 1492, manorial lands alone were worth at £85.[31] As a result of the 1474 arbitration the vicars of Isleworth received only £2 annually in cash but with the inclusion of daily meals and an expensive suit the returns were considerably greater. Those returns appear to have satisfied the incumbents. Only when the Dissolution made it impossible to feed anyone at the "upper table of the hall of the monastery," was the vicar of Isleworth's food and clothing allotment commuted into a lump sum payment of £10.[32]

Syon's wealth and complicated patterns of landholding required, and attracted, some of the era's outstanding legal counsel and men like Richard Lichfield were apt to leave behind some trace of their activities. But when the final decree in a dispute, even a very detailed one, is our only evidence of its settlement we are none the wiser about the role played by advocates and proctors in effecting it. Happily, the complex matter of the appropriation of the parish church of Eltisley by the abbess and nuns of Denney is amply documented, making it a useful source of evidence about this under-explored subject.

This matter was brought before the Bishop of Ely for arbitration in 1512, but difficulties surrounding the appropriation had existed for a very long time before that. One hundred and fifty years earlier, in March of 1362, Edward II had licensed "the abbess and sisters Minoresses of the house of Deneye" to appropriate the church of Eltesle, a church which was "of their advowson and held of John de Moubray."[33] But in the matter of their tenure it seems that the king had been misinformed. A search of the rolls (at whose instigation we do not know) revealed that in 1362 the advowson of Eltisley was not yet held by the Minoresses; it was still in the hands of the founder of Denney, Mary St Pol, making Edward II's grant to the nuns premature. Before the appropriation could be realized, the countess would have to give the advowson to her nuns.

Mary St Pol consequently petitioned for a royal license to alienate the advowson of Eltisley, in mortmain, to Denney, and that request was granted it in 1366. At the same time, indeed, in the same grant, Edward III allowed

31 Aungier, *History*, p. 78; "Heston and Isleworth: Churches," in *A History of the County of Middlesex*, vol. 3: *Shepperton, Staines, Stanwell, Sunbury, Teddington, Heston and Isleworth, Twickenham, Cowley, Cranford, West Drayton, Greenford, Hanwell, Harefield and Harlington* (1962), pp. 122–129. Online at www.british-history.ac.uk/report.aspx?compid=22281 (accessed July 15, 2010).

32 *VCH Middlesex*, vol. 3, p. 122.

33 *CPR 1361–1364*, p. 179.

the abbess and sisters to appropriate the church of Eltisley, explaining that "The king [Edward II] lately granted licence for the abbess and sisters to appropriate the said church, in the belief that it was of their advowson, which licence they have surrendered."[34]

All now seemed to be in order. The Minoresses of Denney had a valid royal license to appropriate Eltisley, the advowson of which they also legally possessed. Nevertheless, they had no luck in securing their right. Since an appropriation involved the transfer of all tithes and endowments of a benefice, the delay certainly had something to do with money. Eltisley was a rich benefice, worth 35 marks in the later part of the fourteenth century, and the land that belonged to the rectory alone would amount to over 100 acres by 1557.[35] As impropriators of the church, the nuns would have had much to gain, and before the early sixteenth century they appear to have had a hard enough time merely asserting their right to present a candidate of their own choosing to this rich living.

Throughout the fourteenth century, the lords of the manor of Eltisley continued to appoint their relatives as rectors of Eltisley.[36] Thomas of Eltisley, rector in 1351 and first master of Corpus Christi College, Cambridge, had gone so far as to present himself when the position stood vacant. By the end of the century, the Minoresses had still been unsuccessful in their attempt to appropriate, and so they appealed to the pope. Boniface IX responded in 1402 and licensed the abbess and convent to appropriate "the church of St Pandwina the Virgin, Eltesle ... to be served by a fit priest appointed and removed at the pleasure of the abbess, with the consent of the ordinaries."[37] Despite being armed with documentary evidence of both royal and papal approval, the Denney appropriation still failed to materialize since the nuns faced opponents whom they were loath to engage.

In the fifteenth century, the rectors of Eltisley were almost always pluralists and highly placed university graduates who used the benefice as a scholarship fund. For the nuns to have challenged the vested interests

34 *CPR 1364–1367*, p. 221.

35 "Parishes: Eltisley," in *A History of the County of Cambridge and the Isle of Ely*, vol. 5 (1973), pp. 46–59. Online at www.british-history.ac.uk/report.aspx?compid=66673 (accessed February 28, 2010).

36 *Ibid.*

37 *CPL*, vol. 5, p. 573. St Pandwina (Pandwyna, Pandonia) of Ettisley was born in Scotland or Ireland and she died c. 904. Pandwina was a nun at Eltisley; her hagiographer Leland records that she was a daughter of a king of the Scots, who fled from those who would deflower her to a kinswoman who was prioress of Eltisley. She was buried near Saint Pandonia Well in Eltisley and was translated into the church there in 1344.

of men like Roger Radcliff, rector from 1457 to 1462, doctor of canon law, and master of Manchester College, would have required considerable time, money, and skill. Nor was Gerard Skipwith, rector until his death in 1508 and fellow of Pembroke College, any less a personage.[38] In addition, as the record of this arbitration will illustrate, there were other influential parties interested in the proceeds from this benefice, notably the archdeacon of Ely and the prior of Ely cathedral church. With the appointment of Dame Elizabeth Throckmorton as Abbess of Denney, however, the situation in which the Minoresses found themselves changed at last. When they set their cause before the Bishop of Ely in 1512, the nuns finally had a redoubtable presence on their own side.

Dame Elizabeth Throckmorton, the last abbess of Denney, was a member of the landed gentry of Warwickshire.[39] Her father, Thomas, had served as Gentleman Usher to Elizabeth of York and her brother had been knighted. She was a woman of considerable learning, admired by Desiderius Erasmus, and curious enough about the changing intellectual climate to secure a copy of Tyndale's *Enchiridion* from a wealthy London supplier.[40] Nor did she lack personal fortitude. After Henry VIII closed Denney, she retired to her family home at Coughton with a couple of like-minded nuns. There she lived a conventual life wearing the habit of her order and observing the rules of enclosure, as far as practicable, until her death in 1547.[41] Elizabeth Throckmorton's willing commitment to the monastic life explains her fidelity to it after the Dissolution and in 1512 that commitment fueled her efforts to make her monastery's theoretical right to Eltisley real at last. Her ability to get James Stanley to act as arbitrator in the matter suggests a happy union of personal conviction and social clout.

Stanley, Bishop of Ely (1506–1515), was the son of the Earl of Derby. He held a doctorate in canon law from Oxford, innumerable benefices and papal licenses to hold even more.[42] The bishop was a man to reckon with and his consistory court, where the Eltisley arbitration began, was one of the most important ecclesiastical courts in late medieval England. It regularly met in the vibrant university town of the diocese, Cambridge, and the fact that the university supplied it with many trained lawyers is amply confirmed by the manuscript record of the Eltisley proceedings.[43]

38 *Ibid.*

39 Bourdillon, *Minoresses*, p. 52.

40 *Ibid.*, p. 80.

41 *Ibid.*, p. 83.

42 *BRUO* vol. 3, p. 1761.

43 Brundage, *Profession and Practice*, pp. 541–560 contains a detailed look at the university

A thirty-two page dossier containing copies of depositions, letters, inspection surveys, and decrees, produced over a period of ten months, details proceedings in the 1512 appropriation of the church of St Pandwina, Eltisley, Cambridgeshire.[44] The volume begins with a January 24 certification of the credentials of the notaries, proctors and commissary officials involved in negotiations. A deposition dated (or perhaps misdated) November 24, 1512, includes stipulations about the settlement which are essentially those of the final concord. More depositions, with additional or alternative monetary stipulations, letters, and notarized land surveys executed in the months between January and June, 1512, account for all but the final pages of the dossier. Those pages contain the final decree, sealed by James Stanley on June 18, 1512, as well as the attestations of the prior and convent of the cathedral church of Ely (June 19), the Archdeacon of Ely (June 20), and Abbess Elizabeth Throckmorton (July 11), expressly agreeing to this settlement.

Throughout the course of the arbitration, the venues change. Depositions were recorded and decrees issued in Bishop Stanley's consistory court, which was held either in the Church of the Blessed Virgin Mary or that of St Michael, Cambridge.[45] Important decrees, including the final concord, were produced in the bishop's palace.[46] Elizabeth Throckmorton set her seal of approval on the decree in the chapter house of Denney and Wiliam [Wiliam Wittlesey, OSB], Prior of the cathedral church of Ely, 1510–1515, approved the decree in his own chapter house.[47]

But no matter where the negotiations took place, notaries and proctors were on hand to represent the interests of their clients. Participating members of the Ely consistory bar included the bishop's official, Richard

graduates who were prominent at the bar of the Ely consistory court in the fourteenth century.

44 EDR G2/5. Alfred Gibbons, *Ely Episcopal Records* (Lincoln: J Williamson, 1891), p. 153 describes the "beautiful MS. volume, written on 32 pages of vellum." It is now housed in Cambridge University Library.

45 Helmholz, *Canon Law*, p. 215 notes the the consistory court of Ely often met in Great St Mary's, Cambridge, and other larger parish churches. On St Michael's see "The City of Cambridge: Churches," in *A History of the County of Cambridge and the Isle of Ely*, vol. 3: *The City and University of Cambridge* (1959), pp. 123–132. Online at www.british-history.ac.uk/report.aspx?compid=66618 (accessed March 1, 2010).

46 "City of Ely: Monastic Buildings and Palace," in *A History of the County of Cambridge and the Isle of Ely*, vol. 4: *City of Ely: Ely, N. and S. Witchford and Wisbech Hundreds* (2002), pp. 77–82. Online at www.british-history.ac.uk/report.aspx?compid=21892 (accessed May 21, 2010).

47 "Priors of Ely," in *Fasti Ecclesiae Anglicanae 1300–1541*, vol. 4: *Monastic Cathedrals (Southern Province)* (1963), pp. 16–17. Online at www.british-history.ac.uk/report.aspx?compid=32713 (accessed March 5, 2010).

Herryson, and his chancellor, Master William Thornburgh, doctor of laws.[48] William Nelson, a notary in the bishop's court, acted as proctor for the nuns of Denney at the outset of proceedings and he was assisted by two other notaries, Oliver Scalis and Galfridus Quarton.[49] In the last stages of the proceedings, the interests of the nuns were also represented by Master Richard Brynkeley, doctor of theology from Oxford, and president of the monastery of Denney, who would soon become Provincial General of the Order of Friars Minor in England.[50] The Archdeacon of Ely, Master Thomas Alcock, was himself a doctor of both laws, and even a member of Doctors' Commons, but he too had the assistance of a proctor, Master William Stevenson, bachelor of laws.[51] The Prior and cathedral chapter of Ely employed Master William Fayrehayre, doctor of civil law, as their proctor.[52]

Before the final concord concerning the appropriation of Eltisley could be signed and sealed, a series of issues had to be addressed, and all interested parties had to be reasonably satisfied with the end result. All of those issues, incidentally, concerned finances. Of course the nuns had to establish their legal right to the church beyond a shadow of a doubt, and William Nelson deposed, more than once, that the Crown had licensed the appropriation. In fact, he produced a copy of a letter from the reigning king, Henry VIII, dated June 21, 1512, and bearing the signature of the Master of the Rolls, John Yonge, for inclusion in the dossier.[53] This letter patent confirmed the grant of the church of Eltisley to the nuns of Denney, in mortmain, provided that they endow a perpetual vicarage and that they set aside a sum of money for distribution as alms to the parish poor.

Henry VIII's confirmation had not mentioned specific amounts, stating only that the endowment be "sufficient to the [vicar's] duties" and that the local ordinary be responsible for deciding what it might be. Part of this arbitration, therefore, involved filling in this proverbial blank check.[54] Proctor Nelson deposed that the nuns would pay 12 marks sterling (£8) to

48 EDR G2/5, pp. 1–2. *BRUC*, p. 290 and p. 584 respectively, for biographical details.

49 *BRUC*, p. 420 for Nelson who appears to have attended, but not received a degree from, King's College.

50 *BRUO 1501*, p. 267.

51 EDR G2/5, p. 6. *BRUC*, pp. 6–7 for Alcock; p. 555 for Stevenson.

52 *BRUC*, p. 222.

53 EDR G2/5, p. 22. Ronald H. Fritze, "Yonge, John (1466/7–1516)," in *ODNB*, www.oxforddnb.com/view/article/30227 (accessed May 21, 2010). The letter can be found in "Henry VIII: June 1512," in *Letters and Papers, Foreign and Domestic, Henry VIII*, vol. 1: *1509–1514* (1920), pp. 567–583 at p. 581. Online at www.british-history.ac.uk/report.aspx?compid=102662 (accessed May 24, 2010).

54 EDR G2/5, p. 16–17.

endow the vicarage, and that they would also be responsible for building a house for the rector at their own expense, upon the death of the incumbent. The exact amount that the sisters were expected to put forward for the provision of alms is mentioned neither here nor in the final concord, but that should not lead us to conclude that such obligations were taken lightly. The establishment of a paupers' table, as it is referred to in the final concord, required no small expenditure and provided genuine benefits to the needy in an era when "monastic alms-giving was the only regular form of poor relief."[55]

Other parties interested in the appropriation included the Prior of the cathedral church of Ely and the Archdeacon of Ely and they next stated their demands. They required the nuns to indemnify them so that they could pay annates, the papal tax levied in the form of a portion of the first year's revenues of a benefice, each time there was a new appointment.[56] James Stanley, as the Bishop of Ely, required 3s. 4d. for himself and his successors to be paid each year at Easter. Following these demands, and acting as a counterweight to them, William Nelson argued that the plague of 1512 made such indemnifications difficult, if not impossible, for the nuns to satisfy. He claimed that the rents and tithes usually collected by Denney had been greatly reduced because of the epidemic. Men and animals had died and fields usually under the plow lay sterile and uncultivated. The monastery and its outbuildings were near ruin, but the sisters lacked the resources either to repair them or to build anew.[57]

Whether or not the plague had wrought as much devastation as Nelson described, it would certainly have affected what the Minoresses could afford to pay in composition for Eltisley tithes since it was a horrible reality for the English in that year and for many to follow. In 1512, for example, the scholars of Merton College, Oxford, purchased a manor house six miles north of the city specifically to serve as a refuge from the plague.[58] Mortality rates in London rocketed when the plague struck that

[55] C. H. Lawrence, *Medieval Monasticism*. 3rd edn (New York: Pearson, 2001), p. 118. Power, *Nunneries*, pp. 120–122. For recent ideas concerning the actual benefits provided by monastic poor relief see Neil Rushton and Wendy Sigle-Rushton, "Monastic Poor Relief in Sixteeth-Century England," *Journal of Interdisciplinary History* 32, no. 2 (Autumn, 2001), pp. 193–216.

[56] W. E. Lunt, *Papal Revenues in the Middle Ages* (New York: Octagon Books, 1965), p. 85. *DMA*, vol. 11, p. 606.

[57] EDR G2/5, p. 18–19.

[58] "Parishes: Hampton Poyle," in *A History of the County of Oxford*, vol. 6 (1959), pp. 160–168. Online at www.british-history.ac.uk/report.aspx?compid=63735&strquery= hampton poyle (accessed May 24, 2010).

city in 1513.[59] And when it struck again just two years later, it claimed the lives of twenty-seven of Denney's co-religious, the Minoresses of Algae.[60]

Nelson's testimony concerning the plague-induced poverty of the monastery constituted his last significant action on behalf of the nuns of Denney. Oversight of the formulation of the final concord which was drawn up in the presence of Bishop Stanley was accorded to "Brother Richard Brynkeley, professor of sacred theology and president of the monastery of Denney." The specifics of that settlement were these: The Eltisley appropriation was agreed to on condition that the nuns of Denney endow a perpetual vicarage at £8 (12 marks) and build a house for the new incumbent, within a year after the living became vacant. They would be obliged to pay 3s. 4 d annually for this appropriation to the Bishop of Ely and his successors, and pay 12d (1 shilling) annually, at the feast of St Michael the Archangel, to the Archdeacon of Ely and his successors for the payment of annates. The Minoresses were also required to distribute perpetual alms to the poor from their appropriated tithes, especially via the annual paupers' table.[61]

In 1518, when the vicarage at last became vacant, Dame Elizabeth Throckmorton and her nuns took possession of Eltisley. Thanks to the arbitration of Bishop Stanley, and the work done in the interest of the nuns by their appointed proctor, William Nelson, a long-ago gift of the Crown was finally theirs to enjoy; until, that is, the Crown decided to take it away again. In October, 1539, as part of his dispersion of lands gleaned from the Dissolution, Henry VIII made a gift of Eltisley, the monastery of Denney, and all of its other possessions, to one Edward Elrington in return for an annual rent of £20 10s.[62] Just twenty-seven years earlier,

59 Paul Slack, *The Impact of Plague in Tudor and Stuart England* (London: Routledge & Kegan Paul, 1985), p. 56. H. D. Traill and James Saumarez Mann, *Social England: A Record of the Progress of the People in Religion, Laws, Learning, Arts, Industry, Commerce, Science, Literature and Manners, from the Earliest Times to the Present Day* (London: Cassell and Co, 1902–1904), vol. 3, pp. 190, 193.

60 "Friaries: The Minoresses without Aldgate."

61 EDR G2/5, pp. 27–32. There is much repetitious material but the essential elements of the accord are listed together at this point.

62 "Letters and Papers: October 1539, 26–31," *Letters and Papers, Foreign and Domestic, Henry VIII*, vol. 14, part 2: *August–December 1539* (1895), pp. 137–160 at p. 159. Online at www.british-history.ac.uk/report.aspx?compid=75895 (accessed May 25, 2010). The entry reads: "Edw. Elryngton. Grant in fee, for 2,500 mks., of the house and site of the late monastery of nuns of St Claire of Denney, Camb.; the steeple and churchyard of the same; the manors of Denney, Waterbeache, Histon, High Hall and Strode, Camb., Beds., Essex, Norf. and Kent; the rectories of Shiston, Eltisley, Byddenham, Roddyswell and Godarston, with the advowsons of the vicarages thereof, in cos. Camb., Beds, Essex and Norf. appropriated and belonging to the

that same king had provided the corroborating evidence which William Nelson used to secure Eltisley for his clients.

late monastery; and all messuages, lands, &c., in the vills, fields, &c., of Denney, Waterbeache, Histon, High Hall, Strode, Cambridge, Chesterton, Fordwere, Milton, Landebeche, Fenedytton, Madyngley, Gorton, Cotton, Paxton Magna, Rampton, Westwartyng, Knapwell, Cottenham, Howsez and Hokyngton, Camb., Beds., Essex, Norf. and Kent. which belonged to the said late monastery of Denney; in as full manner as Eliz. Throgmerton, the late abbess, held the same; with liberties. To hold by a rent of 20l. 10s. Del. Westm., 28 October. 31 Hen. VIII. – S.B. Pat. p. 5, m. 15."

7

Papal Appeals

Delegated Decisions

As the king authorized his judges to dispense royal justice, so the pope delegated the exercise of his juridical power to trusted agents. In England, judgments carrying the approval of the highest ecclesiastical power in Christendom could be secured remotely, in the courts of papal judges delegate. Before the thirteenth century, judges delegate to England were routinely Roman emissaries, but by the later Middle Ages these men were just as regularly drawn from the ranks of the English clergy.[1] English judges delegate could be ad hoc or permanent appointees. The nuns of Waterbeach and the London Minoresses had dealings with the former, while the cause of the nuns of Syon was heard by a distinguished permanent legate on two separate occasions.

We have already observed the nuns of Waterbeach in action when their rights were jeopardized, but the final contest in which they were embroiled would test the mettle of a segment of that community even more than had the dispute with the canons of Barnwell. In this instance, the monastery of Waterbeach was threatened not by jealous or rapacious neighbors but by its own patroness and fellow religious. The papal judges assigned to resolve this bitter internecine quarrel would have to undercut the resistance of a group of well-born nuns whose devotion to place had eclipsed their commitment to their rule. The record testifies to the undesirability of such a commission as well as to the fraught times in which it was issued.

The actions of Mary St Pol, Countess of Pembroke, precipitated the dispute. Related by marriage to the founder of Waterbeach, Denise de Munchensey, the countess too was intensely interested in the house. At some considerable cost – the execution of a variety of quit claims and a payment to the Crown of £250, to be precise – she had transformed her life interest in Denney manor into a holding in perpetuity by 1336. In that same year, she obtained license to alienate that manor, in frankalmoin,

1 Sayers, *Papal Judges Delegate*, pp. 9–30.

to the nuns of Waterbeach.[2] Since Denney Manor was in the parish of Waterbeach and just a mile from the monastery, the Minoresses could conveniently profit from its farmlands and for three years they appear to have done just that. Then the countess rethought the terms of her gift.

Although Pembroke College, Cambridge (1347), was her most famous pious foundation, the monastery of Denney was her first.[3] On April 14, 1339, Mary St Pol successfully petitioned the Crown for permission to transfer the Abbess and sisters of Waterbeach to Denney Manor "and assign to them in mortmain the manor to construct there houses and buildings to dwell in."[4] In the petition, Waterbeach is said to be situated in a place "strait, low and bad and otherwise insufficient for them." While it is true that the site was prone to flooding, Waterbeach does not seem to have been a particularly insalubrious place, but then the countess had made up her mind. By 1342, the monastery buildings, which consisted of a new chapter house, a church "of suitable beauty and houses and other necessary buildings," had been erected at Denney and the Abbess, Katharine de Bolewyk, along with "the greater part of the sisters" of the Waterbeach community had moved in.[5]

According to later accounts, the transfer to Denney had been accomplished "with unanimous consent of the sisters, the provincial minister and the senior and higher brethren of the order in that province."[6] It had also been unanimously decided to leave the rest of the nuns at Waterbeach to look after the place and to make sure that the abbey advowson, which Mary St Pol did not yet possess, would not fall into secular hands. This remnant (estimates vary but there were about a dozen nuns left behind) was to continue to live according to their rule and under obedience to their Abbess Katharine, who was already residing at Denney.

What had started off as a landed bequest to the Minoresses of Waterbeach had been transformed into a new monastery. Canonically founded and possessing more than twice the endowment of Waterbeach (*eciam in duplo plus quam monasterium de Watrebech dotatum existeret* …), the

2 *CPR 1334–1338*, pp. 248 and 250. Bourdillon, *Minoresses*, pp. 19–21, gives a fine summary of major events in the struggle between Waterbeach and Denney, but is mistaken when she says that Mary granted her life interest a year before she had become perpetual owner of the manor of Denney.

3 Jennifer C. Ward, "St Pol, Mary de, Countess of Pembroke (c. 1304–1377)," in *ODNB*, www.oxforddnb.com/view/article/53073 (accessed June 11, 2010).

4 *CPR 1338–1340*, p. 242.

5 *CCR 1349–1354*, p. 237; *CPR 1340–1345*, p. 381.

6 *CCR 1349–1354*, p. 237. Also see Clement VI's commission to his legates in Joseph Henry Parry, ed. *Registrum Johannis de Trillek, Episcopi Herefordensis*, AD MCCCXLIV–MCCCLXI (London: Canterbury and York Society, 1912), pp. 151–152.

"daughter-house" of Denney was destined to take the place of the original foundation. For the nuns who had been left behind as caretakers of the redundant house, that destiny began to seem unacceptable. Within a short time the Waterbeach remnant elected their own abbess, known to us only as Emma, and effectively declared their independence from Denney.[7] They insisted that they would not under any circumstances leave, and proceeded to admit their own novices as a demonstration of how seriously they were committed to the place.

The defection of the Waterbeach nuns had wider ramifications as well. Because Waterbeach and Denney were only about a mile away from each other they held lands that were contiguous and even conjoined. Monastic rivalry spawned quarrels among monastic servants about the distribution of rents and tithes that threatened to get out of hand if a remedy was not speedily applied.[8] When "certain brethren of the order favoring them [the Waterbeach recusants] and defending their willful error" got involved, causing "grave scandal … to the prejudice of the order," Mary St Pol made her first attempt to get the situation under control.[9] She did so by acquiring the Waterbeach Abbey advowson for the nuns of Denney.

When Denise de Munchensley founded Waterbeach Abbey, she had given her manor to the nuns but had kept her life interest in the abbey advowson, passing it down as part of her inheritance. She could do so since, as we know, canon law classified cure of souls as a spiritual duty but common law regarded the right to nominate someone to perform that duty as a separate, marketable, commodity. This commodity was technically referred to as an 'incorporeal hereditament.' Mary St Pol now acquired that hereditament "at great labour and expense," and then got the required royal license to alienate Waterbeach advowson to the Abbess and Minoresses of Denney. In 1346, she did so

> on the condition that they shall find for ever in the said place of Waterbeche a chaplain celebrating divine service for the soul specially of lady Denise de Monte Caniso, foundress of the house, for the souls of the sisters and others buried there, and for the souls of the countess and Aymer de Valencia, Earl of

7 "Houses of Minoresses: Abbey of Waterbeach," in *A History of the County of Cambridge and the Isle of Ely*, vol. 2 (1948), pp. 292–295. Online at www.british-history.ac.uk/report.aspx?compid=40018 (accessed June 15, 2010).

8 *Registrum Johannis de Trillek*, p. 151: "quod terrae et possessiones dictorum monasteriorum sunt vicinae invicem et coniunctae et proinde quia gentes utriusque monasteriorum ipsorum fructus et redditus terrarum et possessionum praefatarum interdum preoccupare contendebant, brigae et scandala inter gentes praedictas et earum sequaces et amicos gravia orta erant et graviora oriri timebantur imposterum nisi super hoc provideretur celeriter de remedio opportuno."

9 *CCR 1349–1354*, p. 237.

> Pembroke, sometime her husband, Guy de Chastellion, sometime count of St Pol, her father, and Mary de Britannia his consort, her mother, and her ancestors and successors.[10]

For good measure, the countess obtained express royal permission for the union of the two houses at the same time.[11]

At this juncture, there could no longer have been any doubt about where the power and the potential for patronage lay. Ecclesiastical concern for the continued occupation of Waterbeach abbey by Franciscans, the reason why a contingent of nuns was left behind in the first place, had been addressed by Mary's grant of the advowson to Denney. As we see from the papal mandates that follow, both the Friars Minor and the pope would appreciate her action. Yet the resilient band at Waterbeach spent three more years resisting any and all attempts to suppress their monastery and to reduce them to obedience to the Abbess of Denney. It was time for papal intervention.

On February 3, 1349, Pope Clement VI dictated replies to two petitions. The first, to the Provincial and Friars Minor of England, allowed them "to receive the monastery of Waterbech wherein can be placed twelve friars, on its being left by the abbess and convent of Minoresses, to whom Mary de Sancto Paulo, Countess of Pembroke has given a new monastery on her manor of Denney."[12] The second, addressed to the Bishop of Hereford (John Trilleck, 1344–1361) on the petition of the Countess of Pembroke and of the abbess, set him the task of compelling "certain Minoresses to obey the said abbess of Waterbech [referring to Katharine, the lawful abbess] and to remove from thence to Denney with their goods and chattels; they having elected a new abbess and received nuns at Waterbech; provided that the monastery and cemetery of Waterbech do not come into lay hands, and that the church thereof is served by a fit priest."[13]

Canon law routinely required that decisions about the disposition of a monastery, even an exempt monastery, be made by the diocesan ordinary. Consequently, Clement VI sent a separate judicial commission to Thomas Lisle, Bishop of Ely (1345–1361), who was then residing at the papal curia in Avignon.[14] Since the pope had made the English friars a gift of Waterbeach Abbey, although it was still occupied by a group of nuns actively hostile to vacating the premises, commissioning Trilleck as

10 *CPR 1350–1354*, p. 73.

11 *CCR 1346–1349*, p. 89; *CPR 1345–1348*, p. 119.

12 *CPP*, vol. 1, p. 160.

13 *Ibid*.

14 *BF*, vol. 6, pp. 223–224.

well as Lisle might have been merely a commonsense move on his part. But it is worth remembering too that the Black Death forced popes as well as lesser prelates throughout Europe to compensate for the appalling mortality rate among the clergy. Before he left for Avignon in October of 1348, for instance, Thomas Lisle himself had made five new appointments to the post of Vicar-General of Ely because of the plague, yet by April of 1349 he had been compelled to replace three more incumbents.[15]

In the event, Lisle did not return to Ely until 1350, leaving John Trilleck, Bishop of Hereford, to act in the matter. A copy of his commission preserved in the episcopal register rehearses the history of the dispute and entrusts him, as papal judge delegate, with the responsibility for its resolution.[16] On May 20, 1350, however, explaining that he was unable to personally execute his apostolic mandate because he was hindered by "various troublesome tasks," Trilleck delegated his duties to others. The first of his designees was Ralph Stratford (1300–1354), then Bishop of London.[17] The Abbot of Walden, unidentified in the commission but known from monastic records to be William Coleman, was also named, along with Master John Ew, canon of Hereford.[18]

As Trilleck was an able and conscientious cleric whose own health, despite the onslaught of the plague, did not seriously decline until 1358, we are left to speculate about his speedy transfer of responsibilities.[19] And by July of 1350, he was required to do so once again. In a commission addressed to the Abbot of West Dereham and others, Trilleck stated that Master John Ew, who had begun hearing the Waterbeach–Denney suit at Cambridge, "had been obliged to adjourn [it]" and he begs for their assistance in the interim.[20] In September, the last-chosen set of delegates was finally empowered to act, although the bishop reserved final judgment to himself.

Lacking the record of proceedings, there is no way of identifying the lawyers who might have represented the interests of the rival communities. But Mary St Pol had many connections with legal professionals, regularly

15 Roy Martin Haines, "Lisle, Thomas (*c.* 1298–1361)," in *ODNB*, www.oxforddnb.com/view/article/16758 (accessed June 7, 2010).

16 *Registrum Johannis de Trillek*, pp. 151–153.

17 Roy Martin Haines, "Stratford, Ralph (*c.* 1300–1354)," in *ODNB*, www.oxforddnb.com/view/article/26647 (accessed June 7, 2010).

18 "Houses of Benedictine Monks: Abbey of Walden," in *A History of the County of Essex*, vol. 2 (1907), pp. 110–115. Online at www.british-history.ac.uk/report.aspx?compid=39831&strquery= (accessed June 7, 2010).

19 D. N. Lepine, "Trillek, John (*c.* 1308–1360)," in *ODNB*, www.oxforddnb.com/view/article/95146 (accessed June 7, 2010).

20 *Registrum Johannis de Trillek*, p. 154.

employing lawyers when out of the country. One of these was a man who would become Archbishop of Canterbury: William de Witlesey [Whittlesey], Archdeacon of Huntingdon at the time, who held a doctorate from Cambridge University in both canon and civil law.[21] Since it was on Witlesey's behalf that the countess petitioned the pope for a dispensation that would allow him to hold an additional benefice, it is reasonable to assume that he helped her in this case.[22] Taken along with Mary St Pol's injunction to the fellows of Pembroke College "to give their best counsel and aid on all occasions to the abbess and sisters of Deney," little doubt remains that she provided those nuns with the best lawyers available.[23]

Before the year was out, the suit had been concluded and the final sentence published. Threatened with excommunication and intervention by secular authorities, the nuns remaining at Waterbeach were to leave for Denney immediately, there to live under obedience to Katharine de Bolewyk. The abbey buildings were to be taken over by twelve friars, and the church served by them. The brothers were to receive their food and clothing from Denney in return for their service.

Immediately, Katharine began to force the remnant to move but as Clement VI's 1351 confirmation of this decision makes clear, even at this late date resistance remained. Their numbers now down to four or five (or as many as sixteen if we consult the calendar of papal petitions for that year), the Waterbeach recusants still contended that the Abbess of Denney had no legal right to force them into another monastery. In response, the pope evoked apostolic plenitude of power which he insisted would compensate for any deficits in law or delegated power.[24] Ultimately, it did.

From the very beginning of this unedifying struggle, Mary St Pol had been determined that the Waterbeach Minoresses, one and all, make a new home for themselves at Denney. But she had also been adamant that Waterbeach Abbey "not remain desolate of divine service or be converted to profane uses."[25] Yet by 1359, Waterbeach Abbey was not only desolate of sacred services but also in ruins.[26] Since the souls of "the sisters

21 *BRUO*, vol. 3, pp. 2040–2041.

22 "Vol. XXI: 10 Clement VI," in *Petitions to the Pope: 1342–1419* (1896), pp. 208–227. Online at www.british-history.ac.uk/report.aspx?compid=92374 (accessed June 17, 2010).

23 J. Bass Mullinger, *A History of the University of Cambridge* (London: Longmans, 1888), p. 38.

24 *BF*, vol. 6, p. 253: "supplentes omnem defectum, si quis propter debitum iuris ordinem non servatum aut propter defectum potestatis transferentium."

25 *CPR 1350–1354*, p. 73.

26 Bourdillon, *Minoresses*, pp. 21–22.

and others buried there" were not being prayed for in the abbey church and their bodies were lying in untended graves in the abbey cemetery, Pope Innocent VI was left with little choice but to license the removal of those bodies to Denney.[27] The twelve friars mandated to occupy Waterbeach had apparently never done so, regardless of the fact that they had been promised food and clothing for their pains. Did the plague cause this result? In the teeth of calamity, the abbey might have been better served by that chauvinistic band of Minoresses so intent on staying in their home.

Unlike the Waterbeach saga, the dispute between the Abbess Joan [Johana] Barton of Aldgate and the rectors of a church in the parish of Wrestlingworth [Wrastlyngworth; Wrestlynworth; Wrastlingworth] has obscure origins.[28] It also lacks the human drama of the preceding saga. But remarkably, this contest over the tithes of a rural parish merited the appointment of no fewer than three papal judges and even more remarkably, given the evanescent nature of ad hoc court decisions, the outcome is documented by an extant final judgment.

In February of 1476, Pope Sixtus IV issued mandates to three men, the Bishop of Lincoln, the Abbot of St Mary's Wardon in the diocese of London, and the Archdeacon of Rochester, ordering them to summon the parties concerned in a tithe dispute "to hear both sides, and taking cognizance of the principal matter also, decide what is just, without appeal, causing their decision to be observed by ecclesiastical censure."[29] The papal mandates were issued at the request of Robert Wilde, rector of the church of Wrestlingworth, Bedfordshire, in the diocese of Lincoln. The Minoresses of Aldgate possessed the advowson of the parish church of Potton [Hatleport], Bedfordshire, in the diocese of Lincoln, which was only three miles distant from Wrestlingworth, and Wilde claimed that they and the rector of Potton had threatened to compel his parishioners to hear Mass and receive the sacraments in that church rather than in his; he also alleged that they had forced Wrestlingworth parishioners to pay their tithes to the nuns rather than to him.[30] This was the 'principal matter' with which the judges delegate were to concern themselves, but Wilde's petition also mentioned *why* Abbess Barton and her nuns had

27 *BF*, vol. 6, p. 321.

28 Paxton, *Nunneries*, pp. 180–181.

29 *CPL*, vol. 12, p. 541.

30 "Parishes: Potton," in *A History of the County of Bedford*, vol. 2 (1908), pp. 237–242. Online at www.british-history.ac.uk/report.aspx?compid=62639 (accessed September 20, 2010). Given the proceedings that follow, and also given the fact that I have found no record of the existence of a church of "Hatleport, alias Beryenhateley" as Sixtus IV's mandate styles it, the church must be that of Potton.

been emboldened to deflect the parishioners of, and oblations due to, the church of Wrestlingworth.

Some time earlier, the Minoresses had filed their own suit concerning tithes which was almost the mirror image of Wilde's. In that case they had charged Wilde's predecessor at Wrestlingworth, Thomas Thorpe, with taking away "certain parishioners and tithes" owed the church of Potton, and, importantly, they had won their case. In the audience court of the Archbishop of Canterbury, Thomas Bourgchier (1454–86), Master Thomas Winterbourne (d. 1478), his auditor of causes, had sanctioned compulsion if necessary to restore the tithes and parishioners to Potton, and thus to the Minoresses of Aldgate.[31] But, according to Wilde's petition, Master Winterbourne had at that time made a procedural error that undermined his sanction – he had failed to take the deposition of a crucial witness.

Although Rector Thomas Thorpe had died by the time Winterbourne pronounced his verdict in the case, Thorpe's successor as rector of Wrestlingworth, William Watson, had still been very much alive. According to Robert Wilde, Master Winterbourne had neglected to summon the said Watson to court to tell his side of the matter. Thus, the auditor "wrongfully proceeding in the cause [had] promulgated *de facto*, an unjust definitive sentence in favor of the said abbess and convent."[32] Wilde therefore asked "that the pope commit the cause of the said appeal, that of the nullity of the whole process and of the sentence of the said auditor, and that of the principal matter, to some upright men in those parts."

This then was not merely a dispute about 'the principal matter,' tithes. Wilde's petition to Sixtus IV complained of an unjust verdict emanating from the court of the highest ecclesiastical authority in England, the Archbishop of Canterbury. Furthermore, the auditor in question, Thomas Winterbourne, was a very distinguished and powerful man. He held a doctorate in canon law from the University of Oxford, and as Archbishop

31 F. Donald Logan, "Archbishop Thomas Bourgchier Revisited," in *The Church in Pre-Reformation Society:Essays in Honour of F. R. H. Du Bouley*, ed. C. M. Barron and C. Harper-Bill (Woodbridge: Boydell, 1985), pp. 177–181; Christopher Harper-Bill, "Winterborne, Thomas (d. 1478)," in *ODNB*, www.oxforddnb.com/view/article/29773 (accessed July 2, 2009).

32 The petition says that the auditor of causes had made his decision without citing the late William Watson, who had succeeded Thomas Thorpe as rector of Wrestlingworth. Consequently, Watson had not been in court to argue his side "not through contumacy."

Bourgchier's *alter ego*, exercised legatine as well as episcopal authority.[33] Investigating the nullity of a sentence which had effectively been handed down by a papal legate could not be left to the faint-hearted, nor to men themselves lacking in prestige. As his commission of 1476 shows, Sixtus IV chose his three judges delegate accordingly. The Bishop of Lincoln at the time was Thomas Rotherham, who also happened to be Chancellor of England (1474–1483).[34] Although we can't be sure who the Abbot of Warden was in 1476, the heads of this prestigious Cistercian house in Bedfordshire had often been commissioned by the papacy to hear highly sensitive cases.[35] The Archdeacon of Rochester might very well have been Thomas Rotherham's much-beneficed brother and doctor of civil law, Roger Rotherham[36]

Faced with sorting out this delicate matter, all the papal judges had a difficult task in front of them. For one of them, it was destined to get even harder. As we just noted, Bishop Rotherham was both Chancellor of England and Bishop of Lincoln in 1476 when he was commissioned to act as judge delegate in the case of Wilde vs. Joan Barton. No sooner had Rotherham received that commission than he was called upon to act *as chancellor* in a case presented by none other than "clerk and parson of the church of Wrestlingworth in the county of Bedford, Robert Wilde."[37] In his complaint to Sixtus IV, Wilde had charged an episcopal auditor with negligence; now, in his petition to Chancellor Rotherham, he accused an abbess of much more.[38]

The rector alleged that it had all begun on September 11 "last past," while the tithes case between himself and Joan Barton had still been pending in the court of the Archbishop of Canterbury (probably 1475, as

33 *Registrum Thomae Bourgchier Cantuarensis Archiebiscopi* AD *1454–1486*, ed. F. R. H. du Boulay (Oxford: Oxford University Press, 1957), pp. 32, 87, 108 record his appointments, and other references throughout the register identify his varied activities. Unfortunately, the register does not contain any record of the suit between Wilde's predecessor and the Minoresses.

34 Rosemary Horrox, "Rotherham, Thomas (1423–1500)," in *ODNB*, www.oxforddnb.com/view/article/24155 (accessed July 2, 2009).

35 "Houses of Cistercian Monks: The Abbey of Warden," in *A History of the County of Bedford*, vol. 1 (1904), pp. 361–366. Online at www.british-history.ac.uk/report.aspx?compid=40036&strquery=warden (accessed July 2, 2009).

36 "Archdeacons: Rochester," in *Fasti Ecclesiae Anglicanae*, vol. 4, pp. 41–42. Online at www.british-history.ac.uk/report.aspx?compid=32725 (accessed July 2, 2009). and see above note 3.

37 C 1/67/163. While this petition is not dated, internal evidence and the fact that it was addressed to the Bishop of Lincoln as chancellor suggest that it was submitted in 1476–1477.

38 See p. 105 for a transcription of this Chancery petition.

Winterbourne had passed judgment in the cause by 1476). He had come to London "to commune with such persons as were of his learned counsel in the spiritual law." William Baker, Abbess Barton's servant, had learned of Wilde's London visit, and convinced the abbess "by means contrary to good conscience," to secure a writ of trespass against the rector so that he would be too afraid and impoverished to continue his tithes suit. The abbess filed a writ accusing Wilde of assaulting William Baker in the parish of Saint Botolph without Aldgate, severely injuring him and making it impossible for him to work. As a result of Barton's writ, Wilde had been arrested and imprisoned by the Sheriff of London.

Wilde was now petitioning the Chancery since he was "not guilty as God knowith" although he could not prove his innocence because all the cards were stacked against him. First, there was the formal allegation of the abbess, whose circle of friends and acquaintances in the City of London underscored the rector's own lack of such connections. Then there was the fact that the London jury picked to try the trespass case against him was made up of Abbess Barton's tenants and assigns, and these jurors had already told Wilde that they would convict him regardless of the evidence. Finally, once they did convict him (and he was sure that they would), he would be powerless to overturn the verdict by writ. Although elsewhere in England one could secure a bill of attaint to initiate common law action against a false jury verdict, the bill was not applicable to verdicts rendered in the City of London.[39]

Wilde's visit to London "to commune with such persons as were of his learned counsel in the spiritual law" might have turned out badly, but the wording of his Chancery petition suggests that he had still had the benefit of good legal counsel. That petition precisely and persuasively argued that Wilde's cause could not be remedied at common law and so belonged in Chancery. Although Thomas Rotherham was obviously adept at dealing with conflicts of interest – a loyal servant of Edward IV, Edward V, *and* Richard III, he still managed to die in his own bed, of natural causes, at the age of seventy-five – Robert Wilde's petition might nevertheless have given him pause. Since Rotherham was not the only, nor even the ordinary, judge in his court, the bishop might merely have recused himself in this instance.[40] Lacking a response to Wilde's Chancery petition we cannot know how he chose to deal with the matter. We do know, however,

39 Surely this statement is evidence that Wilde had found the learned counsel that he had come to London to consult.

40 Richardson, *Medieval Chancery*, p. 29, notes that this would have been true even in Henry V's.

that Chancellor Thomas Rotherham was ultimately not the one to try the case of Wilde vs. the Minoresses of Aldgate as papal judge delegate.[41]

Final sentence in the case was not passed until 1482, and by that time John Russell had replaced Rotherham as Bishop of Lincoln, the latter being translated to York in 1480.[42] Of the two other judges who had been originally appointed by Sixtus IV in 1476, the Abbot of Warden and the Archdeacon of Rochester, we hear nothing. The intervening years had removed the archepiscopal auditor Master Thomas Winterbourne (d. 1478) from active participation as well. But the central issues remained the same, and the care that the new judge delegate, Bishop John Russell, took in sifting through the allegations swirling around them reminds us that one of those issues was the integrity of a judgment passed in the court of the Archbishop of Canterbury.

Bishop Russell's final decree as papal judge delegate was issued in 1482. It began by introducing the parties to the now dated dispute. In all important respects they correspond to those mentioned in Robert Wilde's 1476 papal petition. The perpetual vicar of the church of Potton is cited along with Abbess Joan [Barton] and the convent of the Minoresses without Aldgate, proprietors. The rights claimed by the vicars/rectors of two contiguous parish churches, those of Potton and Wrestlingworth, are the same.

After giving the particulars of the tithe dispute, Bishop Russell's judgment recounted the means by which he had arrived at it. He had enlisted the aid of "upright men of those parts," and taken the depositions of reputable inhabitants, including the lord of Wrestlingworth manor himself. Upon considering the testimony of these worthies, the papal judge then responded to Robert Wilde's demand that, notwithstanding the sentence pronounced by auditor Winterbourne, "certain parishioners and tithes" be restored to him. As might be expected, he crafted a compromise. Russell decreed that all inhabitants, occupants, and tenants of the manor of the lord of Wrestlingworth, present and future, were to regard the church of Potton rather than that of Wrestlingworth as their parish church. These parishioners, consequently, would have all of their sacramental and other spiritual needs, such as Christian burial, served by the perpetual vicar of Potton who, as mentioned, was the appointee of the Minoresses of Aldgate.

But although Wrestlingworth was a small rural parish, it did have inhabitants other than tenants of the manor, and the remainder of John

41 LR 15/213.

42 John A. F. Thomson, "Russell, John (c. 1430–1494)," in *ODNB*, www.oxforddnb.com/view/article/24318 (accessed July 2009).

Russell's decree specified that these people would continue to regard the rector of Wrestlingworth as their pastor. Robert Wilde was to retain his office and to receive annually, for as long as he lived, a portion of the lesser tithes such as would allow him to comfortably sustain himself.[43] To ensure the preservation of this delicate arrangement, the bishop leveled a fiduciary of 26s. 8d. from the parties involved. Apparently John Russell's settlement of this dispute proved a lasting one. At the time of the Dissolution, the Minoresses of Aldgate were still on record as collecting "the corn tithes of the manor of Wrestlingworth within the said parish of Potton," which at that time amounted to £5 6s. 8d.[44]

The nuns of Syon had their own long-standing conflict over tithes. It involved the advowsons of Lancaster Priory; the background to the dispute has already been sketched in relation to a preceding Chancery case.[45] Suffice it to repeat here that by grant of Henry V, the abbess and nuns were to come into possession of the Lancaster Priory estate upon the death of Giles Lovell, its last prior. Until that time, the prior was to pay them £110 yearly. Prior Giles Lovell died in 1428 and in that same year, even before they had formally become the new proprietors, the nuns found their claims challenged. The challenge came from the Archdeacon of Richmond, Master Henry Bowett [Bolbet; Bowet] (1418–1422) and it would be heard by a judge delegated by the pope.[46]

Ordinary jurisdiction prompted Archdeacon Bowett to claim the revenues of Lancaster church which along with the church of Poulton had been a Lancaster Priory church. As local ordinary, Bowett would normally have been responsible for the cure of souls when the provider of same died. Prior Giles Lovell had been that provider and now the position of vicar of Lancaster church was vacant. Bowett argued that he should hold that position until such time as it was canonically filled through election or appointment; he would collect the revenues produced in the interim. Since the thirteenth century, the Archdeacons of Richmond had been responsible for formally instituting the newly elected vicar of the church of Poulton, so Bowett did have a case. He further reinforced his position by

43 As a consequence of this ruling, the Minoresses, their appointed rector and vicar of Potton, would be entitled to the greater or predial tithe, that is a portion of annual crops. But there remained the lesser or small tithes – portions of what resulted from nourishment by the land: cattle, cheese, milk, wool, and portions of what resulted from human industry or occupation: rents, cartwheels, shoes, etc.

44 Tomlinson, *History of the Minories*, p. 62.

45 See Chapter 5, with specific reference to PL 6/1/22.

46 "Archdeacons: Richmond," in *Fasti Ecclesiae Anglicanae 1300–1541*, vol. 6: *Northern Province (York, Carlisle and Durham)* (1963), pp. 25–27. Online at www.british-history.ac.uk/report.aspx?compid=32516 (accessed July 16, 2009).

asserting that Henry V's grant of Lancaster Priory to Syon had "amounted to a fresh appropriation of the churches of Lancaster and Poulton."[47]

Bowett's claims, and the counterclaims of the Abbess of Syon, were weighed by a competent and experienced judge delegate, Archbishop of York, Master John Kempe (1380–1454).[48] A fellow of Merton College, Oxford, Kempe held doctorates in civil law and in divinity. He had spent his early career in the court of the Archbishop of Canterbury and his duties on behalf of the Crown in France ensured that his diplomatic talents were finely honed. When Archbishop Kempe handed down his judgment (September 1, 1428) in the case of Syon vs. Henry Bowett, he was acting as a seasoned and trusted papal legate.

The introductory clauses of the archbishop's judgment, formally addressing the concerned parties, name three individuals aside from Bowett and the nuns of Syon: William Harrington, Thomas Urswik, and John Alnewik, cleric.[49] It is worth noting that William Harrington, labeled a knight, is already familiar to us as one of the executors of the will and testament of Giles Lovell, last Prior of Lancaster.[50] After reviewing the facts – Prior Lovell's death, Bowett's claim to tithes of the church of Lancaster by reason of the vacancy, and the counterclaim of the Abbess and convent of Syon – Kempe awarded the greater or predial tithes of the church to Henry Bowett. These consisted of sheaves of wheat and other unspecified grain. He awarded the lesser or small tithes (an unspecified mix of goods obtained by animal or human production) to the nuns, excepting a portion to be paid to the resident vicar responsible for the maintenance of divine worship and cure of souls.

There was another proviso attached that explains the inclusion of the above-named three men. The tithes awarded to both parties were to be collected by deputies for the litigants. William Harrington (no stranger to the case) and Thomas Urswik were to act on behalf of Bowett, and the cleric, John Alnewik, was deputized to act for the nuns. These deputies were to sell or store the produce they collected and to keep the proceeds in trust for the disputants until a record of their amicable composition had been formally made and recorded.

John Kempe's carefully crafted strategy kept the disputants out of his

47 "Alien House: The Priory of Lancaster," in *A History of the County of Lancaster*, vol. 2 (1908), pp. 167–173. Online at www.british-history.ac.uk/report.aspx?compid=38367&strquery=alien priories (accessed July 17, 2009).

48 R. G. Davies, "Kemp, John (1380/81–1454)," in *ODNB*, www.oxforddnb.com/view/article/15328 (accessed July 13, 2009).

49 E 327/180.

50 See Chapter 5.

court for less than a year. Perhaps the agents deputized in 1428 had proven unreliable, or the parties uncooperative. In any case, the "amicable composition" envisioned by Kempe never materialized. Whatever the cause of renewed hostilities, the archbishop surely wished to stabilize the situation regarding the parishioners of Lancaster and Poulton. On May 14, 1429, he handed down another decision as papal judge delegate, this one pertaining to both the churches of Lancaster and of Poulton. That judgment contained a precise cash award to Henry Bowett and his successors. He decided that the Abbess of Syon, Joan North, and her convent were liable to indemnify the Archdeacon of Richmond and his successors £40 6s. 8d. annually.[51]

Kempe's second decision proved to be more lasting than his first. In fact, it produced the desired effects for nearly fifteen years. In 1430, a perpetual vicarage was finally endowed for the church of Lancaster, and a vicar formally instituted by Archdeacon Bowett. The following year, Lancaster Priory estate was at last conveyed to the nuns of Syon by the trustees who had been appointed by Henry V, and the gift was reconfirmed upon the accession of Edward IV. But then, in 1442, when Henry Bowett resigned as Archdeacon of Richmond, issues concerning Lancaster church tithes re-emerged. Although he would be translated to the see of Canterbury a few years hence, John Kempe was still Archbishop of York when Pope Eugenius IV once again required him to judge a case involving Lancaster church revenues and the nuns of Syon.

In July of 1442, the pope commissioned Kempe to try a case involving Richard Chester, perpetual vicar of Lancaster church. Eugenius explained that some time earlier, Chester had complained to him, claiming that he was being defrauded by the nuns of Syon. In that earlier complaint he alleged that the Bridgettines had assigned him certain tithes "in perpetuity," with the stipulation that he was to use them "for keeping hospitality and for the maintenance of six chaplains to celebrate masses and other divine offices, administer the sacraments in the said church and in the chapels of Stlymyn, Grissyngham and Cayton, dependent on the said priory or church and exercise the cure of souls of the said five [priory and church being separately counted], and for other burdens [specified]."[52] Difficulties emerged when "by reason of pestilences etc." the tithes allotted had become inadequate to support all of the obligations imposed upon him. Yet despite Chester's penury, "the said abbess had for many years, although often asked, neglected to assign to the vicar a sufficient portion

51 E 328/386.

52 *CPL*, vol. 9, p. 268.

for his maintenance and for keeping hospitality and bearing the burdens of the said church."

Eugenius IV had found Chester's complaint convincing and he had consequently responded both to the reported fiscal exigencies of the vicarage, and the wild proliferation of chaplains serving its dependent chantries, by turning back the clock to the time of Giles Lovell. He had granted "all the tithes, fruits, etc. ... within the bounds of the parish churches of Lancaster and Pulton ... to the said church and Richard [Chester] and successors exactly as they had belonged to the said Giles and his predecessors, priors of the then priory." In return, Chester was to pay the Abbess of Syon £110 sterling, just as Lovell had done before the appropriation of the Lancaster Priory.[53]

But now, as the pope explained to Kempe, he was having second thoughts about his decision. He said that these doubts had been occasioned by a recent petition of the Abbess and convent of Syon which stated that what had been alleged in Chester's petition was not true and that the vicar was assigned a yearly portion of 40 marks sterling, and that the pope's decision in favor of Chester was greatly prejudicial to them.

Given the number of infelicities and mistakes that this papal mandate contains, it is not clear whether the nuns' rebuttal had actually listed the vicar's annual stipend at 40 *marks*, or the more likely £40 awarded him in the 1429 arbitration with which we have just dealt. Nevertheless, Eugenius IV went on to appoint Archbishop Kempe, John Stafford, Bishop of Bath and Wells, and the Archdeacon of Exeter, Master Peter Stukeley, bachelor of canon law, to look into the thorny matter.[54] The pope commissioned the judges to bring before them "the said Richard [Chester] and others concerned, and if they find the aforesaid [statements of the abbess and convent] to be true, to revoke and decree null the pope's said ordinance [that is, Eugenius' own] and its consequences, and to restore the said abbess and convent and monastery to the state in which they were before it emanated."[55]

Apparently, this is precisely what John Kempe and his fellow judges did find upon investigation of the principles. Richard Chester got nothing like the generous settlement that Eugenius' first decision would have entailed.

53 *Ibid.*, p. 269.

54 "Bishops," in *Fasti Ecclesiae Anglicanae 1300–1541*, vol. 8: *Bath and Wells Diocese* (1964), pp. 1–3. Online at www.british-history.ac.uk/report.aspx?compid=32141 (accessed July 9, 2010); "Archdeacons: Exeter," in *Fasti Ecclesiae Anglicanae*, vol. 9, pp. 12–15. Online at www.british-history.ac.uk/report.aspx?compid=32243 (accessed July 9, 2010).

55 *CPL*, vol. 9, p. 269.

The clock was not turned back to the days of Giles Lovell. In fact, the entire estate of the former Priory of Lancaster, including the churches of Lancaster and Pulton, was still among the possessions of the nuns of Syon at the time of the Dissolution; it was then worth £216 13s. 8d.[56] It should be noted, however, that even after they had farmed out the priory estates in 1462, the Bridgettines retained the Lancaster church advowson which meant that quarrels with its successive vicars never really ceased. In 1467, for instance, a vicar of Lancaster church, Richard Burton, complained that the "dubious and uncertain wording of a previous composition" that he had made with the Abbess of Syon forced him to come before the arbiter.[57] Somewhat ironically, that arbiter was the Archdeacon of Richmond.[58]

Direct Papal Responses

For late medieval popes struggling to come to terms with a backlog of petitions for legal redress, delegation of decision-making was a popular option, but it was never the only one. Throughout the later Middle Ages, popes continued to respond directly to petitions sent to them from all over Christian Europe. Shortly after their monastery was founded the London Minoresses sent such an appeal to the pope asking him to resolve a dispute that had arisen between them and the Bishop of Coventry and Lichfield. In this instance the pope chose not to delegate the affair to a provincial arbiter. After some lapse of time, he sent the nuns his personal decision concerning the matter.

The dispute which merited such direct papal intervention was occasioned by Edmund, Earl of Lancaster's bequest of an advowson of the church of Hartington, Derby, to the Minories. This gift was formally confirmed in 1295, with these words: "a charter to Edmund the king's brother, granting in frank almoin to the abbess of the order of St Clare, without the walls of London, and to the sisters there, of 10 acres of land of his demesne in the field of Hertindon [Hartington], co. Derby, and the advowson of the church there."[59]

In that same year, and at the request of Edmund and his wife, Blanche of Navarre, the nuns received Pope Boniface VIII's approval to accept this

56 See the full account of the history of the priory in "Alien House: The Priory of Lancaster."

57 E 326/1854: "dubitationes et amiguatates incertis verbis in ipsa compositione."

58 John Shirwode (1465–1484) heard the complaint: "Archdeacons: Richmond."

59 *CPR 1292–1301*, p. 170. The ancient deed of this gift is LR 14/ 1173.

gift. However, he gave that approval without ever naming the church of Hartington. Some of the language of the papal concession is particularly important, given what would shortly transpire. Boniface allowed the nuns use of

> one of the churches of which the said prince holds the right of patronage, and fruits, rents, and proceeds of which amount to the annual value of forty marks sterling; so that when this church shall happen to become vacant by the cession or decease of the rector of the same church, you are at liberty to take it in possession by your own authority, the assent of the diocesan of the place, or any other whatsoever, not being requisite and to retain it to the aforesaid uses in perpetuity.[60]

The pope had sanctioned, however vaguely, the transfer of a spirituality to the Minories. But, as we know, such transfers also involved revenues from landed property and the Crown claimed exclusive jurisdiction over advowsons. Careful to recognize those interests, the Minoresses next applied for a royal patent to validate the pontifically approved grant. They would have to wait for a year and half before the king licensed the gift of both advowson and acreage, but when the Crown finally did so, the Minoresses must have been quite sure of their legal right to the bequest given their meticulous accumulation of requisite deeds.[61] Walter de Langeton, Bishop of Coventry and Lichfield, was not.[62]

The church of Hartington was located in his diocese of Coventry, so the bishop would normally have had a diocesan's control of it. Newly elected in 1296, Walter de Langeton was not pleased to discover that he had lost that control to the nuns of Aldgate. As noted above, Boniface VIII's bull of concession had stipulated that the Minoresses were free to take possession of "one of the churches of which the said prince holds the right of patronage … the assent of the diocesan of the place, or of any other whatsoever, not being requisite." It would have been difficult for de Langeton to challenge such a clear and precise papal statement about the irrelevance of diocesan approval in this matter. Instead, Bishop Langeton chose to make another one of the pope's precise statements, the one about the worth of the advowson, work in his own favor. Claiming that the value of the advowson of the church of Hartington exceeded the 40 marks specified in Boniface VIII's concession, the bishop endeavored to keep the nuns from ever taking seisin.

60 Tomlinson, *History of the Minories*, pp. 19–20.

61 *Ibid.*, p. 28.

62 "Bishops," *Fasti Ecclesiae Anglicanae 1300–1541*, vol. 10: *Coventry and Lichfield Diocese* (1964), pp. 1–3. Online at www.british-history.ac.uk/report.aspx?compid=32256 (accessed June 15, 2009).

Appealing to the pope to decide the issue, the Minoresses were not disappointed with the results, although they had to wait for them. In 1298, Boniface VIII responded to Langeton's claim in no uncertain terms. After recapitulating the particulars of his original bull, his reply to the nuns of Aldgate went to the heart of the matter.

> The church of Hertenden, however, in the diocese of Coventry and Lichfield, of which the said Edmund held the right of patronage, eventually becoming vacant, you endeavored, by our authority, to take possession of the said church at Hertenden but our venerable brother, the bishop of Coventry and Lichfield, the diocesan of the place, and his officials, asserting that the fruits, rents, and proceeds of the said church of Hertenden exceed the value of forty marks, according to their real value, although according to the taxation of ecclesiastical revenues lately made in the kingdom of England they do not exceed the same sum, in many ways annoys and disturbs you respecting the same church. Wherefore you humbly supplicate us to deign to show paternal kindness in this matter. We therefore, desiring to provide for your peace and tranquility, and to enlarge this grant concede to you, by the authority of these presents, that you may retain to your own use the same church of Hertenden, provided that according to the aforesaid taxation, its rents and proceeds do not exceed the annual value of sixty marks, and may take and retain the same by your own authority ... [63]

It is good, sometimes, to be the pope. Boniface VIII effectively quashed the ambitions of Walter de Langeton (whose name he never even mentioned in his response) regardless of which tactic the diocesan might have been tempted to employ in the future. First, citing the valuation of Hartington entered in the *taxatio* of Nicholas IV (1291–1292) "lately made in the kingdom of England," the pope demonstrated that the 40 marks' valuation was not excessive. An extremely thorough assessment of the ecclesiastical property of England and Wales, and one which would became the basis for taxation of the clergy until 1535, the *taxatio* valued Hartington at £26 13s. 4d.[64] Second, possibly to demonstrate to the bishop that things

63 Tomlinson, *History of the Minories*, pp. 28–29. The calendar of papal registers contains this entry for the letter: "Non. Mar. St Peter's (f. 21d.) Grant to the abbess and convent de Domo Gratie, B.M.V., of the order of St Clare [without Aldgate], in the diocese of London, of the church of Hertindon, in the diocese of Coventry and Lichfield, of the advowson of the late Edmund, the king's brother, on their petition that the pope granted them one of his churches on his petition, so that on its voidance the advowson passed to them, but the diocesan and his officials interfered on the ground that the limit of 40 marks, originally fixed, was under its value, although, according to the latest taxation made in England, it is not." "Regesta 49: 1298–1300," in *Calendar of Papal Registers Relating to Great Britain and Ireland*, vol. 1 (1893), pp. 1198–1304, pp. 574–591. Online at www.british-history.ac.uk/report.aspx?compid=96043&strquery=aldgate (accessed June 15, 2009.

64 See the entry for Hartington in the taxation database, which was compiled from the

could get even more humiliating for him, Boniface VIII simply raised the revenue ceiling for the granted advowson to 60 marks.

Forty marks (not to mention 60) was a considerable sum at the close of the thirteenth century. Given the fact that the nuns of Aldgate do not appear to have had any more trouble with the Hartington appropriation, they were doubtless glad that they had sent their appeal all the way to Rome, then bided their time.[65] To the Dominican friars of King's Langley who petitioned the papacy to intervene in their dispute with the nuns of Dartford, upon whom they were financially dependent, the results must at first have seemed equally satisfactory. Only later would it become obvious to them that they had won the battle, but not the war.

Bequests to nunneries often included a stipulation that the recipients dispense alms on a regular basis. Commonly this meant distribution of charity to the nameless poor via the establishment of a paupers' table or similar arrangement. Sometimes the alms were to be given to specific groups or individuals, as when the nuns of Denney had been obliged to feed and clothe the twelve friars who were (theoretically) to inhabit their former abbey at Waterbeach. The material dependence of the friars of King's Langley on the nuns of Dartford, however, was virtually complete.

Dartford Priory existed in order to provide King's Langley Friary with a steady income. Edward II's mother, Eleanor of Castile, had wished to found a house of Dominican nuns in England and her son's fiscal problems with his own foundation of King's Langley were largely what enabled her dream to become a reality. Edward II had founded King's Langley in 1308, but then for years afterward he had been forced to continue making grants of cash to help the friars build and maintain their priory.[66] He had also been obliged to give them gifts of fuel, clothing, and food on a regular basis, all this because the Dominican constitutions at that time prohibited friars from owning lands or rents separate from their churches and priory precincts.[67] While neither as restrictive nor as staunchly defended as the

Taxatio Ecclesiastica Angliae et Walliae Auctoritate Papae Nicholai IV (Record Commission, 1802) at www.hrionline.ac.uk/taxatio/info.html (accessed June 16, 2009). Note the contemporary reckoning of 13s. 4d. to the mark, with 20s. being equal to £1.

65 LR 14/272, dated 1320, records the nuns as granting the rectory for eight years to Sir Robert of Nottingham; LR 14/ 1147 documents an indenture that they made in 1350 with the then vicar, John de Markesby.

66 "Friaries: King's Langley Priory," in *A History of the County of Hertford*, vol. 4 (1971), pp. 446–451. Online at www.british-history.ac.uk/report.aspx?compid=37971 (accessed June 23, 2010); Lee, *Nunneries*, pp. 15–17.

67 William Hinnebusch, *The Early English Friars Preachers* (Rome: S. Sabine 1951), p. 233.

Franciscan notion, the mendicant ideal remained a part of fourteenth-century Dominican spirituality – for men, that is.[68]

As we know, Dominican constitutions mandated personal but not corporate poverty for their cloistered female branches and actually *required* Dominican nunneries to possess endowments. Because the consistency of returns from a landed endowment obviated the need for ad hoc payments (which the friars claimed were not always made when most needed), establishing a nunnery that would support King's Langley was a project that appealed to Edward II and the friars alike. In 1321, the king received papal permission "to found a monastery of Augustinian nuns, living according to the institutes and under the care of the Friars Preachers, in pursuance of the purpose of his mother, Queen Eleanor, who died before she could carry it out."[69]

Unable to fulfill his desire before he was dethroned, the king was fortunate to have a son who was as much interested in the Dominicans as he. In 1349, Edward III received papal confirmation for the foundation of a specific nunnery, Dartford Priory in Kent which, along with King's Langley in Hertfordshire, would "together possess one hundred nuns and friars."[70] Lest there be any confusion, support of the chaplains in residence at Dartford, although also assumed by the nuns, was distinct from their maintenance, at a distance of about 40 miles, of a friary accommodating sixty more men. Dartford Priory, then, fully supported the friars of King's Langley, since the nuns both held and administered their temporalities. For example, a 1356 royal license given to the Prioress of Dartford to acquire in mortmain £300 yearly of lands, rents, and advowsons specifically states that those bequests are for the sustenance of forty nuns and sixty friars; even the grant of a pension to the prior of King's Langley was licensed "out of the issues of lands of Dartford Priory."[71]

But the link between Dartford and King's Langley was not merely fiscal. As far back as Pope John XXII's license granting Edward II the right to found a Dominican nunnery anywhere in England, it was assumed that the spiritual care and direction of the nuns would be provided by the Friars Preachers. Dartford's foundation charter of November 19, 1356, specifically named the Dominicans of King's Langley as providers of that care and guidance.

68 On earlier notions of corporate poverty of the friars, see C. H. Lawrence, *The Friars* (London: Longman, 1994), pp. 69–73.

69 *CPL*, vol. 2, p. 217.

70 *CPP*, vol. 1, p. 187.

71 Lee, *Nunneries*, p. 17.

> Whereas the King has founded upon his land at Dartford a monastery of sisters of the order of Preachers with houses, cloisters and enclosures to be a priory and dwelling for a prioress and thirty-nine sisters to be there enclosed, to be under the rule and habit of S. Augustine and the obedience of the priory of Langeleye of the said order, and also for the said prior of Langeleye and his vicar when they shall come thither, and for the brethren of that house who shall abide in the said priory by the orders of the prior and minister to the prioress and nuns in divine service.[72]

Mention that Dartford Priory should be the abode "for the said prior of Langeleye and his vicar when they shall come thither" refers to the regular visitations conducted to ensure discipline. Visitation of Dominican convents was the responsibility of the provincial prior who might delegate that duty to the prior of a neighboring priory or even to the superior of the friars resident in the house to be visited.[73] The wording of the foundation charter might mean that the prior of King's Langley had such a duty delegated to him. Because all records of the English province of the Dominican order have been lost to us, there is no way of knowing how many visits by the prior of King's Langley and his vicar, or by the Provincial General, were made before the fifteenth century.[74] We do know that one visit, conducted by the Provincial General himself and formally slated for the summer of 1415, brought discord in its wake.

On July 20, 1415, Henry V issued this letter patent:

> Commission to Master John Aylmere and Master Richard Alkyrton to assist the provincial of the order of Friars Preachers in England at his proposed visitation of the house or monastery of nuns of Derteford, of the said order, in augmentation of lapsed religion, reformation of due obedience and strengthening of its foundation, as it is of the foundation of the king's progenitors and of the king's patronage; with full power to enquire into and punish with the said provincial any defects, excesses and trespasses in these things and to reduce all the sisters to obedience according to the form of apostolic bulls and letters patent dated 10 November, 30 Edward III.[75]

This sternly worded directive referring to lapsed practice and reformation of due obedience strongly suggests that the Dartford nuns had not been scrupulously honoring all of the provisions of their foundation charter. That charter had stated that the sisters be under the "obedience of the priory of Langeleye of the said order," and there are signs that they had

[72] B. E. R. Formoy, *The Dominican Order in England before the Reformation* (London: Macmillan, 1925), pp. 126–17 reproduces the charter. See also Lee, *Nunneries*, pp. 23–24.

[73] Hinnebusch, *History of the Dominican Order*, vol. 1, p. 393.

[74] Lee, *Nunneries*, p. 7. Formoy, *The Dominican Order*, p. xiii.

[75] *CPR 1413–1416*, p. 359.

given into their desire for increased independence from the friars. In 1393, for instance, two Dartford nuns received papal permission to choose their own confessors, although the chaplains resident at the priory were there to provide such spiritual care.[76] It is not difficult to imagine why the sisters might have felt justified in asserting their autonomy from King's Langley. The senior friar chaplain in residence at Dartford had authority over the friars' chaplain but only the prior of King's Langley had the authority over the nuns, and he lived at some distance (42 miles). Day-to-day running of the monastery and discipline of the nuns, as well as the administration of the temporal affairs of two separate communities, fell to the Prioress of Dartford. This was not a situation that was likely to foster submissiveness.

Understandable or not, Henry V's commission was aimed at stopping Dartford's move away from the direct oversight of King's Langley. His willingness to provide Church authorities with the services of two respected aides testifies to his seriousness. John Alymere [Elmer, Ailemer, Aylemer] held a doctorate in canon law from Oxford, had been an advocate in the court of Canterbury, commissioner of appeals in cases from the king's courts of admiralty and chivalry, and in 1415, he was the official of the Bishop of Winchester.[77] Richard Alkyrton [Alkrynton] while less publically active, held an Oxford doctorate in theology and was a notable preacher.[78]

Did the nuns of Dartford ultimately, if grudgingly, admit these distinguished commissioners, the visiting provincial, and his aides? There is no surviving evidence of that visit nor of any other made to Dartford, so it is impossible to say. The sisters must have remained intractable on some issues, however, since both the Provincial General and the prior of King's Langley next petitioned Pope Martin V to intervene. The unambiguous papal response came in July of 1418.[79]

The bulk of the pope's rescript was an account of the foundation of Dartford, beginning with the pious wishes of Queen Eleanor and culminating in the endowment of a monastery of nuns "living under the care and according to the Institutes of the Friars Preachers ... under the rule of the prior of King's Langley." Throughout the body of the bull, the pope employed this phrase or a variant, preparing the reader for his concluding judgment. The nuns of Dartford were ordered under pain of ecclesiastical censures, to live under obedience to the prior of King's Langley and to

76 Formoy, *The Dominican Order*, pp. 130–131.

77 *BRUO*, vol. 1, p. 635.

78 *Ibid.*, p. 25.

79 *Bull. O.P.*, vol. 2, pp. 548–549.

continue to administer their endowments as prescribed in their foundation charter.

Referring to the 1415–1418 dispute between Dartford and King's Langley, Bede Jarrett wrote "Just once … the nuns protested against the visitation of the Prior and Provincial, but otherwise the relations between friars and sisters seem to have worked out well."[80] For the nineteenth-century historian of Dartford Priory, the Reverend Palmer, Pope Martin V's decision was actually a watershed after which "the friendly relations between Dartford and Kings-Langley were fully and permanently established."[81] The fact that the nuns continued to administer the holdings of King's Langley until the Dissolution lends credibility to both these assessments; there can be no doubt that relations between the two houses improved. But the reasons for that improvement have little to do with the tractability of the nuns of Dartford.

One reason why friars and nuns cooperated in the later part of the fifteenth century was that Dominican policy about corporate poverty for friars had changed. "The Order's strict concept of poverty was gradually modified, and more certain sources of revenue were secured. This mitigation set in about the middle of the thirteenth century and progressed until in 1475 the Order completely changed its attitude toward possessions."[82] In that year, the Dominican friars were granted papal permission to directly accept properties and rents. And even before then, the friars of King's Langley had been recipients of outside revenues, thus decreasing their reliance on the Dartford nuns as feoffees.

Another reason for the improved relations between the two houses is the steady decrease in numbers at King's Langley.[83] This meant that although popes and provincial generals granted more and more indults to the nuns of Dartford, allowing them to choose their own confessors and eventually permitting the abbess to do so for the entire community, the show of independence was not interpreted as an affront to the friars of King's Langley. Rather, it was acceptable to nuns and friars alike. Were the nuns to have continued to rely completely on King's Langley to provide their chaplains, the burden on the remaining brothers might have been onerous indeed.

Just a few years after Martin V had replied to the Provincial of the English Dominicans regarding the controversy at Dartford, he was asked

80 B. Jarrett, *The English Dominicans* (London: Burns, Oates and Washbourne, 1921), p. 10.

81 Palmer, "History of the Priory of Dartford," p. 257.

82 Hinnebusch, *The Early English Friars Preachers*, p. 237.

83 Lee, *Nunneries*, pp. 34, 38–39.

decide another issue involving a house of cloistered nuns. This time, however, the appeal was made in person. When a papal decision was truly crucial to the resolution of a dispute, and when money for travel, lodging, and legal fees was plentiful, it was advisable not to wait for Rome to come to you. The situation in which the Bridgettines of Syon found themselves in 1422 qualified on all counts. Faced with the imminent loss not of a single property or privilege but of their very monastery, the issue was indeed 'time sensitive' and Syon, by all accounts the richest nunnery in England, had no cash-flow problems. Bridgettine brothers had to travel to Rome to secure it (or rather to hire the lawyers who would secure it), but the decision that they received from Pope Martin V was more important to Syon than any made before the Dissolution. A short retrospective is required to contextualize it.

The monastery of St Savior, Syon, was not only the last fully enclosed nunnery to be founded in medieval England, it was also the most idiosyncratic of these foundations. Like its mother house of Vadstena and its sister foundations throughout Europe, Syon embodied the unique vision of St Bridget of Sweden (1303–1373).[84] Governed by an abbess, and admitting a fixed number of priests (thirteen), deacons (four), and lay brothers (eight) to serve the daily liturgical needs of sixty sisters, it was structured to evoke the memory of that golden era in Church history when "the church had been headed by a woman, the Lord's mother."[85] Not everyone, even those who were themselves Bridgettines, found the practical expression of Bridget's vision congenial.

Some critics within the order, the brothers of Vadstena for example, hesitated to think of themselves as mere helpmates to the nuns; some critics in the Curia rejected the theological basis of the Bridgettine constitutions, the notion that the Virgin Mary had ever been head of the Church.[86] Others suggested that the proximity of monks and nuns violated sound ecclesiastical practice, the heyday of enthusiasm for double monasteries having long since passed.[87] The parlous state of the papacy in the

84 Morris, *St Birgitta of Sweden*, is a good overview.

85 Jelsma, "The Appreciation of Bridget of Sweden," p. 168.

86 Hans Cnattingius, *Studies in the Order of St Bridget of Sweden I: The Crisis in the 1420s* (Stockholm: Almquist and Wiksell, 1963), p. 126 notes the continued criticism of the notion that Mary "fuit caput et domina post ascensum Christi apostolorum." Morris, *St Birgitta*, pp. 168–169 mentions the tensions at Vadstena.

87 Cnattingius, *Studies*, pp. 9–26, provides a good survey of the decline of enthusiasm for foundations such as Fontevrault in France and the Gilbertine houses in England. He also explores the ways in which the concept of the double monastery appealed to Bridgettine monks in particular.

years directly following the death of St Bridget enabled all those critics to thrive.

Coming as it did during the Great Schism, from a pope whom not all Christians recognized as such, Urban VI's approval of the Bridgettine rule (1379) was far from unassailable. The actions of subsequent popes toward individual monasteries and the order as a whole are most uneven, with privileges rescinded and organizational alterations made and then unmade.[88] Such unsettled conditions notwithstanding, plans went ahead for the establishment of the first English house, structured in accordance with the statutes of the Bridgettine order. Henry V laid its cornerstone in 1415 and obtained Martin V's approval for his foundation in 1418. On April 1, 1420, twenty-seven sisters, five priests, two deacons, and four lay brothers took their vows, marking "the real foundation day of the abbey."[89] Just two years later, this fledgling establishment along with all the other monasteries of the order faced extinction.

Reacting in part to a politically charged situation involving the admission of nuns to the (theoretically) Bridgettine monastery of Scala Celi in Genoa, Martin V used all the authority of a newly invigorated papacy to rule against the continued existence of the order in the form envisioned by its founder.[90] On February 13, 1422, he issued a bull denying the right of the Bridgettines to establish any more monasteries. Additionally, since he classified those already established as 'double monasteries,' he instructed bishops to oversee the separation of the nuns and monks living in them, allowing the nuns to remain and compelling the monks to find or to construct new buildings for themselves.[91]

Understandably outraged by Martin V's so-called 'bull of separation,' the brothers and sisters of Vadstena implored their royal patrons and influential friends to send letters and envoys to Rome. Objections to the pope's decision were raised at the highest levels – Queen Philippa of Sweden writing to the pope as well as to her brother the King of England. It was the latter contact which was to bear the best fruit. In 1423, an English delegation arrived in Rome headed by a man who had been Henry V's confessor and who now held the office of Confessor General of Syon. The man's name was Thomas Fishbourne (d. 1428) and he would harness

88 Cnattingius, *Studies*, details several such actions, the most drastic of which involved Martin V's suspension of all Bridgettine privileges in the town and diocese of Valencia, p. 44.

89 David Knowles, *The Religious Orders of England*, vol. 2 (Cambridge: Cambridge University Press, 1955), p. 179.

90 Cnattingius, *Studies*, pp. 115, 126–127. Chapters 2 and 3 detail the conflict between the conservator general of the Bridgettines and the *pater* of Scala Celi.

91 *Ibid.*, pp. 122–25.

the not insignificant legal talent available to him in Rome to successfully overturn Martin V's bull of separation.

Thomas Fishbourne's role as champion of Bridgettine interests in Rome was long remembered by the nuns of Syon, who ordered that solemn mass be celebrated annually and perpetually for this counselor and confessor who had "labored strenuously for the continuous increase, spiritual as well as temporal, of this order and monastery, as well at the court of Rome as in this kingdom and monastery."[92] It was not, however, the first significant role Fishbourne had played in his life. A member of the landed gentry of northern England, he had been a wealthy squire serving as steward of William Heyworth, Abbot of St Albans from 1401 to 1420.[93] He then gave up his worldly life, was ordained a priest, and from his hermitage of St German acted as spiritual director to the nuns of Sopwell. King Henry V had met him there and he became the royal confessor, also advising the king about the Syon project. It was Fishbourne, in fact, who took receipt of the official papal approval of the foundation in 1418, after which he was duly elected Confessor General of Syon replacing its titular confessor, William Alnwick.

When he arrived in Rome in August of 1423, the first people Fishbourne enlisted to aid him were legal professionals already known to the order. As a royal foundation and the recipient of extensive and valuable papal privileges that required monitoring, Syon retained standing proctors in Rome.[94] Bridgettine communities on the continent also depended upon resident proctors and advocates with whom they had repeated contacts and good working relationships.[95] To one of these, an Englishman known only as "*dominus Riccardus advocatus noster*," Fishbourne entrusted a full set of documents that bolstered the reputation of St Bridget and her order. He next paid eight ducats, to "our advocate Ardecinus."[96]

This *jurisperitus* was Ardicino della Porta senior (d. 1434), doctor of both laws and advocate in the papal consistory.[97] A seasoned ecclesiastical

92 Aungier, *History*, p. 55.

93 Knowles, *Religious Orders*, p. 180. See also Cnattingius, *Studies*, pp. 131–32.

94 Power, *Nunneries*, p. 2 estimates the gross annual income of the house as £1,943.

95 One very valuable privilege was the indulgence affording pilgrims who gave alms to Syon the same liberal terms as those granted visitors to the exalted church of S. Pietro in Vincoli in Rome. W. E. Lunt, *Financial Relations of the Papacy with England* (Cambridge, MA: Mediaeval Academy of America, 1939–1962), vol. 2, p. 492.

96 Cnattingius, *Studies*, pp. 132–133. If we use a 1436 value of 3s. 5d. per ducat, the retainer in sterling would be about £1 4s. See Peter Spufford, *Handbook of Medieval Exchange* (London: Boydell, 1986), p. 201.

97 S. Miranda, *The Cardinals of the Holy Roman Church*. Digital resource, Florida International University Library. Online at www.fiu.edu/%7Emirandas/cardinals.htm.

practitioner, della Porta would be made a cardinal in 1426. For Fishbourne to have such a lawyer and papal favorite at his side was an advantage, but he was determined to succeed and had come to Rome prepared to spend largely for large results. In short order, and with "fresh distributions of money," he and Ardicino convinced the pope to entrust the question of the Bridgettine future to legal experts *extra collegium cadinalium*.[98] Two Rota auditors, Petrus Nardi and Johannes de Opizis, were then selected as judges by consent of the parties. Criteria for appointment as an auditor of the Rota had reached elevated heights by this time, and Martin V's own decree on this matter made it a certainty that only well-known doctors of the law would occupy those posts.[99] If the opinions of any privately retained consultants were to sway Nardi and Opizis, they would have to come from men of equal distinction. Consequently, Fishbourne solicited *consilia* from two of the most eminent legal minds of the day.

The first of these was a professor at the University of Bologna teaching that year at Siena, Nicholas de Tudeschis (1386–1445). Better known as Panormitanus, since he later held the office of Archbishop of Palermo, he was one of the most eminent canonists of the fifteenth century.[100] For a fee of 10 ducats, Panormitanus produced a certified legal opinion upholding the canonical legitimacy of the Bridgettine Order.[101] We know the exact fee, since Fishbourne's traveling companion and fellow religious, Simon Wynter of Syon, personally delivered it to Panormitanus in Siena.[102]

As formal briefs designed to provide advice on complex points of law or procedure, *consilia* generally followed a standard form. Arguments *contra*, those which would ultimately be rejected, were refuted point by point. Since it was expertise in law as learned at university that clients and judges sought from their consulting jurists, arguments both *pro* and *contra* were buttressed by citations of proof texts. These supporting sources were drawn from canon and civil law, scripture, and other doctrinal authori-

98 Cnattingius, *Studies*, p. 134.

99 Brundage, *Medieval Origins*, p. 376.

100 Kenneth Pennington, "Nicholaus de Tudeschis," in *Niccolo Tedeschi (Abbas Panormitanus) e i suoi Commentaria in Decretales* (Rome: Libri de Erice 25, 2000), pp. 9–36 supplies biographical details that take most recent scholarship into account. Also see, Charles Lefebvre, "Panormitain," *DDC*, vol. 6 (1957): 1195–1216; Schulte *QL*, vol. 2, pp. 312–314.

101 This *consilium*, numbered VII, appears in many printed editions of Panormitanus' collected opinions. I cite the collection published at Lyon in 1500, Hain #7187. Cnattingius, *Studies*, pp. 138–141 discusses the content of Panormitanus' opinion in some detail. So too does Walter Ullmann, "The Recognition of St Bridget's Rule by Martin V," *Revue Bénédictine* 3–4 (1957): 190–201, although the author misdates it.

102 Cnattingius, *Studies*, p. 139. Aungier, *History*, p. 52, lists Simon Wynter as a priest at Syon as of the year 1428.

ties.[103] Because Martin V's bull of separation had been issued largely on the basis of canonical pronouncements against double monasteries, it was especially important that such negative proof texts be cited in a consulting opinion, but then, somehow, shown to be irrelevant to the case at issue. Panormitanus did just that.

Without denying that double monasteries were banned by canon law, and adducing the legal citations to illustrate the fact, he demonstrated that *de iure* Bridgettine monasteries did not qualify as such. St Bridget founded an order *per mulieres primo et principaliter* and Bridgettine houses were therefore convents for nuns whose spiritual care was entrusted to individual clerics residing nearby. The priests and monks of the order did not constitute an official *collegium*, and did not have their own corporate monastic identity, but were merely assistants to the nuns. Bridgettine communities were not double monasteries in the strict sense of the term then, and so did not violate canonical regulations. As for Martin V's bull of separation, the crucial factor in this case, Panormitanus pointed out that even the pope can make a mistake. If the Supreme Pontiff made a ruling based on misinformation – and clearly Martin V had been wrongly informed about the Bridgettines – that ruling was flawed. An erroneous judgment, even if it took the form of a papal bull, was not binding on the faithful and might be rescinded.

Thomas Fishbourne had spent Syon funds wisely in securing the expert counsel of Panormitanus, and he had not finished spending in the Bridgettine cause. Since independent judges had been appointed to hear this case, in the manner of an arbitration, Fishbourne was free to solicit a second *consilium* to bolster Syon's position. Again he chose wisely, hiring none other than the distinguished canonist and Auditor General of the Rota, Dominicus de Sancto Geminiano.[104] If we correctly interpret Fishbourne's 'gift' presented to him at a papal audience in August, Dominicus' fee was 6 ducats.[105] Although he produced nothing like the *tour de force* composed by Panormitanus, the former Bologna law professor did what

103 See, for examples, Julius Kirshner, "Consilia as Authority in Late Medieval Italy: The Case of Florence," in *Legal Consulting in the Civil Law Tradition*, ed. Marior Ascheri *et al.* (Berkeley: University of California Press, 1999), pp. 107–138. By the end of the thirteenth century, the authoritative cache of contemporary jurists like Bartolus de Saxoferrato, Baldus de Ubaldis, Oldradus de Ponte, Johannes de Imola, Petrus de Ancharano, Antonius de Butrio, and Panormitanus. was so great that their opinions too began to be cited as proof texts.

104 Schulte *QL*, vol. 2, pp. 294–96 provides biographical details. For some illustrations of Dominicus' work as a canonist, see Makowski, *Canon Law and Cloistered Women*, pp. 83–88 and "Cloister Contested."

105 Cnattingius, *Studies*, p. 133.

was required of him.[106] He too argued for the canonically acceptable status of the Bridgettines based on the ancillary position of the monks and priests of the order. Like Panormitanus, he emphasized that the abbess alone was head of a Bridgettine monastery. In making this second point he went further than his colleague, however, by stressing that, unlike the nuns of the order, Bridgettine brethren owed their primary obedience to the confessor general and not to the abbess. Dominicus markedly reinterpreted the ideas of St Bridget with this emphasis, although that reinterpretation did not undercut the immediate utility of his brief.

Both of these *consilia* supporting the perpetuation of existing Bridgettine practice were completed sometime in early October, 1423; in a remarkably short space of time they were handed over to the curial judges Petrus Nardi and Johannes de Opizis. By November of that year Martin V acted on the opinion of those judges and issued a decree revoking his bull of separation insofar as it concerned the English Bridgettines. Although limited in scope, this was only the first in a series of decrees by which the bull would eventually be nullified. Thomas Fishbourne earned the perpetual gratitude of his order for a reason. With two well-crafted *consilia* that allowed a pope to reverse his original position without losing face, the Confessor General succeeded where costly envoys and royal petitions had failed.

For over a hundred years Syon would thrive as the unique English embodiment of Bridgettine spirituality. Even the 1442 inroads into the monastery's holdings occasioned by Henry VI's zeal for his new foundation of King's College, Cambridge, would not seriously imperil its institutional existence.[107] The events of 1442 do signify, however, in our final papal appeal that issued from Syon, this one made by the brethren alone.

Sometime near the middle of his term in office, Martin V's successor, Pope Eugenius IV (1431–1447) received a petition from several disaffected Syon brothers. They complained of the imperious attitude of their abbess, Maud Muston (1434–1447), reporting that her high-handed treatment of the priests and monks at Syon had caused some of them to wish to leave the house. They also claimed that Abbess Muston's conduct toward the brethren was seriously diminishing the number of new male recruits to the monastery.[108] Pope Eugenius responded to this petition by delegating the matter to the Archbishop of Canterbury. He ordered the archbishop to

106 It is published in L. M. Bååth, ed., *Acta Pontificum Suevica*, vol. 1: *Acta Cameralia* II (Stockholm: P. A. Norstedt 1957) as no. 1539, pp. 686–690.

107 See Chapter 4 for the details of Syon's loss to the masters and scholars of King's.

108 T. M. Höjer, *Studier i Vadstena Klosters Och Birgittinordens Historia Intill Midten Af 1400–Talet* (Uppsala: Almqvist & Wiksells, 1905), p. 258. Unfortunately, there is no

inquire into the matter, find out if the complaints against Abbess Muston were justified, and, if so, to discipline her.[109] Newly entered into his office, and owing his unimpeded institution to the pontiff who now required his services, Archbishop John Stafford (1443–1452) could scarcely have declined the request.[110] Therefore, he instructed his officials to summon Abbess Muston to the court of Canterbury to answer the charges leveled by the Syon brethren. As for the charges themselves, a man who moved in John Stafford's circles would have known what had occasioned them.

One member of Archbishop Stafford's circle of friends and confidants was James Fiennes (Lord Saye). Upon his elevation to the see of Canterbury, Stafford had appointed Fiennes steward for life of the episcopal estates.[111] Since this is the same Lord Saye named by deponents in the case of Syon vs. King's College, the same courtier who with "menacings and utterances in the king's name" had forced Maud Muston to surrender monastic holdings to Henry VI's new foundation of King's College in 1442, we can be sure that the archbishop knew the details of that event when he summoned Abbess Muston to his court on orders from Eugenius IV. And we can guess that his knowledge made him sanguine about the outcome of that summons. A beleaguered Maud Muston, required to make newly reduced supply fill existing demand in her community might be ill-tempered, but she would surely be amenable to discipline. She would know better than anyone that new recruits to a monastery so recently despoiled by the king might be limited, and would not wish to further imperil the future of her house. What John Stafford had not realized was

reference to papal documentation in this source and I have not been able to locate the petition in question.

109 "Religious Houses: House of Bridgettines," in *A History of the County of Middlesex*, vol. 1: *Physique, Archaeology, Domesday, Ecclesiastical Organization, The Jews, Religious Houses, Education of Working Classes to 1870, Private Education from Sixteenth Century* (1969), pp. 182–191. Online at www.british-history.ac.uk/report.aspx?compid=22119 (accessed July 27, 2010).

110 "On 10 April 1442 Archbishop Chichele wrote to Pope Eugenius IV asking to be allowed to retire and nominating Stafford as his successor. The king supported this proposal, but the pope refused to let the old man go, recognizing him as a stalwart supporter against the Council of Basel. However, Chichele's death on 12 April 1443 allowed for Stafford's smooth promotion; he was elected on 20 May but had in fact been papally provided as early as the 13th. Clearly this vacancy, too, had been well prepared for, and the pope had no objections to Stafford in himself. Stafford received the temporalities on 25 June, the pallium on 23 August, and was enthroned on 22 September during a one-week visit to his diocese proper." R. G. Davies, "Stafford, John (d. 1452)," in *ODNB*, www.oxforddnb.com/view/article/26209 (accessed October 28, 2010).

111 *Ibid.*

that it was precisely *because* the king had recently despoiled Syon that he was now prepared to prove himself its special protector.

By July of 1444 when he personally intervened in the case that the pope had delegated to Archbishop Stafford, Henry VI had already issued two in a series of compensatory grants to Syon. On March 11, 1444, "in consideration of the devotion of Henry V to that house," he had granted the Abbess and convent of Syon "exemption from any tenth, subsidy or quota from goods spiritual and ecclesiastical granted by the clergy of either province," along with further exemptions from taxes that might be demanded from them by regional or even papal authority.[112] On June 8, he had allowed a manor that had been part of the alien priory of Caen to be given in frank almoin to the abbess and convent.[113] And then, upon complaint from Abbess Maud Muston, he issued a letter patent on July 16 of that year. Issued from Sheen Manor, it appointed two proctors, Master Robert Rokke and the priest, John Wynter, to represent Maud, the Abbess, and the convent of the Monastery of St Savior, Syon, in the court of the Archbishop of Canterbury. The lawyers were to appear in the Canterbury court, but *not* to defend Maud Muston from charges leveled against her by disgruntled brethren. Henry VI assigned Rokke and Wynter specifically to oppose the archbishop's right to summon her (through her proctor) to his court at all! Abbess Muston, he declared, was "exempt from all jurisdiction inferior to the apostolic see" and "the abbess [was] being brought before the officials of the court of Canterbury contrary to the privileges of her house." The lawyers assigned her by the Crown were to address this violation.[114]

Henry VI's answer to John Stafford – or, shall we say, Maud Muston's answer – must have stung the pride of the newly appointed archbishop. As papal legate *natus*, the Archbishop of Canterbury technically possessed jurisdiction that was in no way inferior to that of the apostolic see. Yet Henry VI appeared uninterested in technicalities at this juncture. He had appointed two proctors to assert the right of the Abbess of Syon to be judged by the pope alone, not his agent, however exalted. As we hear no more about the dispute, it seems likely that king took bishop in this particular match.

112 *CPR 1441–1446*, p. 255.

113 *Ibid.*, p. 272.

114 *Ibid.*, p. 274; Aungier, *History*, p. 58. Both proctors remain unidentified.

Conclusion

This book has been concerned with legal activity engaged in by professional lawyers on behalf of English mendicant and Bridgettine nuns. It has focused exclusively on the late medieval period since, before the end of the thirteenth century, substantial numbers of professional lawyers of cloistered nuns did not exist in England. I have argued that the successful establishment of the latter was closely related to the emergence of the former; that the evolution of a class of legal professionals directly affected the ability of strictly cloistered communities to survive for more than two hundred years, a time during which the English experienced the worst fiscal exigencies that war, famine, and plague could inflict. Now I would like to review some of the supporting evidence for my thesis and to underscore its relevance to the study of religious women.

The origins of the legal profession in England, as well as on the continent, have been exhaustively documented by historians. They have described how lawyers were trained in university law schools and at the Inns of Court. They have compiled lists of attorneys licensed to practice in specific courts, and even garnered choice bits from the anti-lawyer literature that had begun to flourish as professional lawyers became more numerous. Most importantly, legal historians have confirmed that the intricacies of courtroom procedure in late medieval society made professional lawyers indispensable agents in the courts of Church and Crown. Yet, in topical studies based on the records of those courts, lawyers often become invisible, leaving readers with the unqualified image of litigants personally pleading their cases at the bar.

Sometimes, when it is the law *per se* that is under discussion, there is no real need to redress this image. When the topic is trespass, or bastardy, or the development of contract law, the consequences are negligible. But failure to consider the role of the lawyer can lead to interpretive problems when litigants as well as the law are at issue. These problems have surfaced in investigations of women and the law in late medieval England.

It is quite true, for example, to say that Englishwomen rarely made personal appearances in the courts of that era; it is also true to say that when they directed and guided their legal undertakings they did so privately, outside of the courtroom. To suggest that women engaged in behind-the-scenes oversight of their litigation because it was the only kind allowed them in a patriarchal society is less true. To posit that gentlewomen had to guide their cases remotely because they were constrained by societal notions of appropriate behavior (notions that limited their activities to the private sphere) ignores the fact that men, who were certainly not so constrained, employed the same sort of 'extra-curial' oversight of their litigation.[1] With the advent of legal professionalization, men, too (unless they themselves were lawyers), left the actual conduct of their suits to hired professionals. Some nuance is therefore required: Men, like women, rarely presented their own cases in court but men, unlike women, could come to court regularly to keep abreast of their suits without incurring any social stigma. And, of course, men could, and did, become lawyers.

With these facts in place, it becomes the physical absence of women from the courtroom, whether as professional lawyers (which they could not hope to become) or as interested observers (which would have been 'inappropriate' to their sex), and not the indirect methods by which they litigated, that reflects patriarchal conceptions of gendered public and private spheres. The distinction is not merely academic. Acknowledging the ubiquity of professionals who did the forensic work for their female as well as male clients highlights an area in which late medieval Englishwomen escaped the legal and social limitations imposed upon them generally.

To leave out the lawyers when dealing with mendicant and Bridgettine nuns poses an even more significant problem. Unable to appear in person because they were women, even more so because they were enclosed, the clients themselves become invisible. Without the lawyers, a suit brought in the name of an abbess or prioress of a cloistered house risks being classified as evidence of what her 'handlers,' male patrons and religious superiors, undertook to do in her best interests. The enforced exclusion of cloistered nuns from the courtroom ceases to be a legal liability only when we acknowledge that other litigants who were fully able to enter the courtroom *chose* not to do so. When the Prior of Durham, Oxford scholar and experienced defender of his monastery's legal privileges, John Wessington, is observed hiring a cadre of lawyers to plead cases in his stead, and when Prioress Margery de Honyland of the far-from-enclosed monastery of Bishopsgate is glimpsed suing through an attorney rather than appearing at a London assize, then a suit launched in the name of an Abbess of Syon or Aldgate takes on new significance: It illustrates the

1 This is the position taken by Emma Hawkes, "'[S]he will … protect and defend her rights boldly by law and reason': Women's Knowledge of Common Law and Equity Courts in Late Medieval England," in *Medieval Women and the Law*, ed. N. Menuge (Woodbridge: Boydell Press, 2000), pp. 145–161.

head of a cloistered house overseeing the legal affairs of that house, as would any other religious superior.

No small part of that oversight involved finding the money to pay the lawyers who worked for them. Cloistered nuns undoubtedly benefitted from occasional *pro bono* work; counsel given by Syon's Richard Lichefeld, Oxford-educated civilian and official principal of the Ely consistory, is a case in point. But when they actually went to law, mendicant and Bridgettine nuns became paying clients, just like all other litigants. When they hired members of the bar in the Court of Common Pleas or Chancery, they paid the fees established for practitioners in that particular court. When they availed themselves of expert outside opinion, they paid the *jurisperitus* who provided it what he required – 10 gold ducats for a jurist as important as Panormitanus. When their communities were wealthy enough to retain a number of lawyers, they reimbursed them in the same way that the monks of Westminster paid their proctors, advocates, and trusted serjeants at law, via monastic pensions or annuities.

Payment for services rendered made cloistered nuns less vulnerable to the vagaries of volunteerism and secured for them the kind of impartiality essential to the professional practice of law. It made them clients, pure and simple, possessing the same advantages and disadvantages as secular litigants. So it was a not uncommon event when Common Pleas' serjeant at law, Edmund Chelre, pleaded for the nuns of Dartford in 1365, and argued against them in a case four years later when he had been hired by the opposition.

When recruiting the lawyers who would serve them, the nuns relied on family ties and parochial or regional connections. Demonstrated expertise in the kind of legal work most commonly required by a particular monastery also brought clients and lawyers together. As landlords with considerable interest in London property, the Minoresses of Aldgates used the attorneys licensed by the city who represented other proprietors and businesspeople there: Robert fitzRobert, attorney for the Minories, had the Grocers of London as additional corporate clients. Sometimes the nuns made common cause with lay proprietors and so shared the legal fees incurred. When Abbess Eleanor Scrope, timbermonger John Bythewod, and vintner, John Michell, had charges brought against them in the 1382 London Assize of Nuisance, they were all represented by the same attorney.

As members of the social elite, mendicant and Bridgettine nuns had access to lawyers of the highest caliber. The above-mentioned Robert fitzRobert acted for the Earl of Ormond as well as for the Minoresses of Aldgate, and Inner Temple lawyer Sir Richard Sutton was Syon Abbey's lawyer and steward in addition to being a counselor to Henry VII. Dartford

Priory attorney Michael Skillyng served as King's Attorney in the Court of Common Pleas from 1361 to 1377, and another Dartford attorney, Serjeant at Law John Martyn, was named a Justice of Common Pleas.

The nuns were similarly fortunate in the caliber of their representation when their cases came before ecclesiastical judges. In the consistory court of the Bishop of Ely, which regularly met in Cambridge, they were served by the many university-trained lawyers in the city. At the time that Dame Elizabeth Throckmorton of Denney filed suit there, participating members of the Ely consistory bar included the bishop's official, Richard Herryson, and his chancellor, Master William Thornburgh, doctor of laws. Master Robert Kent, who was named "proctor in all suits" for Syon Abbey in 1455, practiced in the Court of Arches where he worked for some other notable clients, such as John Paston. Mary St Pol's injunction to the fellows of Pembroke College, Cambridge, "to give their best counsel and aid on all occasions to the abbess and sisters of Deney," helped those nuns to retain the best ecclesiastical lawyers available. And for some of the stormiest years in Syon's history, any suit bearing the abbey name that came before the papal curia would have been overseen by the man whom Fishbourne styled 'our advocate Ardecinus': Ardicino della Porta senior (d. 1434), doctor of both laws, advocate in the papal consistory, and cardinal by 1426.

With respect to venues, cloistered nuns were in very much the same position as other members of the propertied classes. Whether abbots or wealthy gentry, clients from that social stratum litigated chiefly about land and property rights, and consequently frequented Exchequer and Common Pleas. They petitioned Chancery when the king's courts provided no remedy (or no further remedy), or when an adversary's influential connections allegedly made him or her immune to common law restraints. When litigation involved a specifically ecclesiastical right, landholding religious all availed themselves of episcopal arbitration or papal appeals.

Lawyers who represented cloistered nuns appear to have labored just as doggedly on their behalf as they did for their other clients. Bridgettine attorneys persistently reasserted Syon's claim to alien priory lands in a decades-long battle and, as late as 1535, Dartford attorneys were still filing objections to a suit lodged against the Prioress of Dartford by virtue of the Statute of Farms. As clients, cloistered nuns appear to have acted very much like their secular counterparts. Allowing for the fact that legal briefs are phrased to present the plaintiff in the best (and the defendant in the worst) possible light, the nuns appear to have been just as capable as other litigants of succumbing to base instincts. We need only review two Chancery petitions to illustrate the fact.

In 1470, the Abbess of Denney petitioned Chancellor Robert Stillington to take action against the executors of Thomas Burgoyn, erstwhile Justice of the Peace and lord of the manor of Impington. She alleged that for over twenty years the decedent, whose property lay next to the abbey's own manor of Histon, had misused his powers, both those that naturally flowed from his local personal prominence and those conferred upon him as a representative of the king's justice, to visit a series of injuries upon them, vexing their servants with false writs of trespass, indictments, and false arrests.[2] Their neighbor's gross subversion of local justice also involved keeping tenants and servants from attending their manorial courts, impeding their officials from taking strays and occupying fens owned by the convent – actions which over the course of many years had cost the convent an estimated £883.

But in 1476, the proctor of the much disputed church of Wrestlingworth, Robert Wilde, petitioned Chancellor Rotherham, accusing Abbess Joan Barton of a similar misuse of power and privilege.[3] The rector alleged that while a tithes case between himself and Barton had been pending in the court of the Archbishop of Canterbury, he had come to London to seek legal counsel only to find that William Baker, Abbess Barton's servant, had convinced her "contrary to good conscience" to secure a writ of trespass against him, thus rendering him too afraid and impoverished to continue his tithes suit. In the writ, the abbess accused Wilde of assaulting William Baker in the parish of Saint Botolph without Aldgate; as a result of the charge he had been arrested and imprisoned by the Sheriff of London. Wilde was now petitioning Chancery since he was "not guilty as God knowith" but could not *prove* his innocence because all the cards were stacked against him. First, there was the formal allegation of the abbess, whose circle of friends and acquaintances in the City of London underscored the rector's own lack of such connections. Then there was the fact that the London jury picked to try the trespass case against him was made up of Abbess Barton's tenants and assigns, and these jurors had already told Wilde that they would convict him regardless of the evidence.

Similar comparison could be drawn in debt cases, since reluctance to honor an alleged monetary obligation was no respecter of the habit. For example, the executors of Giles Lovell may have resisted paying the nuns of Syon mortuary fees and income due them from Lancaster priory, but then the nuns of Waterbeach were alleged to have violated the final stipulation in an episcopal settlement by refusing to pay the large tithes owed

2 C 1/40/30. This particular segment is also transcribed in Bourdillon, *Minoresses*, p. 31.

3 C 1/67/163. The case which occasioned his petition is dealt with in Chapter 7.

to Barnwell Priory. And there is the case, meticulously documented by the plaintiff, of Aldgate's defrauded attorney, Henry Manpas [Maupas]. In his writ for the collection of debt before the justices of Common Pleas, Henry claimed that Abbess Margaret Helmystede had stopped payment of his annuity and produced a copy of the contract for same, bearing the seal of the abbess – evidence that convinced the defendant to concede victory by pleading (through her new attorney) no contest.

Henry Manpas' writ is something of an exception to the rule. It is a model of clarity, describes a rather surprising chain of events, and even records the outcome of the suit. But even writs like his have their limitations. Court rolls, no matter how substantial, are no substitute for cartularies, and Chancery petitions cannot compete with chronicles as literary evidence. Public legal records can tell us little about daily life at the Minories, or at Syon or Dartford for that matter; they reveal virtually nothing at all about the spiritual round within these cloisters. Luckily for the history of women religious in England, other scholars have used the lamentably few alternative sources that remain to provide insight into both these matters. What I have attempted to demonstrate is what legal records are more than capable of substantiating – namely, the extent to which the material and spiritual health of mendicant and Bridgettine communities depended upon the work done by professional lawyers on their behalf.

Appendix

Lawyers Employed by the Nuns

Dates in parentheses are those of the first, or only, known appointment for the respective monasteries. For common law jurists, dates for elevation to serjeant at law and appointment as King's Attorney or justice of the bench are from J. H. Baker, *The Order of Serjeants at Law*; information about City of London appointments is drawn from Penelope Tucker, *Law Courts and Lawyers in the City of London, 1300–1550*. Information about canonists and civilians is taken from the *BRUC*, *BRUO*, *BRUO 1501*, *ODNB*, and *Medieval Canonists: A Bio-Bibliographical Listing* online at http://faculty.cua.edu/pennington/biobibl.htm.

Dartford

Sir Robert Belknap [Bealknap] (1365) Created serjeant in 1362.
Edmund de Chelre (1365) Created serjeant in 1354; Justice of King's Bench 1371–1372.
Roger Digg (1367–1370)
Walter Perle (1368) Created serjeant in 1371; King's Attorney 1375–1376.
Michael Skillyng (1368 ff.) King's Attorney in King's Bench and Common Pleas.
Walter Durant (1370 ff.)
John Videlew (1371 ff.)
Nicholas Heryng (1375) King's Attorney.
Thomas Sherdelowe [Shardlow] (1375) King's Attorney in King's Bench.
John Bretton (1381–1384) Possibly a Domincan friar at Cambridge in the 1350s.
William Makenade (1387 ff.)
John Martyn (1400) Created serjeant in 1418; Chief Justice of Common Pleas 1420–1436.
William Gonorby (1415).
Robert Kendale (1415)
John Depyng (1425) Possibly Cambridge bachelor of canon law by 1427.
John Pecche (1426)

John White (1459) Possibly at Cambridge in 1424.

John Baker (1534) Inner Temple bencher by 1517, he was Recorder of London from 1526 to 1535 and served as Chancellor of the Exchequer in 1540.

Thomas Golde, William Waller of Gray's Inn, and John Wyseman: All three were granted annuities in 1538 for previous service, dates unknown.

Denney

Richard Brynkeley (1512)

William Nelson (1512) Possibly at Cambridge in 1484.

The Minories

Peter de Shordich (1303)

John de Colecestre (1306)

Cambin Fulbert (1309)

Roger de Hortone (1314)

Nicholas de Cranle (1328) City of London attorney of record in 1331.

Thomas Atteponde (1358)

James Lovet (1382)

Henry Maupas: A senior Chancery clerk under Henry IV and during the first two years of Henry V's reign, he is recorded as being an attorney in Chancery by 1382. He was much beneficed, and was granted an annuity by the nuns of Aldgate in 1402 for previous service, dates unknown.

William Aunger (1402)

John Stafford (1424)

Robert fitzRobert (1426) Active as a City of London attorney, described as "a man of law" by his company, the Grocers, in 1428.

Sir Thomas Frowyk: Dates of service unknown. Member of the Inner Temple and created serjeant in 1495, he served as Chief justice of Common Pleas 1502–06.

John Marten (1518)

Roger Higham (1531)

Syon

Ardicino della Porta, senior (1423) Doctor *utroque iure*, was a consistorial advocate and a cardinal by 1426.

Nicolaus de Tudeschis (Panormitanus) (1423) Called the most influential jurist of the fifteenth century, he was a student and then professor of canon law at the University of Bologna. He also taught in Parma (1411–1418), Siena, until 1430, and probably at Florence. He was famous for his commentaries as well as his consultations and diplomatic work. He was created Archbishop of Palermo in 1434 and a cardinal in 1440.

Dominicus de Sancto Geminiano (1423) Student at the University of Bologna where he became a professor of canon law by 1409; auditor of the Apostolic Camera, eminent jurist and commentator.

John Seton (1424–1425)

Richard Skot (1424–1425)

Robert Rokke (1444)

John Wynter (1444) Oxford University bachelor of canon law by 1439.

Richard Lichfield (1450) Oxford University doctor of canon law by 1458.

Robert Kent (1455) Oxford University bachelor of canon law, and proctor in Court of Arches, he served as a Paston family lawyer in their dispute over the will of John Fastolf, 1459–1466.

William Laken [Laicon] (1456, 1460). Created serjeant in 1453 he was promoted to Justice of King's Bench in 1465.

Sir Richard Sutton (1460–1524) Member of the Inner Temple by the 1480s, he was a judge in Court of Requests from 1497, and Syon steward from 1513.

Thomas Turneye (1462)

Thomas Jan (dates of service unknown)

William Lardner (1496)

Waterbeach

Thomas de Redeswelle (1298)

Hugh le Taillur [Tayllur, Taylur, Tayllour] (1298)

Robert Barnard (1305)

Stephan de Clopton (1305)

Select Bibliography

Manuscript Sources

Cambridge, King's College Archive Centre

SYO/4 Dispute	Details of dispute between Syon and King's concerning St Michael's Mount.
SYO/5 Extracts	Extracts from Exchequer memoranda rolls concerning Syon's claim to former alien priory lands.

Cambridge, University Library

EDR G2/5	Ely Diocesan Records

National Archives (Public Records Office), UK

Chancery Petitions
C 1/40/30
C 1/67/163
C 1/168/41
C 1/189/5
C 1/471/20
C 1/427/20
C 1/534/1
C 4/10/80
C 81/1792

Exchequer Memoranda Rolls
E 135/22/80
E 211/417
E 326/386
E 326/1854
E 326/3871
E 327/180
E328/48
E 328/143

Records of the Auditors of Land Revenues
LR 14/1175
LR 15/213

Records of the Palatinate of Lancaster
PL 6/1/22

Primary Sources

Annales Minorum Seu Trium Ordinum a S. Francisco Institutorum, ed. Luke Wadding, 3rd edn. Florence: Ad Claras Aquas (Quaracchi), 1931.

Bullarium Franciscanum, ed. Konrad Eubel. Rome: Typis Vaticanis, 1898.

Bullarium Ordinis FF. [i.e. Fratrum] Prædicatorum: Sub Auspiciis SS. D.N.D. Benedicti XIII, Pontificis Maximi, Ejusdem Ordinis, ed. Thomas Ripoll. Rome: Ex Typographia Hieronymi Mainardi, 1729–1740.

Calendar of Entries in the Papal Registers Relating to Great Britain and Ireland: Papal Letters, ed. William Henry Bliss. London: HMSO, 1893.

Calendar of Entries in the Papal Registers Relating to Great Britain and Ireland: Petitions to the Pope, AD 1342–1419, ed. William Henry Bliss. London: Eyre and Spottiswoode, 1896.

Calendar of the Close Rolls Preserved in the Public Record Office. London: HMSO, 1886–.

Calendar of the Patent Rolls Preserved in the Public Record Office. London: HMSO, 1891–.

Calendars of the Proceedings in Chancery, in the Reign of Queen Elizabeth: to which are Prefixed Examples of Earlier Proceedings in that Court, Namely, from the Reign of Richard the Second to that of Queen Elizabeth, Inclusive, ed. John Bayley. London: Printed by G. Eyre and A. Strahan, 1827–1832.

Cockburn, J. S., King, H. P. F., and McDonnell, K. G. T. *A History of the County of Middlesex*, vol. 1. The Victoria History of the Counties of England. London: Oxford University Press, 1969.

Des Augustinerpropstes Iohannes Busch Chronicon Windeshemense und Liber De Reformatione Monasteriorum. Geschichtsquellen Der Provinz Sachsen und Angrenzender Gebiete 8. Farnborough: Gregg International, 1968.

Documents Illustrating the Rule of Walter De Wenlok, Abbott of Westminster, 1283–1307, vol. 2, ed. Barbara F. Harvey. London: Royal Historical Society, 1965.

Dominicus, de Sancto Geminiano, *Dominici Geminiani Consilia: Eminentissimi i.v. Monarchae … Consiliorum Opus Integritati Suae Nunc Restitutum Ac … Domini Felini … Annotationibus … Auctum, Summarijsq [ue] … Nuperrimè Locupletatum*. Lyon: Iacobus Giunta, 1541.

Donahue, Charles and Working Group on Church Court Records. *The Records of the Medieval Ecclesiastical Courts*. Comparative Studies in Continental and Anglo-American Legal History 6. Berlin: Duncker & Humblot, 1989.

Emden, Alfred Brotherston. *A Biographical Register of the University of Cambridge to 1500*. Cambridge: Cambridge University Press, 1963.

—— *A Biographical Register of the University of Oxford to AD 1500*. Oxford: Clarendon Press, 1957–1959.

—— *A Biographical Register of the University of Oxford*, AD *1501 to 1540*. Oxford: Clarendon Press, 1974.

—— *A Survey of Dominicans in England Based on the Ordination Lists in Episcopal Registers (1268 to 1538)*. Institutum Historicum Ff. Praedicatorum Romae ad S. Sabinae. Dissertationes Historicae 18. Rome: S. Sabina, 1967.

Eye Priory Cartulary and Charters, ed. Vivien Brown. Woodbridge: Boydell Press, 1992.

Francis and Clare: The Complete Works, ed. Regis J. Armstrong and Ignatius C. Brady. New York: Paulist Press, 1982.

Gibbons, Alfred W. *Ely Episcopal Records. A Calendar and Concise View of the Episcopal Records Preserved in the Muniment Room of the Palace at Ely*. Lincoln: J. Williamson, 1891.

Hardy, Thomas D. "A Catalogue of Lords Chancellors, Keepers of the Great Seal, Masters of the Rolls, and Principal Officers of the High Court of Chancery." H. Butterworth. Online at www.gale.com/ModernLaw. Note: Available to subscribing institutions.

Harvey, Barbara F. *The Obedientiaries of Westminster Abbey and their Financial Records, c. 1275–1540*. Westminster Abbey Record Series 3. Woodbridge: Boydell Press, 2002.

Letters and Papers, Foreign and Domestic, of the Reign of Henry VIII, Preserved in the Public Record Office, the British Museum, and Elsewhere, ed. J. S. Brewer, Robert Henry Brodie, and James Gairdner. 2nd edn. Vaduz: Kraus Reprint, 1965.

Liber Memorandum Ecclesie De Bernenwelle [Barnwell], ed. J. W. Clark and F. W. Maitland. Cambridge: Cambridge University Press, 1907.

Mackman, Jonathan and Matthew Stevens, eds. *Court of Common Pleas: The National Archives, CP40: 1399–1500*. London: Institute of Historical Research. Online at www.british-history.ac.uk/report.aspx?compid=118035.

Miranda, Salvador. *The Cardinals of the Holy Roman Church*. Digital resource, Florida International University Library. Online at www.fiu.edu/%7Emirandas/cardinals.htm.

Oldradus de Ponte de Laude. *Consilia Seu Responsa, Et Quaestiones Aureae*. Venice: 1571.

Owen, Dorothy Mary. *Ely Records: A Handlist of the Records of the Bishop and Archdeacon of Ely*. Chichester: Marc Fitch Fund, 1971.

Page, William. *The Victoria History of the County of Kent*, vol. 2. The Victoria History of the Counties of England. London: Institute of Historical Research, 1974.

—— *The Victoria History of the County of Suffolk*. The Victoria History of the Counties of England. London: Constable, 1907.

—— *The Victoria History of London: Including London within the Bars, Westminster and Southwark*, vol. 1. The Victoria History of the Counties of England. London: Institute of Historical Research, 1974.

Panormitanus [Niccolò Tedeschi]. *Consiliorum Abbatis Primum Volumen (Cum Ludovici Bolognini Tabula)*. Lyon: J. Siberti, 1500.

The Paston Letters: A Selection in Modern Spelling, ed. Norman Davis. The World's Classics 591. Oxford: Oxford University Press, 1963.

Registers of the Archbishops of Canterbury in Lambeth Palace. London: Lambeth Palace Library, 1974.

Registers of the Bishops of London, 1304–1660, pt 5. Brighton: Harvester Press Microform Publications, 1984.

The Registers of Robert Stillington, Bishop of Bath and Wells, 1466–1491, and Richard Fox, Bishop of Bath and Wells, 1492–1494, ed. Sir Henry Churchill Maxwell-Lyte. Somerset Record Society 52. London: Printed for subscribers only, 1937.

Registrum Hamonis Hethe Diocesis Roffensis AD *1319–1352*, ed. Charles Johnson. The Canterbury and York Society 48–[49]. Oxford: Oxford University Press, 1948.

Registrum Johannis De Trillek, Episcopi Herefordensis, AD MCCCXLIV–MCCCLXI *[i.e.* MCCCLX*]*, ed. Joseph Henry Parry. Canterbury and York Society 8. London: Canterbury and York Society, 1912.

Registrum Roberti Winchelsey Cantuariensis Archiepiscopi AD *1294–1313*, ed. Rose Graham. Canterbury and York Society 51, 52. Oxford: Oxford University Press, 1952–1956.

Registrum Thomae Bourgchier Cantuarensis Archiebiscopi AD *1454–1486*, ed. F. R. H. du Boulay. Canterbury and York Society 54. Oxford: Oxford University Press, 1957.

Roach, John, L. F. Salzman, and R. B. Pugh. *The Victoria History of the County of Cambridgeshire and the Isle of Ely*. The Victoria History of the Counties of England. London: Dawsons of Pall Mall for the Institute of Historical Research, 1967.

Salzman, L. F. *The Victoria History of the County of Cambridgeshire and the Isle of Ely*. The Victoria History of the Counties of England. Oxford: Oxford University Press, 1938.

Seipp, David, and Carol Lee. *Legal History, the Year Books Medieval English Legal History: An Index and Paraphrase of Printed Year Book Reports, 1268–1535*. Online resource, Boston University School of Law. Online at www.bu.edu/law/seipp.

Select Cases in Chancery, AD *1364 to 1471*, ed. W. Paley Baildon. Publications of the Selden Society 10. London: Bernard Quaritch, 1896.

Select Cases in the Court of King's Bench, ed. G. O. Sayles. Publications of the Selden Society 55, 57, 58, 74, 76, 82, 88. London: Bernard Quaritch, 1936–1971.

Select Cases from the Ecclesiastical Courts of the Province of Canterbury c. *1200–1301*, ed. Norma Adams and Charles Donahue. Publications of the Selden Society 95. London: Selden Society, 1981.

Sources of English Constitutional History: A Selection of Documents from AD 600 *to the Present*, ed. Carl Stephenson and Tr. Frederick George Marcham. Harper's Historical Series. New York: Harper & Bros, 1937.

Spufford, Peter, Wendy Wilkinson, and Sarah Tolley. *Handbook of Medieval Exchange*. Royal Historical Society Guides and Handbooks 13. Woodbridge: Boydell Press, 1986.

The Statutes of the Realm (1225–1713) from Original Records and Authentical Manuscripts. London: Record Commission, 1810.

Strayer, Joseph R. *Dictionary of the Middle Ages*. New York: Scribner, 1982–1989.

Supplementum ad Bullarium Franciscanum Continens Litteras Romanorum Pontificum Annorum 1378–1484 pro Tribus S.P.N. Francisci Ulterius Obtentas: Appendice Hierarchica Addita, ed. Cesare Cenci. Grottaferrata: Editiones Collegii S. Bonaventurae ad Claras Aquas, 2002–2003.

University of London, Institute of Historical Research and History of Parliament Trust (Great Britain). *British History Online*. Digital resource at www.british-history.ac.uk.

Valor Ecclesiasticus Temp. Henr. VIII. Auctoritate Regia Institutus, ed. John Hunter Caley. London, 1976.

Year Books of Edward II, vol. 26, part 1 and part 2: *The Eyre of London, 14 Edward II*, AD *1321*, ed. Helen Maud Cam. Publications of the Selden Society 85 and 86. London: Bernard Quaritch, 1968–1969.

Zabarella, Francesco. *Consilia ... Francisci Zabarellae ...: Quibus ... Accesserunt Collegiorum Bononiensis, Paduani & Ferrariensis & Baptistae Cacialupi à S. Severino, De Dignitate & Praerogativa Monachorum Consilia Singula: Vna Cum Dialogo ... & Annnotationibus Eodem Pertinentibus: Bartholomaei Beneventan. in Causa Matrimoniali Consilium Unum*. Venice: apud Ioannem Baptistam a Porta, 1581.

Secondary Sources

Arnold, Matthew. *Essays, Letters, and Reviews*, ed. Fraser Neiman. Cambridge, MA: Harvard University Press, 1960.

Aungier, George James. *The History and Antiquities of Syon Monastery: The Parish of Isleworth, and the Chapelry of Hounslow*. London: J. B. Nichols and Son, 1840.

Avery, Margaret. "The History of the Equitable Jurisdiction of Chancery before 1460." *Bulletin of the Institute of Historical Research* 42, no. 106 (November 1969): 9–144.

Baker, John Hamilton. *An Introduction to English Legal History*. 2nd edn. London: Butterworth, 1979.

—— *Judicial Records, Law Reports, and the Growth of Case Law*. Comparative Studies in Continental and Anglo-American Legal History 5. Berlin: Duncker & Humblot, 1989.

—— "Lawyers Practising in Chancery 1474–1486." *Journal of Legal History* 4, no. 1 (1983): 54–76.

—— *The Legal Profession and the Common Law: Historical Essays*. London: Hambledon Press, 1986.

—— *Monuments of Endlesse Labours: English Canonists and Their Work, 1300–1900*. London and Rio Grande, OH: Hambledon Press, with the Ecclesiastical Law Society, 1998.

—— *The Order of Serjeants at Law: A Chronicle of Creations, with Related Texts and a Historical Introduction*. Selden Society, Supplementary Series 5. London: Selden Society, 1984.

—— *The Oxford History of the Laws of England*. Vol. 6, *1483–1558*. Oxford: Oxford University Press, 2003.

Barron, Caroline M., and Harper-Bill, Christopher. *The Church in Pre-Reformation Society: Essays in Honour of F. R. H. du Boulay*. Woodbridge: Boydell Press, 1985.

Bell, David N. *What Nuns Read: Books and Libraries in Medieval English Nunneries*. Cistercian Studies Series 158. Kalamazoo, MI: Cistercian Publications, 1995.

Berman, Constance H. *Women and Monasticism in Medieval Europe: Sisters and Patrons of the Cistercian Reform*. Documents of Practice Series. Kalamazoo, MI: Published for TEAMS (The Consortium for the Teaching of the Middle Ages) by Medieval Institute Publications, 2002.

Biancalana, Joseph. "The Legal Framework of Arbitration in Fifteenth-Century England." *American Journal of Legal History* 47, no. 4 (2005): 347–382.

Birks, Peter. *The Life of the Law: Proceedings of the Tenth British Legal History Conference, Oxford, 1991*. London: Hambledon Press, 1993.

Bourdillon, Anne Francis Claudine. *The Order of Minoresses in England*. British Society of Franciscan Studies 12. Manchester: Manchester University Press, 1926.

Brand, Paul. "Courtroom and Schoolroom: The Education of Lawyers in England prior to 1400." *Historical Research* 60 (1987): 147–165.

—— *The Origins of the English Legal Profession*. Oxford: Blackwell, 1992.

Brundage, James A. *Medieval Origins of the Legal Profession: Canonists, Civilians, and Courts*. Chicago: University of Chicago Press, 2008.

—— *The Profession and Practice of Medieval Canon Law*. Variorum Collected Studies Series CS797. Aldershot: Ashgate, 2004.

—— "The Profits of the Law: Legal Fees of University-Trained Advocates." *American Journal of Legal History* 32, no. 1 (1988): 1–15.

Clay, William Keatinge. *A History of the Parish of Waterbeach in the County of Cambridge*. Cambridge Antiquarian Society. Octavo Publications 4. Cambridge: Deighton, Bell, 1859.

Cnattingius, Hans Jacob. *Studies in the Order of St Bridget of Sweden*. Acta Universitatis Stockholmiensis. Stockholm Studies in History 7. Stockholm: Almqvist & Wiksell, 1963.

Coss, Peter R. *The Moral World of the Law*. Past and Present Publications. Cambridge: Cambridge University Press, 2000.

Dobson, R. B. *Durham Priory, 1400–1450*. Cambridge Studies in Medieval Life and Thought, 3rd series, 6. Cambridge: Cambridge University Press, 1973.

Dugdale, W. *Monasticon Anglicanum*. London, 1693.

Dunning, R. "The Muniments of Syon Abbey: Their Administration and Migration in the Fifteenth and Sixteenth Centuries." *Bulletin of the Institute of Historical Research* 37, no. 95 (1964): 103–111.

Ellis, Roger. Viderunt Eam Filie Syon*: The Spirituality of the English House of a Medieval Contemplative Order from Its Beginnings to the Present Day*. Salzburg: Institut für Anglistik und Amerikanistik, 1984.

Elton, G. R. *The Tudor Revolution in Government: Administrative Changes in the Reign of Henry VIII*. Cambridge: Cambridge University Press, 1953.

Field, Sean L. *Isabelle of France: Capetian Sanctity and Franciscan Identity in the Thirteenth Century*. Notre Dame, IN: University of Notre Dame Press, 2006.

Formoy, Beryl E. R. *The Dominican Order in England before the Reformation*. Studies in Church History. London: Macmillan, 1925.

Gee, Loveday Lewes. *Women, Art, and Patronage from Henry III to Edward III, 1216–1377*. Woodbridge: Boydell Press, 2002.

Gies, Joseph, and Mary Gies. *Merchants and Moneymen: The Commercial Revolution, 1000–1500*. New York: Crowell, 1972.

Gumbley, Walter. "Provincial Priors and Vicars of the English Dominicans, 1221–1916." *English Historical Review* 33, no. 130 (1918): 243–251.

Hanawalt, Barbara. *The Wealth of Wives: Women, Law, and Economy in Late Medieval London*. Oxford: Oxford University Press, 2007.

Harvey, Margaret. *The English in Rome, 1362–1420: Portrait of an Expatriate Community*. Cambridge Studies in Medieval Life and Thought. 4th series. Cambridge: Cambridge University Press, 1999.

Haskett, Timothy S. "The Medieval English Court of Chancery." *Law and History Review* 14, no. 2 (1996): 245–313.

Helmholz, R. H. *The Canon Law and Ecclesiastical Jurisdiction from 597 to the 1640s*. Oxford History of the Laws of England 1. Oxford: Oxford University Press, 2004.

—— *The Spirit of Classical Canon Law*. Athens, GA: University of Georgia Press, 1996.

Hinnebusch, William A. *The Early English Friars Preachers*. Institutum Historicum FF. Praedicatorum Romae ad S. Sabinae. Dissertationes Historicae 14. Rome: Ad S. Sabinae, 1951.

—— *The History of the Dominican Order*. Staten Island, NY: Alba House, 1966.

Höjer, Torvald Magnusson. *Studier i Vadstena Klosters Och Birgittinordens Historia Intill Midten Af 1400–Talet*. Uppsala: Almqvist & Wiksells, 1905.

Ives, E. W. *The Common Lawyers of Pre-Reformation England: Thomas Kebell, a Case Study*. Cambridge Studies in English Legal History. Cambridge: Cambridge University Press, 1983.

Jacob, E. F. *Essays in Later Medieval History*. Manchester: Manchester University Press, 1968.

Jarrett, Bede. *The English Dominicans*. London: Burns, Oates and Washbourne, 1921.

Kanner, Barbara. *The Women of England from Anglo-Saxon Times to the Present: Interpretive Bibliographical Essays*. Hamden, CT: Archon Books, 1979.

Kerr, Bernice M. *Religious Life for Women from the Twelfth Century to the Middle of the Fourteenth Century with Special Reference to the English Foundations of the Order of Fontevraud*. Oxford: Oxford University Press, 1995.

Kingsford, Charles Lethbridge. *The Grey Friars of London: Their History, with the Register of Their Convent and an Appendix of Documents*. Aberdeen: Aberdeen University Press, 1965.

Lawrence, C. H. *The Friars: The Impact of the Early Mendicant Movement on Western Society*. The Medieval World. London and New York: Longman, 1994.

Lee, Paul. *Nunneries, Learning, and Spirituality in Late Medieval English Society: The Dominican Priory of Dartford*. York: York Medieval Press, 2001.

Lehfeldt, Elizabeth A. "Discipline, Vocation, and Patronage: Spanish Religious Women in a Tridentine Microclimate." *Sixteenth Century Journal* 30, no. 4 (1999): 1009–1030.

Lekai, Louis Julius. *The Cistercians: Ideals and Reality*. Kent, OH: Kent State University Press, 1977.

Little, A. G. *The Grey Friars in Oxford*, part 1: *A History of the Convent*; part 2: *Biographical Notices of the Friars, Together with Appendices of Original Documents*. Oxford Historical Society 20. Oxford: Clarendon Press, 1892.

Logan, F. Donald. *Runaway Religious in Medieval England, c. 1240–1540*. Cambridge Studies in Medieval Life and Thought, 4th series, 32. Cambridge: Cambridge University Press, 1996.

—— *The Medieval Court of Arches*. The Canterbury and York Society 95. Woodbridge: Boydell Press, 2005.

Lund, Thomas. "The Modern Mind of the Medieval Lawyer." *Texas Law Review* 64 no. 7 (1986):1267–1289.

Lunt, William E. *Financial Relations of the Papacy with England*. Mediaeval Academy of America. Publication 33, 2 vols, Cambridge, MA: Mediaeval Academy of America, 1939–1962.

—— *Papal Revenues in the Middle Ages*. Records of Civilization: Sources and Studies 19. New York: Octagon Books, 1965.

Makowski, Elizabeth M. *Canon Law and Cloistered Women:* Periculoso *and Its Commentators, 1298–1545*. Studies in Medieval and Early Modern Canon Law 5. Washington, DC: Catholic University of America Press, 1997.

—— "Cloister Contested: *Periculoso* as Authority in Late Medieval *Consilia*." *The Jurist* 71, no. 2 (2011): 334–348.

—— *A Pernicious Sort of Woman: Quasi-Religious Women and Canon Lawyers in the Later Middle Ages*. Studies in Medieval and Early Modern Canon Law 6. Washington, DC: Catholic University of America Press, 2005.

Menuge, Noël James, ed. *Medieval Women and the Law*. Woodbridge: Boydell Press, 2000.

Mlynarczyk, Gertrud. *Ein Franziskanerinnenkloster im 15. Jahrhundert: Edition und Analyse von Besitzinventaren aus der Abtei Longchamp*. Pariser Historische Studien 23. Bonn: L. Röhrscheid, 1987.

Morris, Bridget. *St Birgitta of Sweden*. Studies in Medieval Mysticism 1. Woodbridge: Boydell Press, 1999.

Mullinger, J. Bass. *A History of the University of Cambridge*. Epochs of Church History. London: Longmans, Green, and Co, 1888.

Musson, Anthony, and W. M. Ormrod. *The Evolution of English Justice: Law, Politics, and Society in the Fourteenth Century*. British Studies Series. New York: St Martin's Press, 1999.

Oliva, Marilyn. *The Convent and the Community in Late Medieval England: Female Monasteries in the Diocese of Norwich, 1350–1540*. Studies in the History of Medieval Religion 12. Woodbridge: Boydell Press, 1998.

Palmer, C. F. R. "History of the Priory of Dartford." *Archaeological Journal* 36 (1879): 241–271.

Parker, David. "Three Models of Self-Government: Medieval English Translations of Latin Rules for Nuns." *Magistra* 7 (2001): 100–125.

Paxton, Catherine. "The Nunneries of London and Its Environs in the Later Middle Ages." D.Phil. thesis, Oxford University, 1992.

Pike, L. Owen. "An Action at Law in the Reign of Edward III: The Report and the Record." *Harvard Law Review* 7, no. 5 (1893): 266–280.

Pollock, Sir Frederick, and F. W. Maitland. *The History of English Law before the Time of Edward I*. 2nd edn reissued; with a new introduction and select bibliography by S. F. C. Milsom. Cambridge: Cambridge University Press, 1968.

Power, Eileen Edna. *Medieval English Nunneries* c. *1275 to 1535*. Cambridge Studies in Medieval Life and Thought. Cambridge: Cambridge University Press, 1922.

Ramsay, Nigel. "Retained Legal Counsel, *c.* 1275–*c.* 1475: The Alexander Prize Essay." *Transactions of the Royal Historical Society* 35 (1985): 95–112.

Richardson, Malcolm. *The Medieval Chancery under Henry V*. List and Index Society (special series) 30. London: List and Index Society, 1999.

Richmond, Colin. *The Paston Family in the Fifteenth Century: Fastolf's Will*. Cambridge: Cambridge University Press, 1996.

Roberts, Clayton, David Roberts, and Douglas R. Bisson. *A History of England*. 5th edn. Upper Saddle River, NJ: Pearson Prentice Hall, 2009.

Rushton, Neil S. and Wendy Sigle-Rushton. "Monastic Poor Relief in Sixteenth-Century England." *Journal of Interdisciplinary History* 32, no. 2 (2001): 193–216.

Sayers, Jane E. *Law and Records in Medieval England: Studies on Medieval Papacy, Monasteries and Records*. Aldershot: Ashgate, 1988.

—— *Papal Judges Delegate in the Province of Canterbury, 1198–1254: A Study in Ecclesiastical Jurisdiction and Administration.* Oxford: Oxford University Press, 1971.

Schulte van Kessel, Elisja, *Women and Men in Spiritual Culture, XIV–XVII Centuries: A Meeting of South and North.* The Hague: Netherlands Government Publications Office, 1986.

Slack, Paul. *The Impact of Plague in Tudor and Stuart England.* London and Boston: Routledge & Kegan Paul, 1985.

Snape, Robert Hugh. *English Monastic Finances in the Later Middle Ages.* New York: Barnes & Noble, 1968.

Squibb, G. D. *Doctors' Commons: A History of the College of Advocates and Doctors of Law.* Oxford: Clarendon Press, 1977.

Stöber, Karen. *Late Medieval Monasteries and Their Patrons: England and Wales,* c. *1300–1540.* Studies in the History of Medieval Religion 29. Woodbridge: Boydell Press, 2007.

Tait, M. B. "The Brigittine Monastery of Syon (Middlesex) with Special Reference to Its Monastic Usages." D.Phil. thesis, Oxford University, 1976.

Tierney, Brian. *The Crisis of Church and State, 1050–1300.* Englewood Cliffs, NJ: Prentice-Hall, 1964.

Tomlinson, Edward Murray. *A History of the Minories, London.* London: Smith, Elder, 1907.

Tout, T. F. *Historical Essays by Members of the Owens College, Manchester: Published in Commemoration of Its Jubilee (1851–1901).* London: Longmans, 1902.

Traill, H. D., and James SaumarezMann. *Social England: A Record of the Progress of the People in Religion, Laws, Learning, Arts, Industry, Commerce, Science, Literature and Manners, from the Earliest Times to the Present Day.* 6 vols. London: Cassell and Co, 1902–1904.

Tucker, Penelope. *Law Courts and Lawyers in the City of London, 1300–1550.* Cambridge Studies in English Legal History. Cambridge: Cambridge University Press, 2007.

Ulmann, Walter. "The Recognition of St Bridget's Rule by Martin V." *Revue Bénédictine* 3–4 (1957): 190–201.

Vodola, Elisabeth. *Excommunication in the Middle Ages.* Berkeley: University of California Press, 1986.

Walker, Sue Sheridan. "Litigant Agency in Dower Pleas in the Royal Common Law Courts in Thirteenth- and Early Fourteenth-Century England," *Journal of Legal History* 24, no. 3 (2003): 1–22.

Warren, Nancy Bradley. *Spiritual Economies: Female Monasticism in Later Medieval England.* The Middle Ages Series. Philadelphia: University of Pennsylvania Press, 2001.

Waugh, Scott and Peter Diehl, eds. *Christendom and Its Discontents.* Cambridge: Cambridge University Press, 1996.

Winston-Allen, Anne. *Convent Chronicles: Women Writing about Women and Reform in the Late Middle Ages*. University Park: Pennsylvania State University Press, 2004.

Woodcock, Brian Lindsay. *Medieval Ecclesiastical Courts in the Diocese of Canterbury*. Oxford Historical Series. Oxford: Oxford University Press, 1952.

Wunderli, Richard M. *London Church Courts and Society on the Eve of the Reformation*. Speculum Anniversary Monographs 7. Cambridge, MA: Medieval Academy of America, 1981.

Index

Note: page numbers in bold refer to the appendix; references to footnotes are indicated by n. and the footnote number after the page number.

Other Volumes in
Studies in the History of Medieval Religion

I: Dedications of Monastic Houses in England and Wales 1066–1216
Alison Binns

II: The Early Charters of the Augustinian Canons of Waltham Abbey, Essex, 1062–1230
Edited by Rosalind Ransford

III: Religious Belief and Ecclesiastical Careers in Late Medieval England
Edited by Christopher Harper-Bill

IV: The Rule of the Templars: the French text of the Rule of the Order of the Knights Templar
Translated and introduced by J. M. Upton-Ward

V: The Collegiate Church of Wimborne Minster
Patricia H. Coulstock

VI: William Waynflete: Bishop and Educationalist
Virginia Davis

VII: Medieval Ecclesiastical Studies in honour of Dorothy M. Owen
Edited by M. J. Franklin and Christopher Harper-Bill

VIII: A Brotherhood of Canons Serving God: English Secular Cathedrals in the Later Middle Ages
David Lepine

IX: Westminster Abbey and its People c.1050–c.1216
Emma Mason

X: Gilds in the Medieval Countryside: Social and Religious Change in Cambridgeshire c.1350–1558
Virginia R. Bainbridge

XI: Monastic Revival and Regional Identity in Early Normandy
Cassandra Potts

XII: The Convent and the Community in Late Medieval England: Female Monasteries in the Diocese of Norwich 1350–1540
Marilyn Oliva

XIII: Pilgrimage to Rome in the Middle Ages: Continuity and Change
Debra J. Birch

XIV: St Cuthbert and the Normans: the Church of Durham 1071–1153
William M. Aird

XV: The Last Generation of English Catholic Clergy: Parish Priests in the Diocese of Coventry and Lichfield in the Early Sixteenth Century
Tim Cooper

XVI: The Premonstratensian Order in Late Medieval England
Joseph A. Gribbin

XVII: Inward Purity and Outward Splendour:
Death and Remembrance in the Deanery of Dunwich, Suffolk, 1370–1547
Judith Middleton-Stewart

XVIII: The Religious Orders in Pre-Reformation England
Edited by James G. Clark

XIX: The Catalan Rule of the Templars:
A Critical Edition and English Translation from Barcelona,
Archito de la Corona de Aragón, 'Cartes Reales', MS 3344
Edited and translated by Judi Upton-Ward

XX: Leper Knights:
The Order of St Lazarus of Jerusalem in England, c.1150–1544
David Marcombe

XXI: The Secular Jurisdiction of Monasteries
in Anglo-Norman and Angevin England
Kevin L. Shirley

XXII: The Dependent Priories of Medieval English Monasteries
Martin Heale

XXIII: The Cartulary of St Mary's Collegiate Church, Warwick
Edited by Charles Fonge

XXIV: Leadership in Medieval English Nunneries
Valerie G. Spear

XXV: The Art and Architecture of English Benedictine Monasteries, 1300–1540:
A Patronage History
Julian M. Luxford

XXVI: Norwich Cathedral Close: The Evolution of the
English Cathedral Landscape
Roberta Gilchrist

XXVII: The Foundations of Medieval English Ecclesiastical History
Edited by Philippa Hoskin, Christopher Brooks and Barrie Dobson

XXVIII: Thomas Becket and his Biographers
Michael Staunton

XXIX: Late Medieval Monasteries and their Patrons:
England and Wales, c.1300–1540
Karen Stöber

XXX: The Culture of Medieval English Monasticism
Edited by James G. Clark

XXXI: A History of the Abbey of Bury St Edmunds, 1182–1256:
Samson of Tottington to Edmund of Walpole
Antonia Gransden

XXXII: Monastic Hospitality:
the Benedictines in England, c.1070–c.1250
Julie Kerr

XXXIII: Religious Life in Normandy, 1050–1300:
Space, Gender and Social Pressure
Leonie V. Hicks

XXXIV: The Medieval Chantry Chapel: An Archaeology
Simon Roffey

XXXV: Monasteries and Society in the British Isles
in the Later Middle Ages
Edited by Janet Burton and Karen Stöber

XXXVI: Jocelin of Wells: Bishop, Builder, Courtier
Edited by Robert Dunning

XXXVII: War and the Making of Medieval Monastic Culture
Katherine Allen Smith

XXXVIII: Cathedrals, Communities and Conflict in the Anglo-Norman World
Edited by Paul Dalton, Charles Insley and Louise J. Wilkinson

Printed and bound by CPI Group (UK) Ltd, Croydon, CR0 4YY

13/09/2026

14961003-0001